ZOMBIE TALES

GOOD EATIN'

ANDREW COSBY
ROSS RICHIE
founders

MARK WAID
editor-in-chief

ADAM FORTIER
vice president,
new business

CHIP MOSHER
marketing &
sales director

MATT GAGNON
managing editor

ED DUKESHIRE
designer

Zombie Tales: Good Eatin' — published by Boom! Studios. Zombie Tales is copyright © Boom Entertainment, Inc. HEADSHOT is copyright Boom Entertainment and Monte Cook. Boom! Studios™ and the Boom! logo are trademarks of Boom Entertainment, Inc., registered in various countries and categories. All rights reserved. The characters and events depicted herein are fictional. Any similarity to actual persons, demons, anti-Christs, aliens, vampires, face-suckers or political figures, whether living, dead or undead, or to any actual or supernatural events is coincidental and unintentional. So don't come whining to us.

Office of publication: 6310 San Vicente Blvd, Ste 404, Los Angeles, CA 90048-5457.

First Edition: January 2009

10 9 8 7 6 5 4 3 2 1
PRINTED IN KOREA

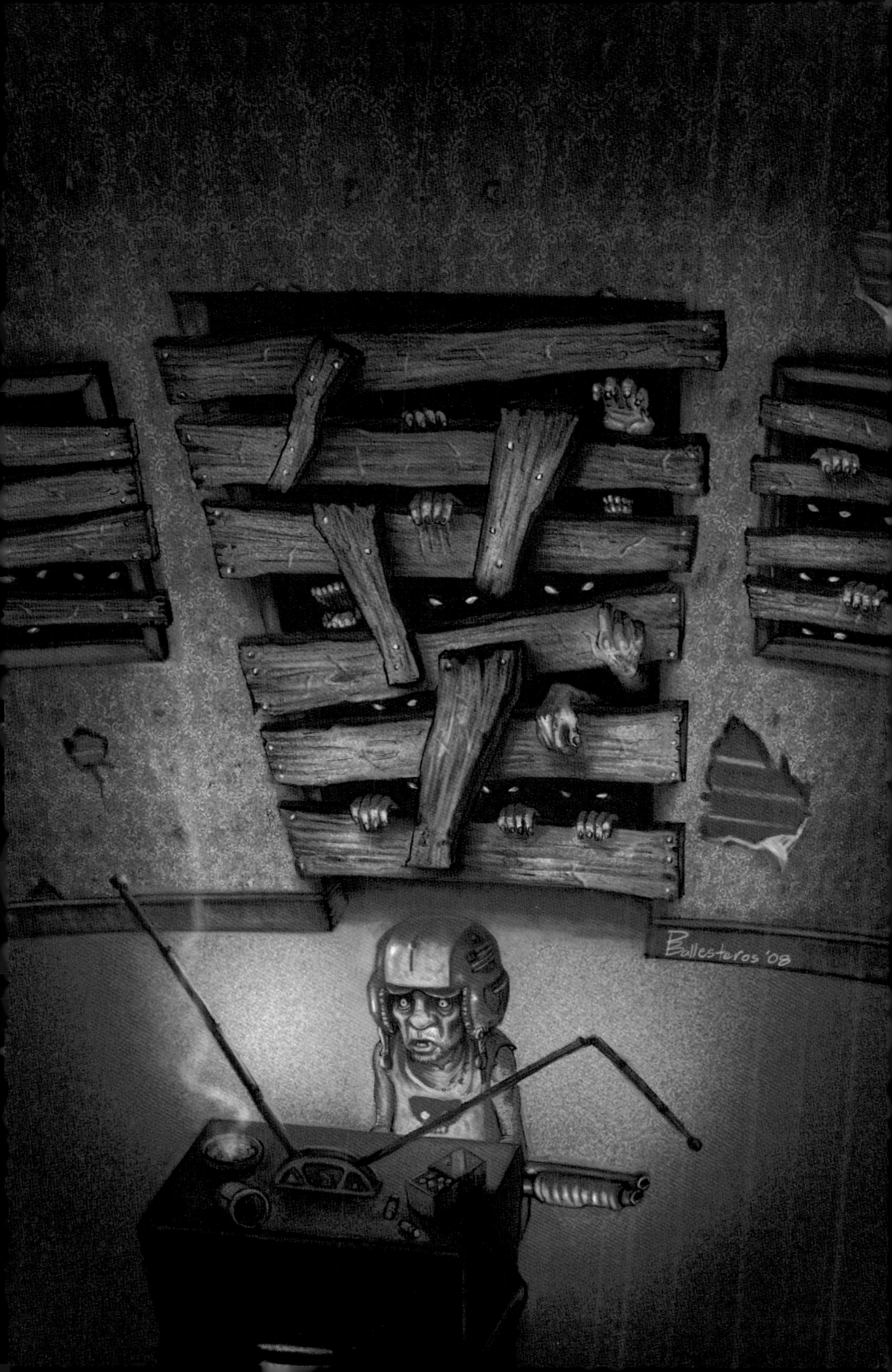
Ballesteros '08

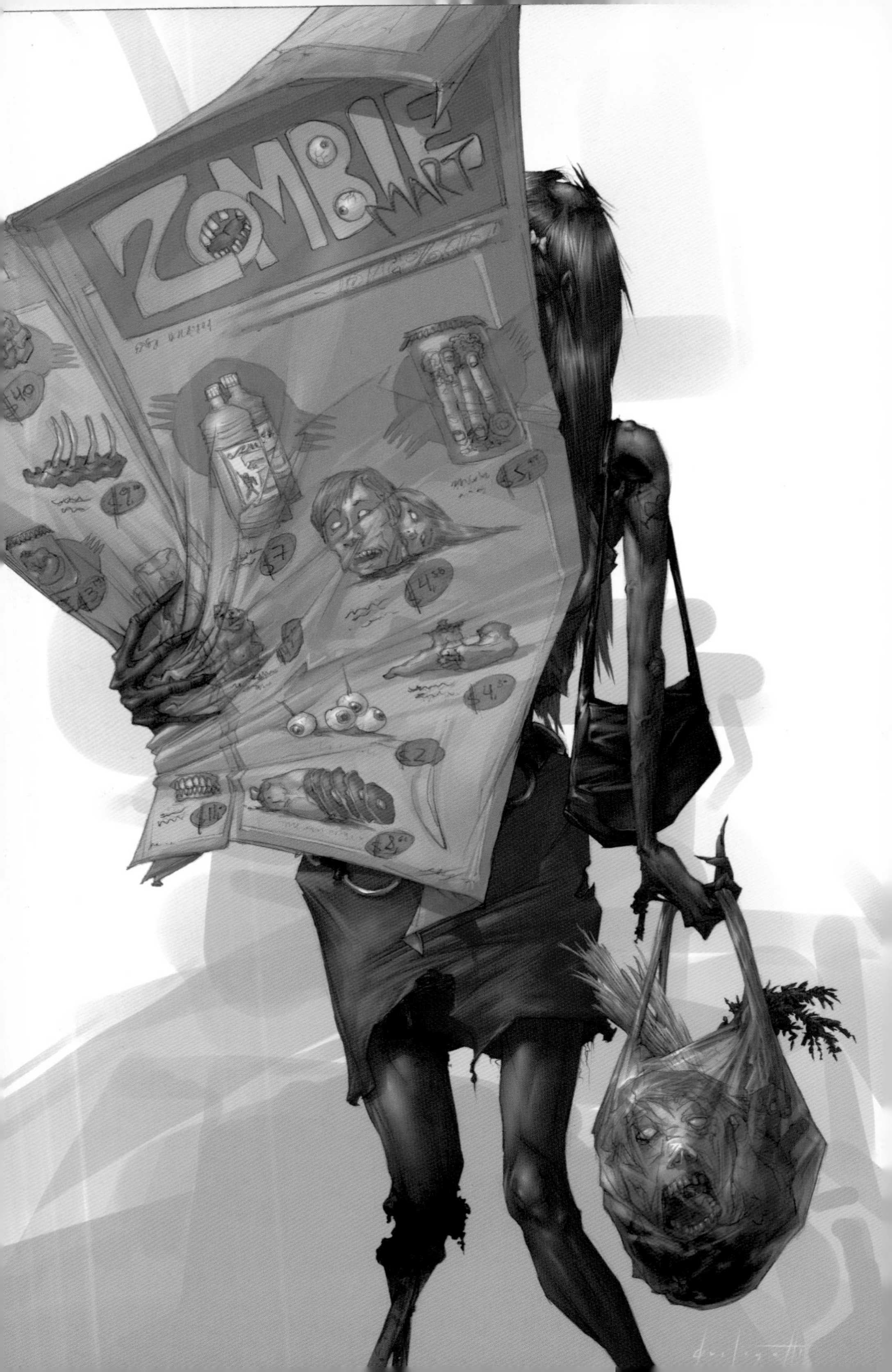
ZOMBIE
MART
$40
$7
$2

HE AIN'T HEAVEN, HE'S MY BROTHER

Story: William Messner-Loebs
Art: Matt Cossin

SANCTUARY

Story: Brian Augustyn
Art: Leno Carvalho

BAIT

Story: Ian Brill
Art: Jason Ho

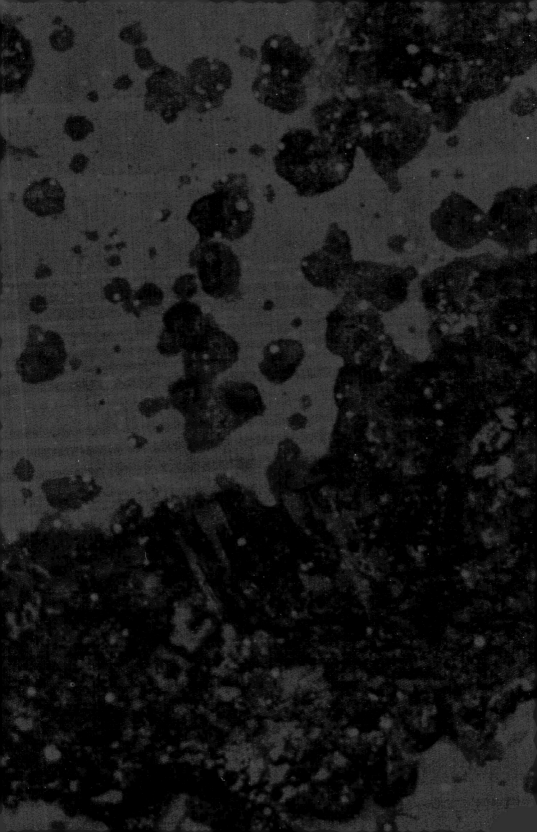

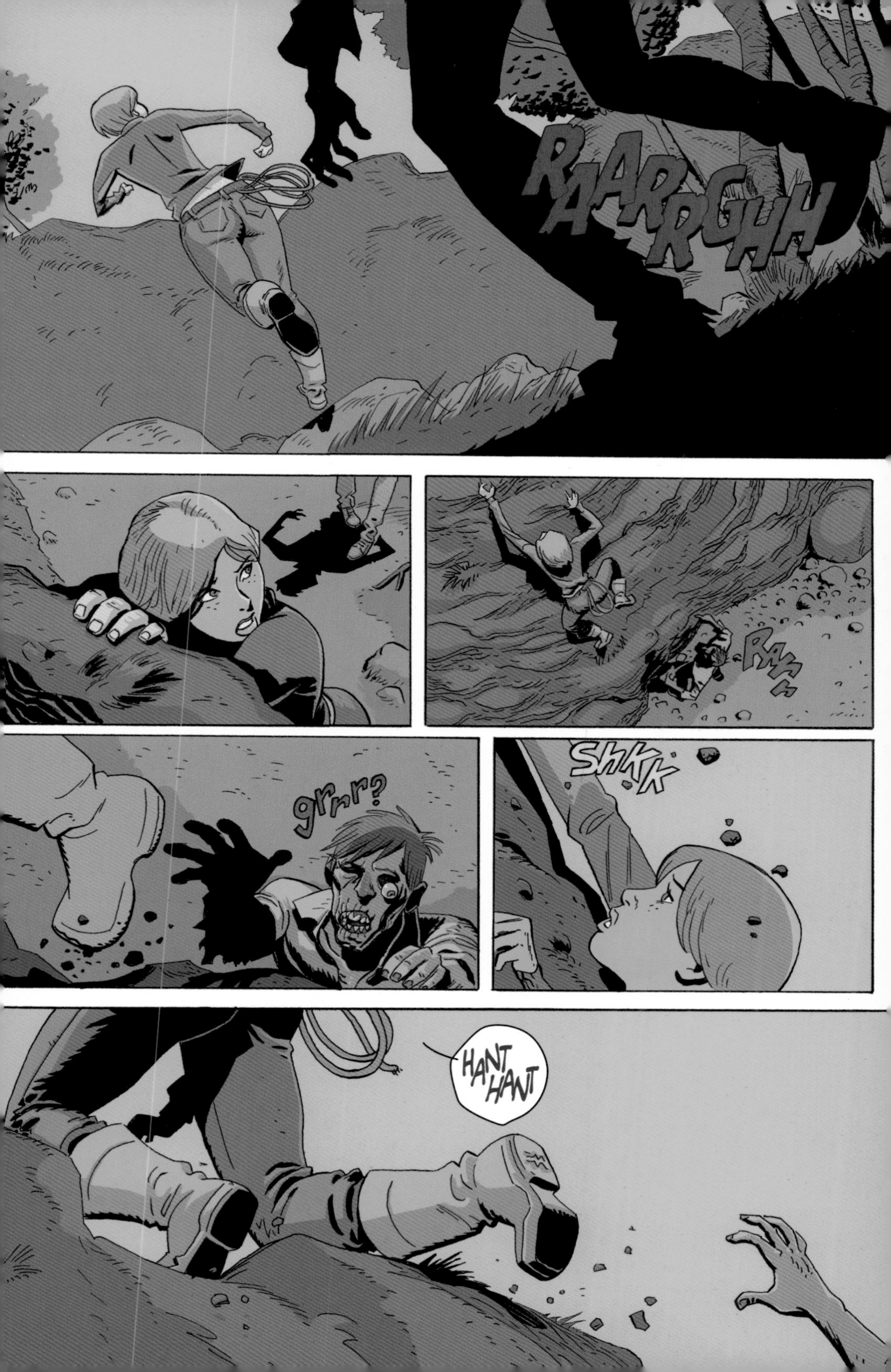
RAARRGHH
RAAR
grrr?
SHKK
HANT HANT

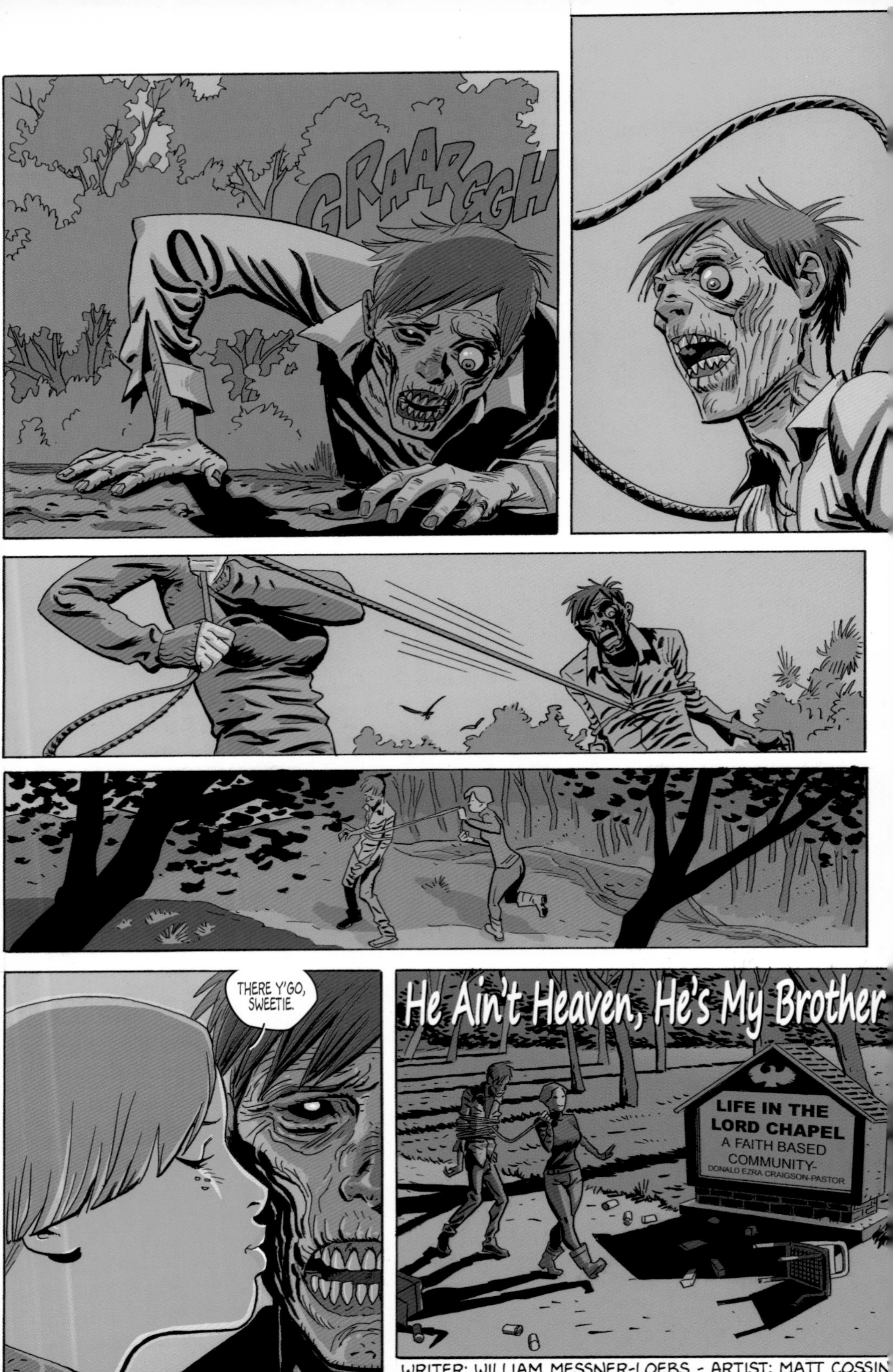
GRAARGGH
THERE Y'GO, SWEETIE.
He Ain't Heaven, He's My Brother
LIFE IN THE LORD CHAPEL
A FAITH BASED COMMUNITY-
DONALD EZRA CRAIGSON-PASTOR

WRITER: WILLIAM MESSNER-LOEBS - ARTIST: MATT COSSIN
COLORIST: MIKEY COSSIN - LETTERER: MARSHALL DILLON

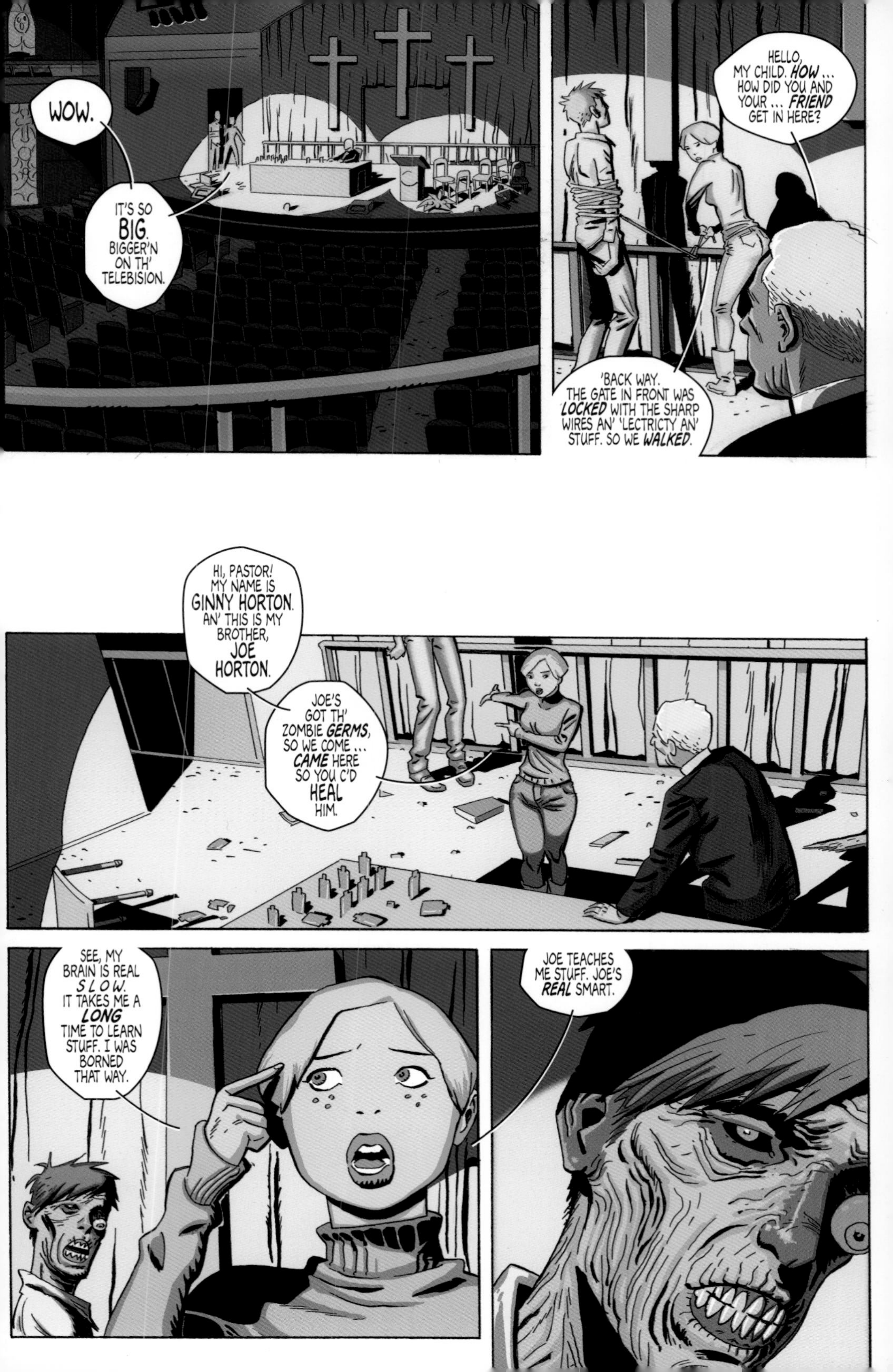
WOW.
IT'S SO BIG. BIGGER'N ON TH' TELEBISION.
HELLO, MY CHILD. HOW... HOW DID YOU AND YOUR... FRIEND GET IN HERE?
'BACK WAY. THE GATE IN FRONT WAS LOCKED WITH THE SHARP WIRES AN' 'LECTRICTY AN' STUFF. SO WE WALKED.
HI, PASTOR! MY NAME IS GINNY HORTON. AN' THIS IS MY BROTHER, JOE HORTON.
JOE'S GOT TH' ZOMBIE GERMS, SO WE COME... CAME HERE SO YOU C'D HEAL HIM.
SEE, MY BRAIN IS REAL SLOW. IT TAKES ME A LONG TIME TO LEARN STUFF. I WAS BORNED THAT WAY.
JOE TEACHES ME STUFF. JOE'S REAL SMART.

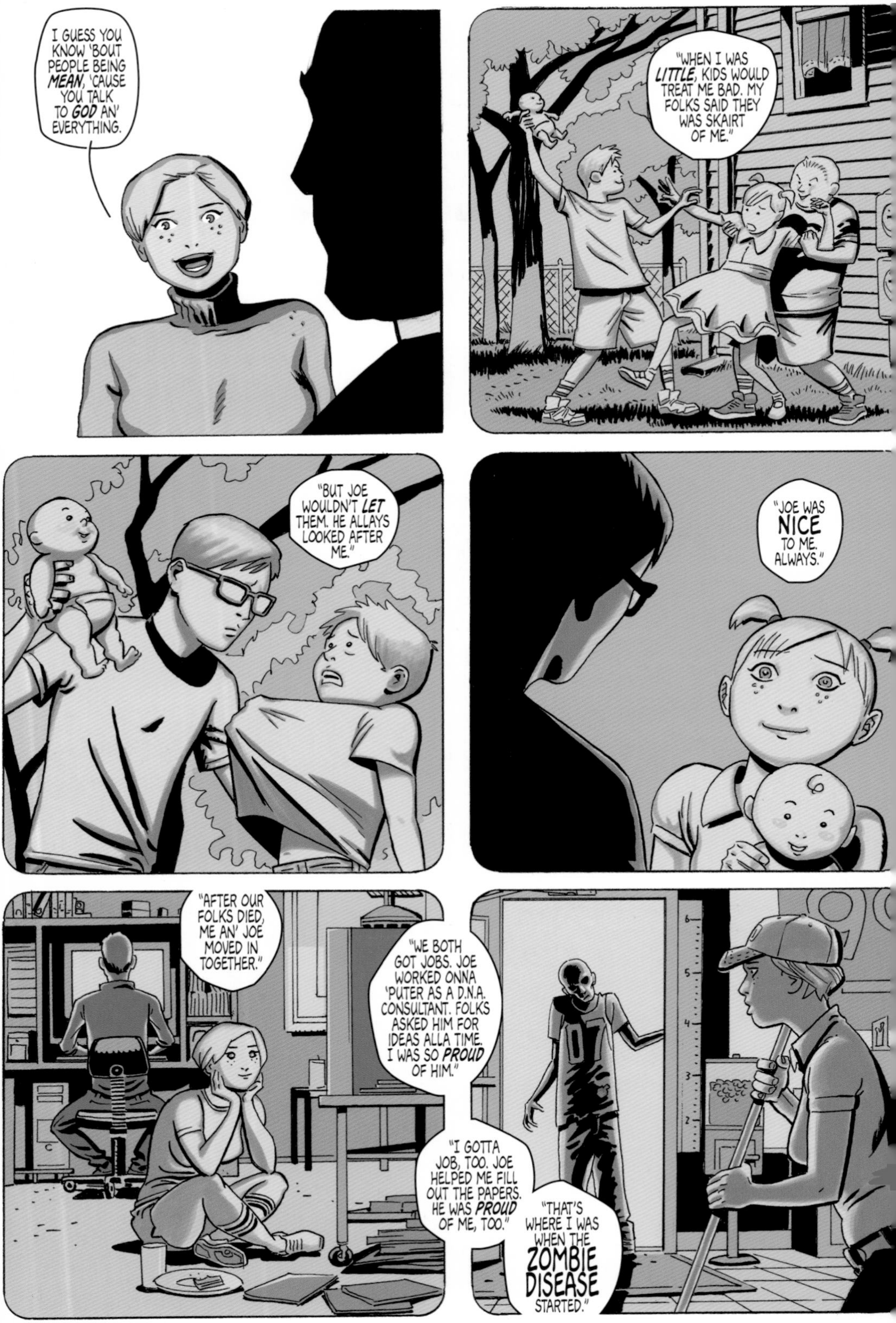
I GUESS YOU KNOW 'BOUT PEOPLE BEING MEAN, 'CAUSE YOU TALK TO GOD AN' EVERYTHING.
"WHEN I WAS LITTLE, KIDS WOULD TREAT ME BAD. MY FOLKS SAID THEY WAS SKAIRT OF ME."
"BUT JOE WOULDN'T LET THEM. HE ALLAYS LOOKED AFTER ME."
"JOE WAS NICE TO ME. ALWAYS."
"AFTER OUR FOLKS DIED, ME AN' JOE MOVED IN TOGETHER."
"WE BOTH GOT JOBS. JOE WORKED ONNA 'PUTER AS A D.N.A. CONSULTANT. FOLKS ASKED HIM FOR IDEAS ALLA TIME. I WAS SO PROUD OF HIM."
"I GOTTA JOB, TOO. JOE HELPED ME FILL OUT THE PAPERS. HE WAS PROUD OF ME, TOO."
"THAT'S WHERE I WAS WHEN THE ZOMBIE DISEASE STARTED."

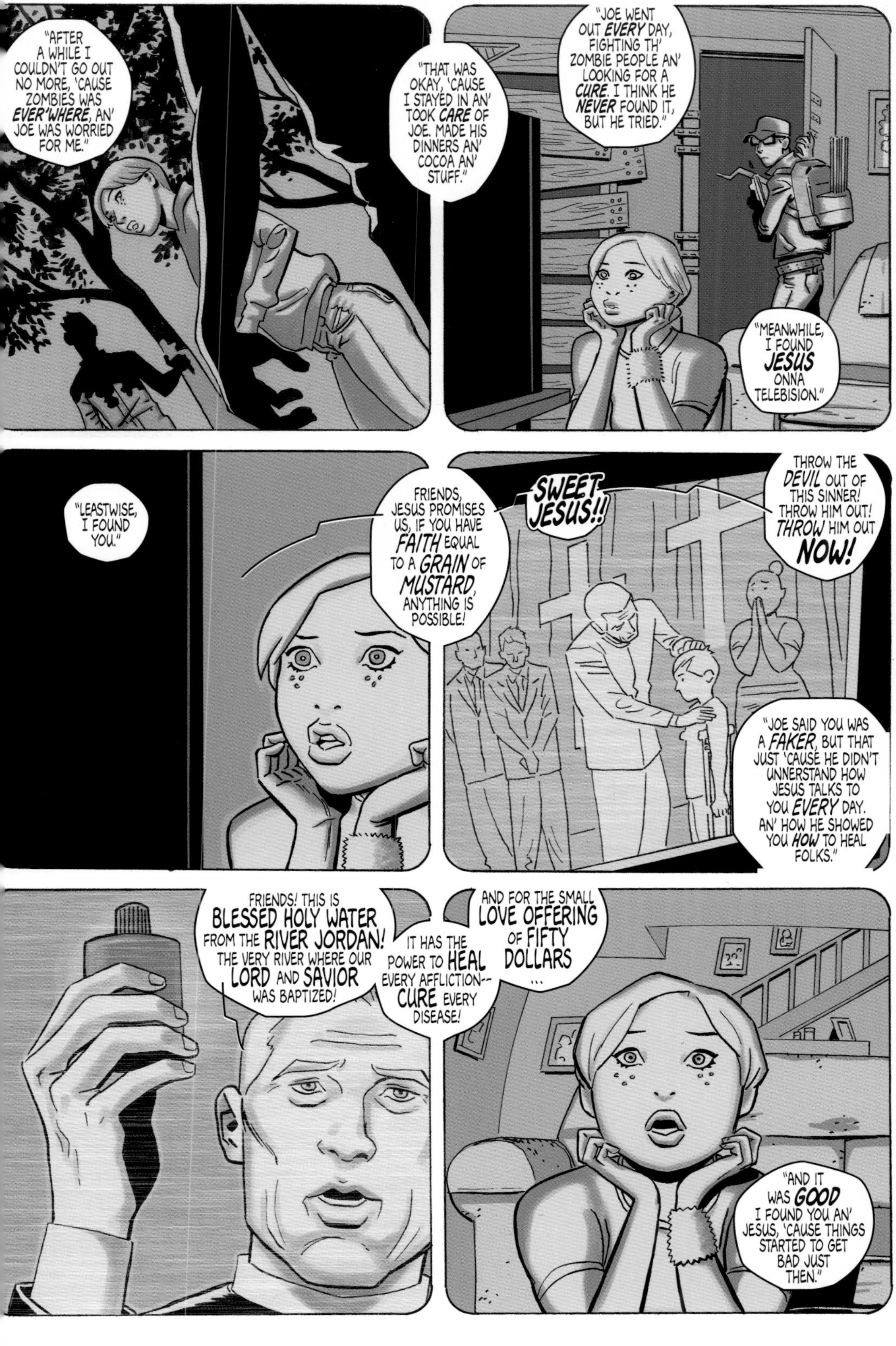
"AFTER A WHILE I COULDN'T GO OUT NO MORE, 'CAUSE ZOMBIES WAS EVER'WHERE, AN' JOE WAS WORRIED FOR ME."
"THAT WAS OKAY, 'CAUSE I STAYED IN AN' TOOK CARE OF JOE. MADE HIS DINNERS AN' COCOA AN' STUFF."
"JOE WENT OUT EVERY DAY, FIGHTING TH' ZOMBIE PEOPLE AN' LOOKING FOR A CURE. I THINK HE NEVER FOUND IT, BUT HE TRIED."
"MEANWHILE, I FOUND JESUS ONNA TELEBISION."
"LEASTWISE, I FOUND YOU."
FRIENDS, JESUS PROMISES US, IF YOU HAVE FAITH EQUAL TO A GRAIN OF MUSTARD, ANYTHING IS POSSIBLE!
SWEET JESUS!!
THROW THE DEVIL OUT OF THIS SINNER! THROW HIM OUT! THROW HIM OUT NOW!
"JOE SAID YOU WAS A FAKER, BUT THAT JUST 'CAUSE HE DIDN'T UNNERSTAND HOW JESUS TALKS TO YOU EVERY DAY. AN' HOW HE SHOWED YOU HOW TO HEAL FOLKS."
FRIENDS! THIS IS BLESSED HOLY WATER FROM THE RIVER JORDAN! THE VERY RIVER WHERE OUR LORD AND SAVIOR WAS BAPTIZED!
IT HAS THE POWER TO HEAL EVERY AFFLICTION-- CURE EVERY DISEASE!
AND FOR THE SMALL LOVE OFFERING OF FIFTY DOLLARS ...
"AND IT WAS GOOD I FOUND YOU AN' JESUS, 'CAUSE THINGS STARTED TO GET BAD JUST THEN."

SEE, JOE GOT BIT, AN' HE TRIED REALLY, REALLY HARD *NOT* TO TURN INTO A ZOMBIE BUT HE DID ANYHOW. AN' I HID HIM INNA HOUSE, BUT HE WANTED TO GET OUT SO HE C'D *FEED.* AN' HE WAS REALLY HUNGRY. AN' I DIDN'T KNOW WHAT TO DO ...

THEN I 'MEMBERED HOW YOU AN' JESUS *HEAL* PEOPLE. SO I BROUGHT *JOE* AN' I BROUGHT *FIFTY DOLLARS* ...

UM, PASTOR ... ?

HAHAHAHAAAAHA

YOU WORTHLESS LITTLE *FOOL!* WHAT MAKES YOU THINK THERE'S A *GOD?* THERE IS **NO** GOD!!

ONE OF THOSE DAMNED *THINGS* GOT IN HERE... *BIT ME!* BIT US *ALL!*

MY BEAUTIFUL *MANSIO* MY OFF-SHORE *ACCOUNTS!* WHAT DO ANY OF IT MATTER? LIFETIME OF BLATHERI *NONSENSE* TO *IDIOT.* ALL COME TO NOTHIN

MY *LOYAL* STAFF ALL TURNED TO ZOMBIES! THEY WANTED THE *WATER,* TOO ... THE *HOLY TAP WATER!*

I LACED IT WITH *RAT POISON! THEY* WON'T EAT ME *ALIVE!!* HEH HEH HEH!

BUT... THIS IS THE WATER *GOD BLESSED.* IT'S *JESUS WATER* ... I SAW IT ON TH' TELEBISION.

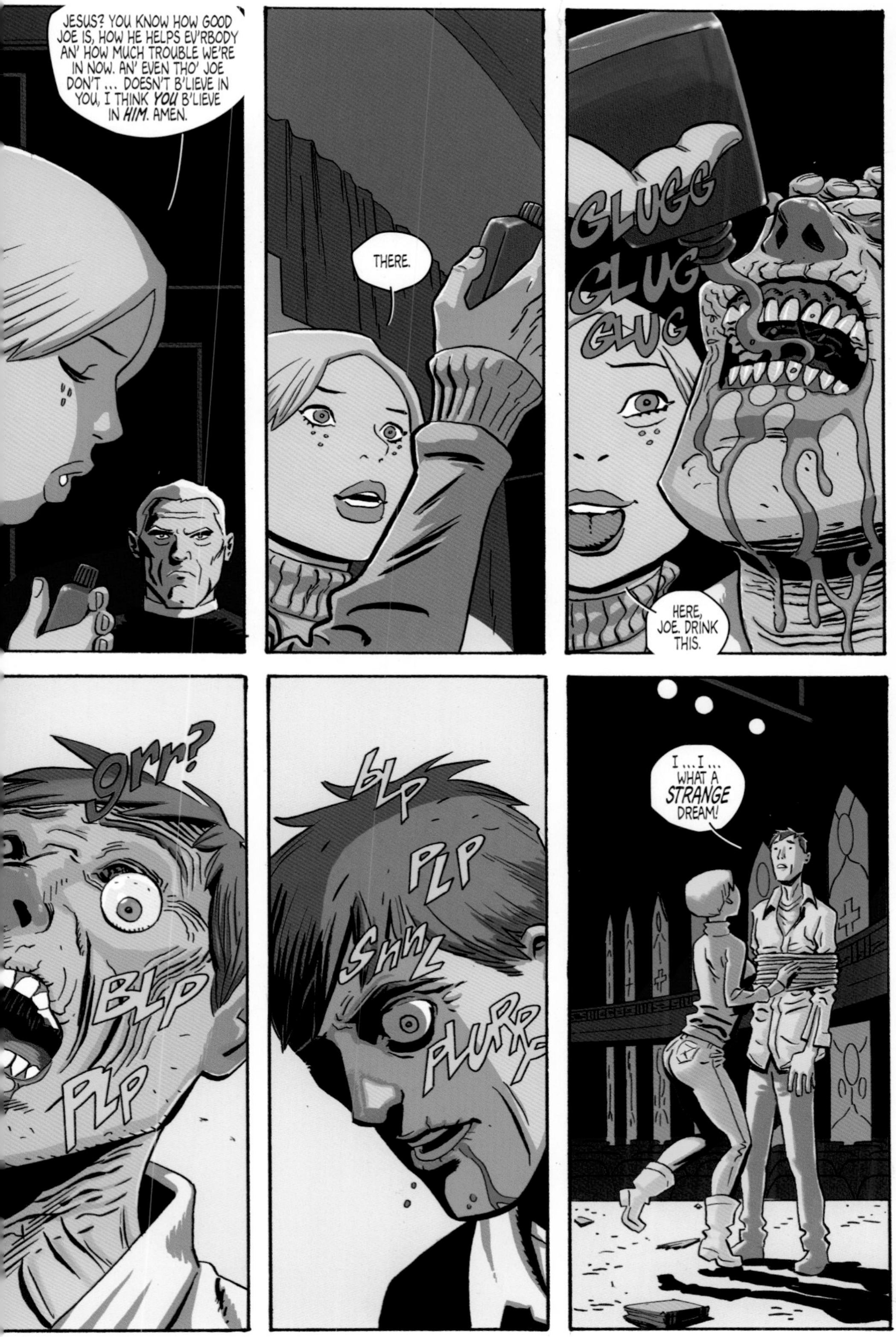

JESUS? YOU KNOW HOW GOOD JOE IS, HOW HE HELPS EV'RBODY AN' HOW MUCH TROUBLE WE'RE IN NOW. AN' EVEN THO' JOE DON'T ... DOESN'T B'LIEVE IN YOU, I THINK YOU B'LIEVE IN HIM. AMEN.
THERE.
GLUGG
GLUG
GLUG
HERE, JOE. DRINK THIS.
grrr?
BLP
PLP
bLP
PLP
SHNL
FLURP
I ... I ... WHAT A STRANGE DREAM!

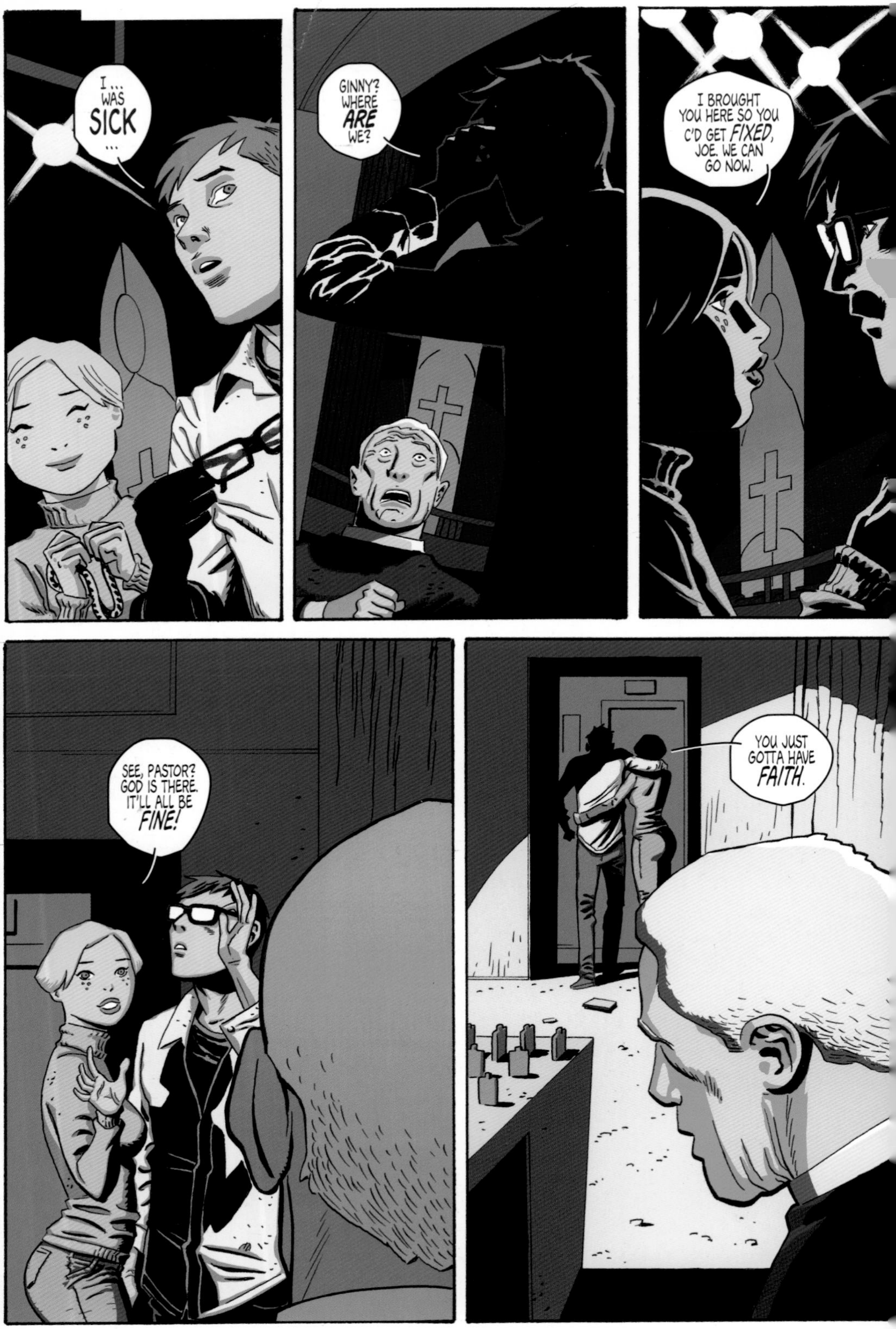
I... WAS SICK ...
GINNY? WHERE ARE WE?
I BROUGHT YOU HERE SO YOU C'D GET FIXED, JOE. WE CAN GO NOW.
SEE, PASTOR? GOD IS THERE. IT'LL ALL BE FINE!
YOU JUST GOTTA HAVE FAITH.

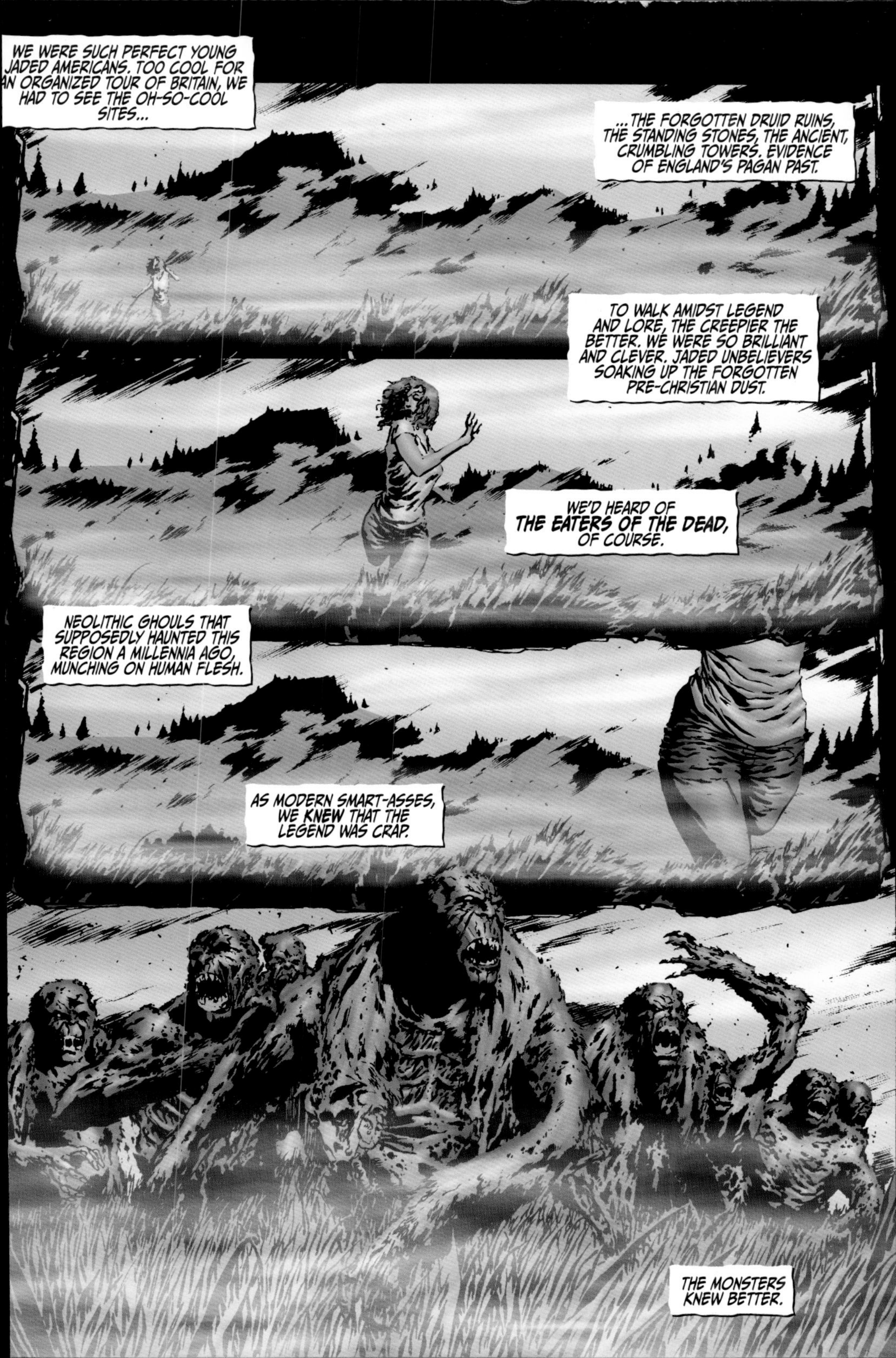
WE WERE SUCH PERFECT YOUNG JADED AMERICANS. TOO COOL FOR AN ORGANIZED TOUR OF BRITAIN, WE HAD TO SEE THE OH-SO-COOL SITES...
...THE FORGOTTEN DRUID RUINS, THE STANDING STONES, THE ANCIENT, CRUMBLING TOWERS. EVIDENCE OF ENGLAND'S PAGAN PAST.
TO WALK AMIDST LEGEND AND LORE, THE CREEPIER THE BETTER. WE WERE SO BRILLIANT AND CLEVER. JADED UNBELIEVERS SOAKING UP THE FORGOTTEN PRE-CHRISTIAN DUST.
WE'D HEARD OF **THE EATERS OF THE DEAD,** OF COURSE.
NEOLITHIC GHOULS THAT SUPPOSEDLY HAUNTED THIS REGION A MILLENNIA AGO, MUNCHING ON HUMAN FLESH.
AS MODERN SMART-ASSES, WE *KNEW* THAT THE LEGEND WAS CRAP.
THE MONSTERS KNEW BETTER.

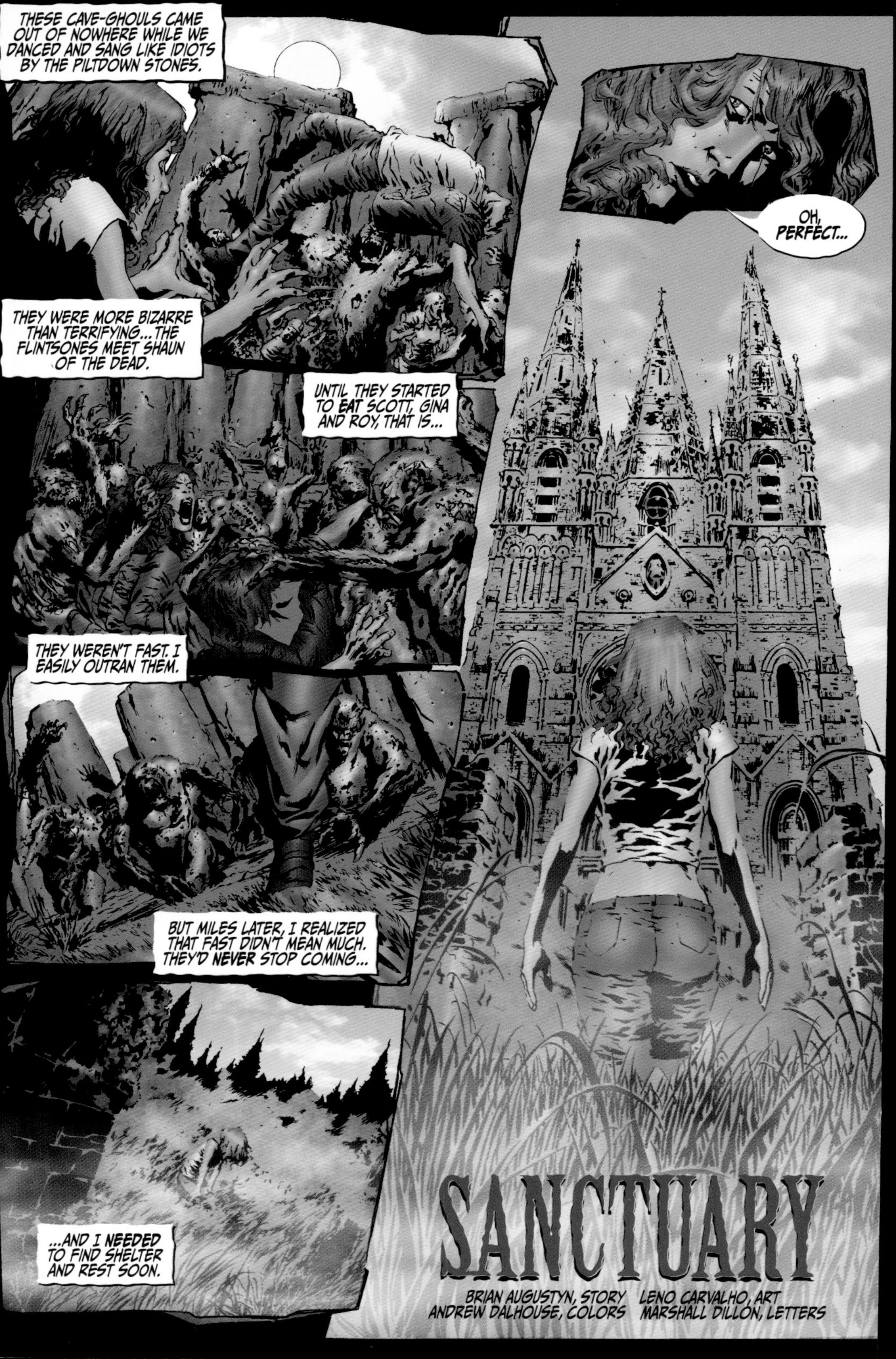
THESE CAVE-GHOULS CAME OUT OF NOWHERE WHILE WE DANCED AND SANG LIKE IDIOTS BY THE PILTDOWN STONES.
THEY WERE MORE BIZARRE THAN TERRIFYING...THE FLINTSONES MEET SHAUN OF THE DEAD.
UNTIL THEY STARTED TO EAT SCOTT, GINA AND ROY, THAT IS...
THEY WEREN'T FAST. I EASILY OUTRAN THEM.
BUT MILES LATER, I REALIZED THAT FAST DIDN'T MEAN MUCH. THEY'D NEVER STOP COMING...
...AND I NEEDED TO FIND SHELTER AND REST SOON.
OH, PERFECT...
SANCTUARY
BRIAN AUGUSTYN, STORY LENO CARVALHO, ART
ANDREW DALHOUSE, COLORS MARSHALL DILLON, LETTERS

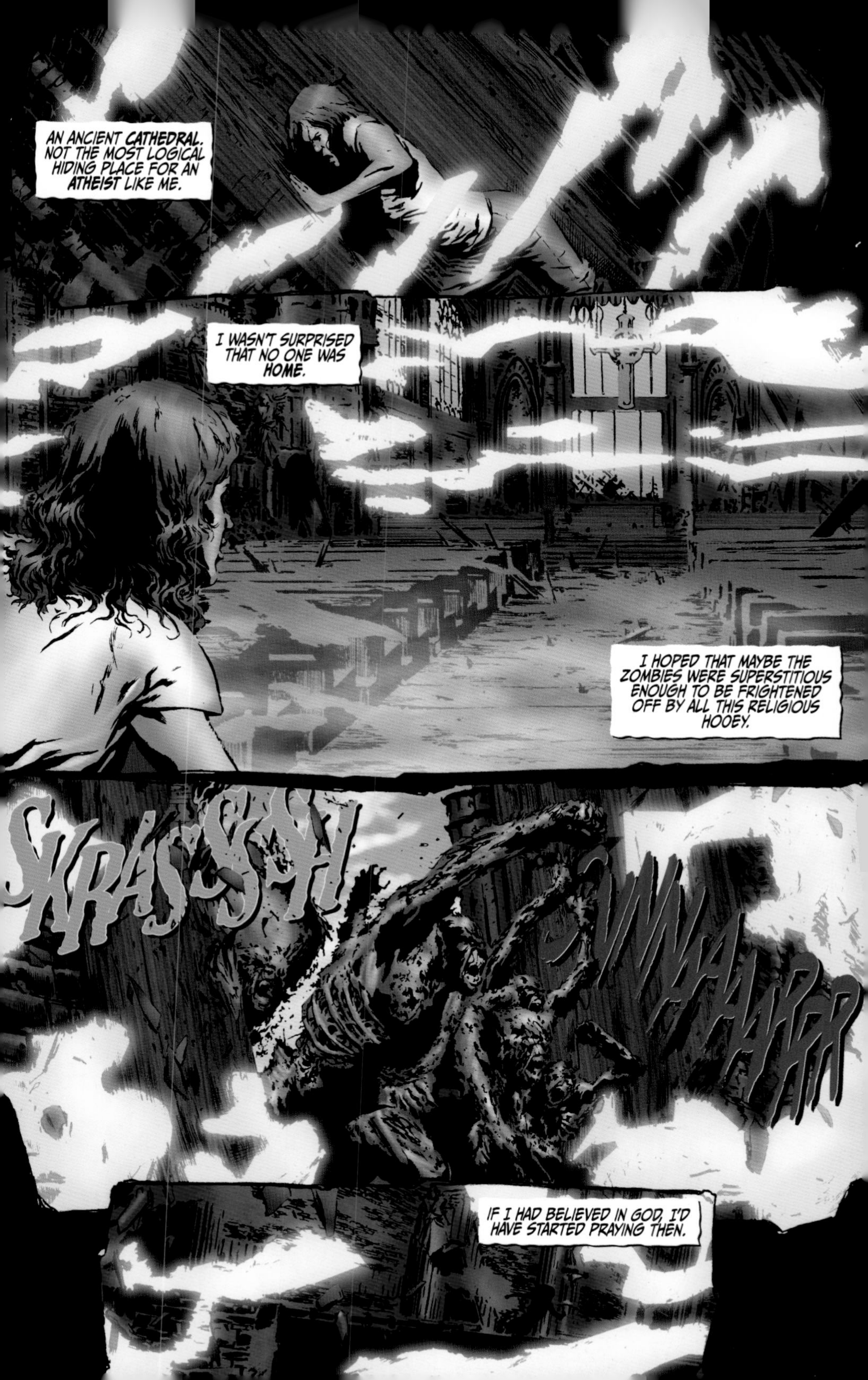
AN ANCIENT CATHEDRAL. NOT THE MOST LOGICAL HIDING PLACE FOR AN ATHEIST LIKE ME.
I WASN'T SURPRISED THAT NO ONE WAS HOME.
I HOPED THAT MAYBE THE ZOMBIES WERE SUPERSTITIOUS ENOUGH TO BE FRIGHTENED OFF BY ALL THIS RELIGIOUS HOOEY.
SKRASSSH
UNNAAARRR
IF I HAD BELIEVED IN GOD, I'D HAVE STARTED PRAYING THEN.

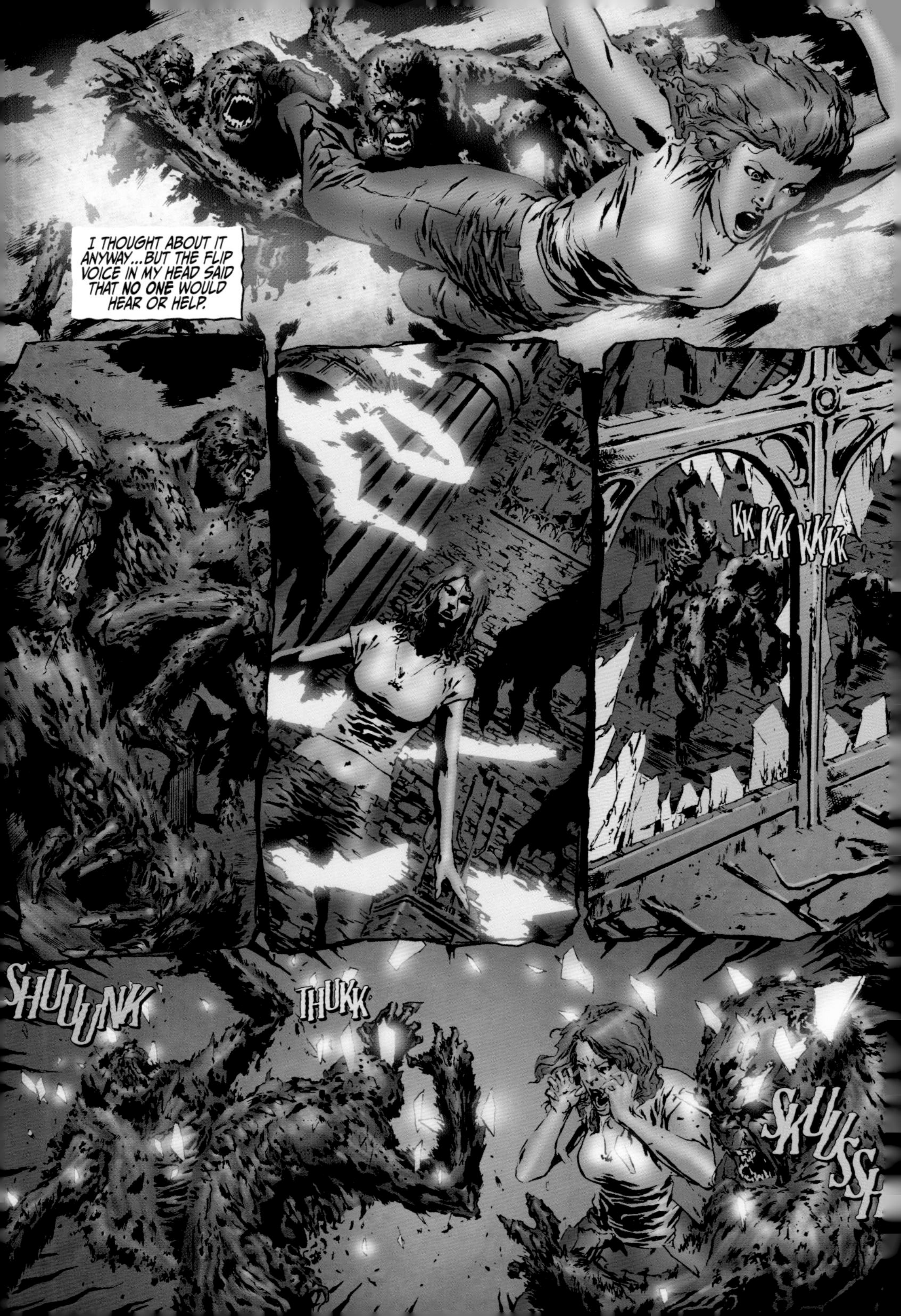
I THOUGHT ABOUT IT ANYWAY...BUT THE FLIP VOICE IN MY HEAD SAID THAT NO ONE WOULD HEAR OR HELP.
KKKKKKKKK
SHUUUNK
THUKK
SKUSSH

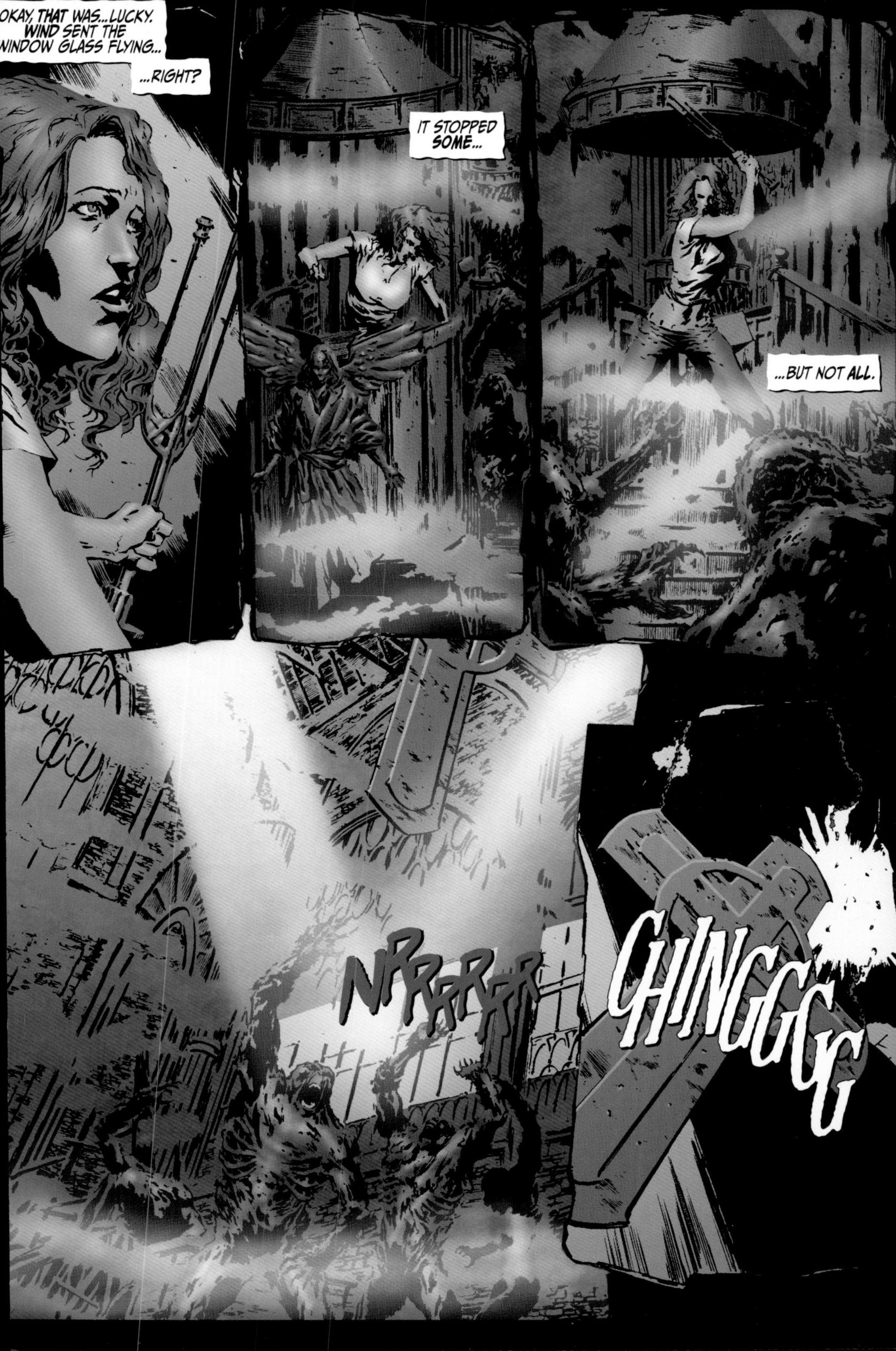
OKAY, THAT WAS...LUCKY. WIND SENT THE WINDOW GLASS FLYING...
...RIGHT?
IT STOPPED SOME...
...BUT NOT ALL.
NRRRRRR
CHINGGGG

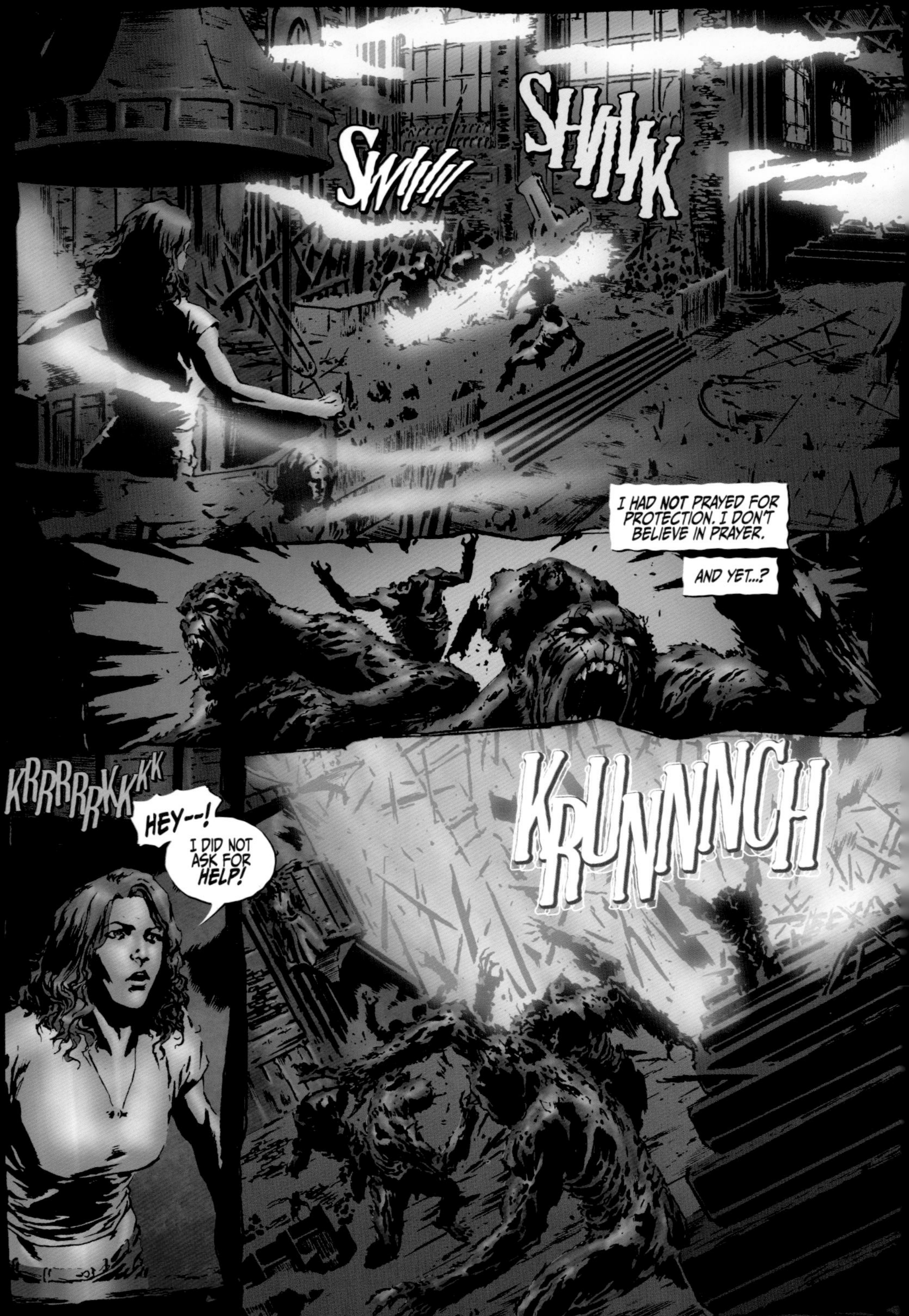
SWIIIII
SHNNK
I HAD NOT PRAYED FOR PROTECTION. I DON'T BELIEVE IN PRAYER.
AND YET...?
KRRRRRRKKKKK
HEY--!
I DID NOT ASK FOR HELP!
KRUNNNCH

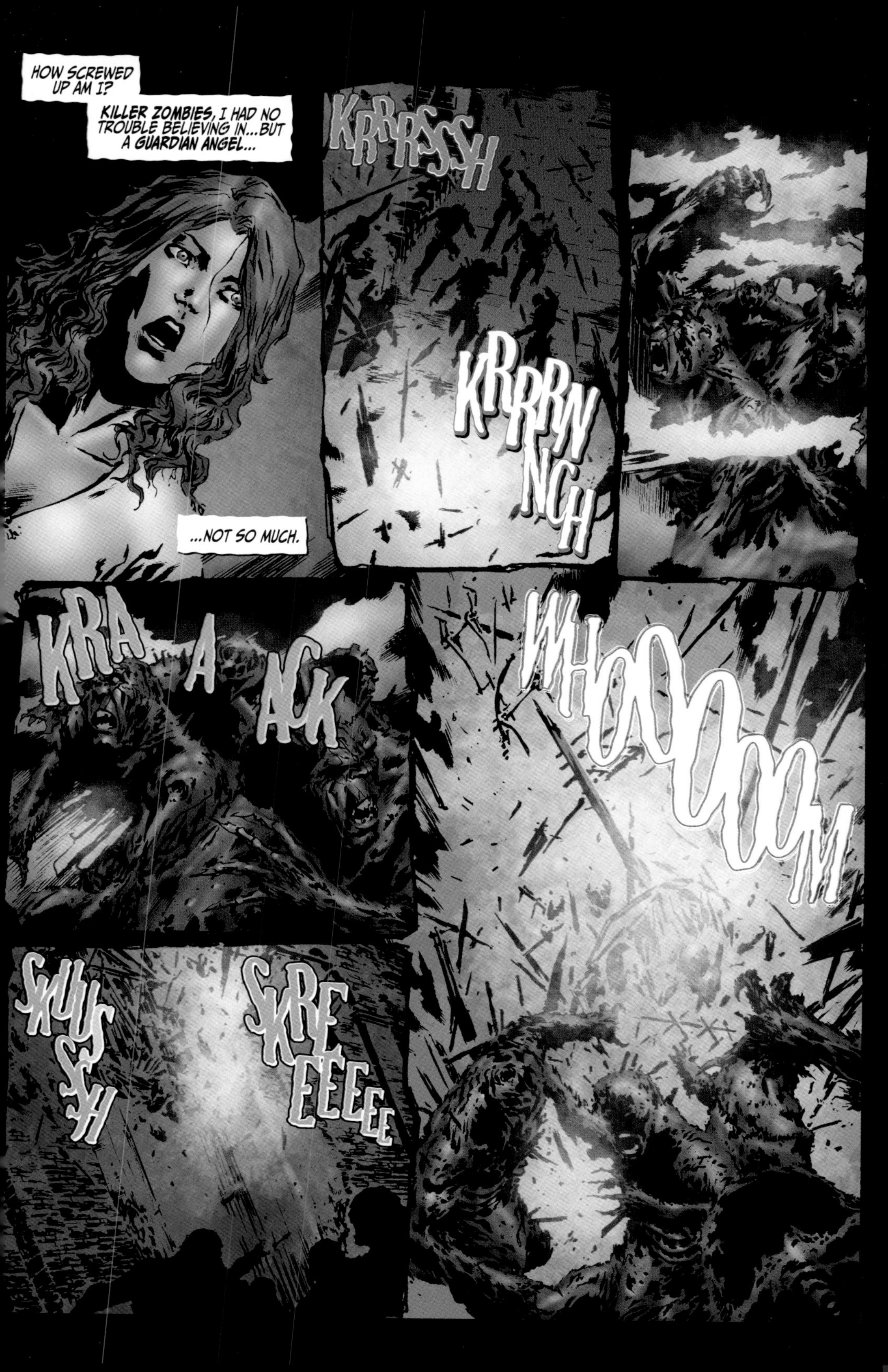
HOW SCREWED UP AM I?
KILLER ZOMBIES, I HAD NO TROUBLE BELIEVING IN...BUT A GUARDIAN ANGEL...
...NOT SO MUCH.
KRRRSSSH
KRRRRNNCH
KRAAACK
WHOOOOOOM
SKUUSSSH
SKREEEEEE

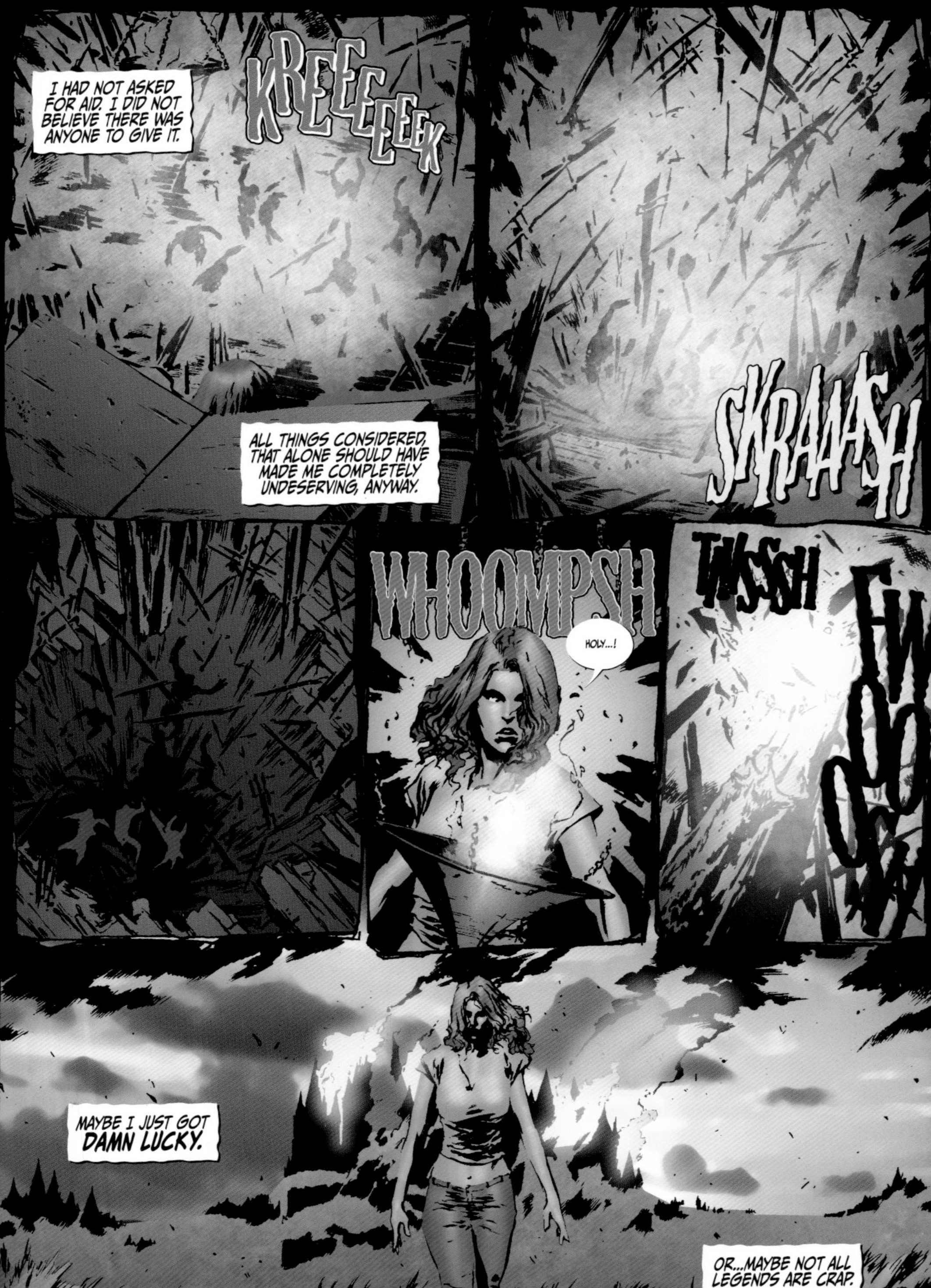
I HAD NOT ASKED FOR AID. I DID NOT BELIEVE THERE WAS ANYONE TO GIVE IT.
KREEEEEEK
ALL THINGS CONSIDERED, THAT ALONE SHOULD HAVE MADE ME COMPLETELY UNDESERVING, ANYWAY.
SKRAAASH
WHOOMPSH
HOLY...!
TWSSH
MAYBE I JUST GOT DAMN LUCKY.
OR...MAYBE NOT ALL LEGENDS ARE CRAP.

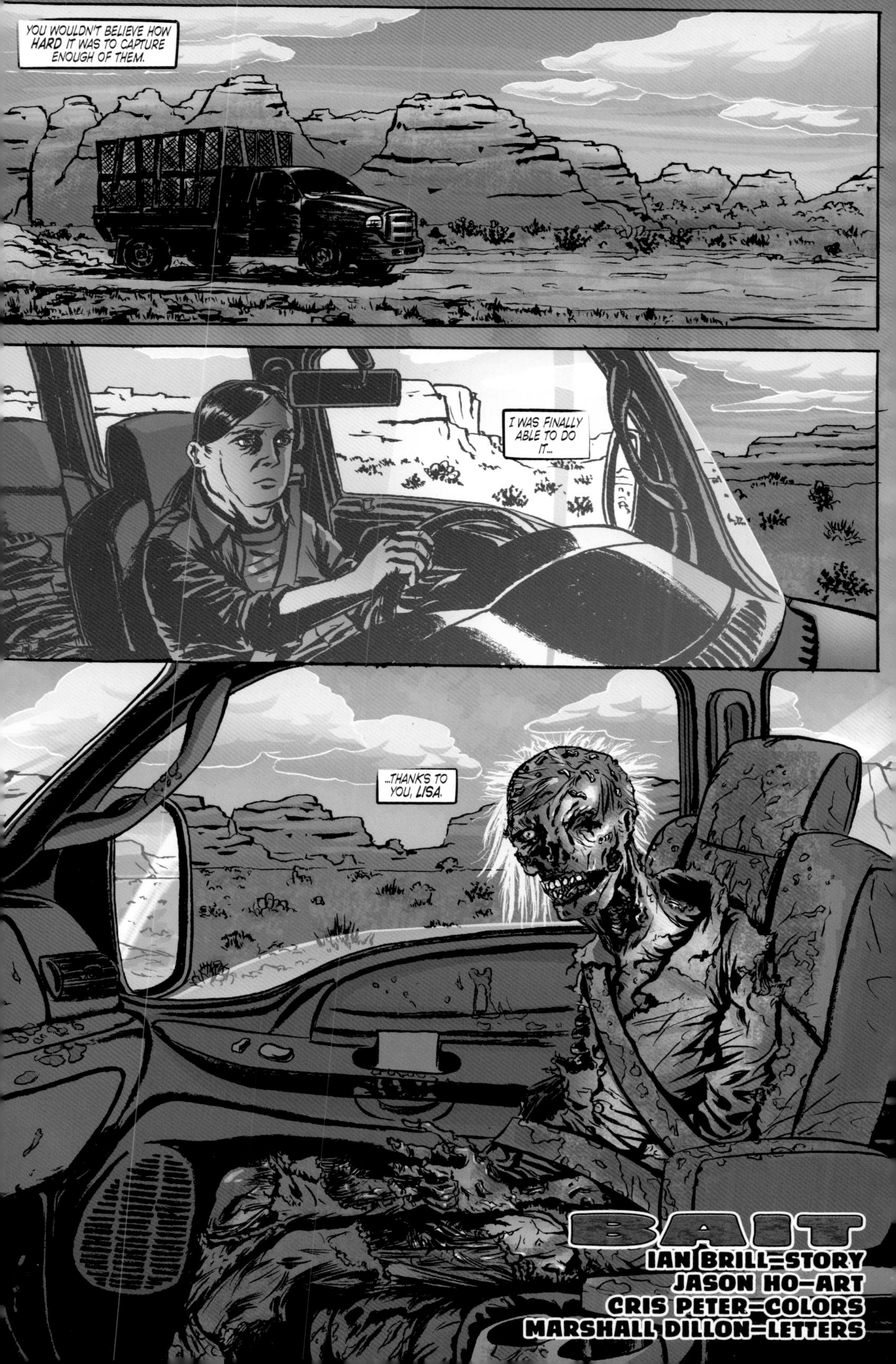
YOU WOULDN'T BELIEVE HOW HARD IT WAS TO CAPTURE ENOUGH OF THEM.
I WAS FINALLY ABLE TO DO IT...
...THANKS TO YOU, LISA.
BAIT
IAN BRILL–STORY
JASON HO–ART
CRIS PETER–COLORS
MARSHALL DILLON–LETTERS

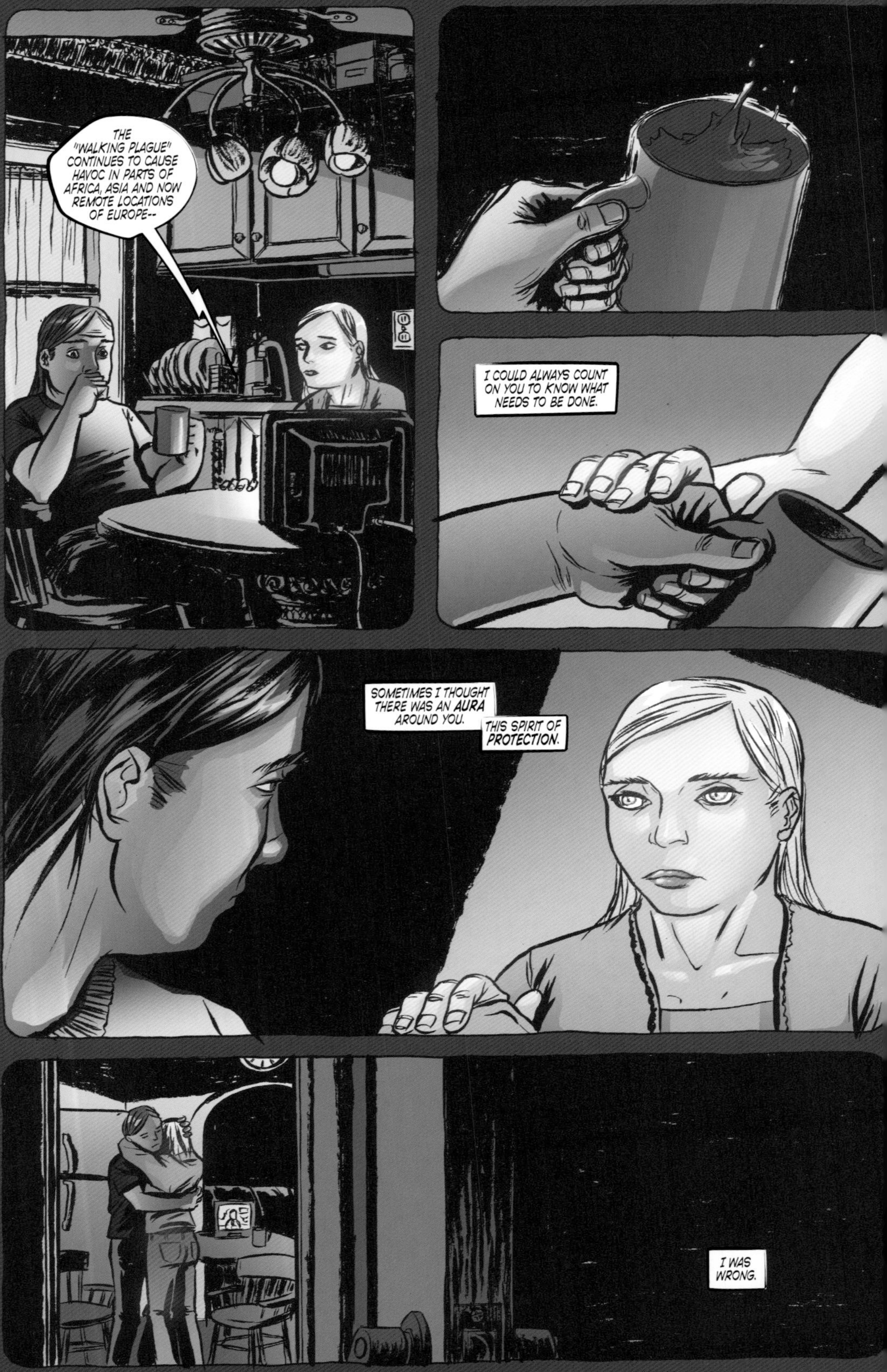
THE "WALKING PLAGUE" CONTINUES TO CAUSE HAVOC IN PARTS OF AFRICA, ASIA AND NOW REMOTE LOCATIONS OF EUROPE--
I COULD ALWAYS COUNT ON YOU TO KNOW WHAT NEEDS TO BE DONE.
SOMETIMES I THOUGHT THERE WAS AN AURA AROUND YOU.
THIS SPIRIT OF PROTECTION.
I WAS WRONG.

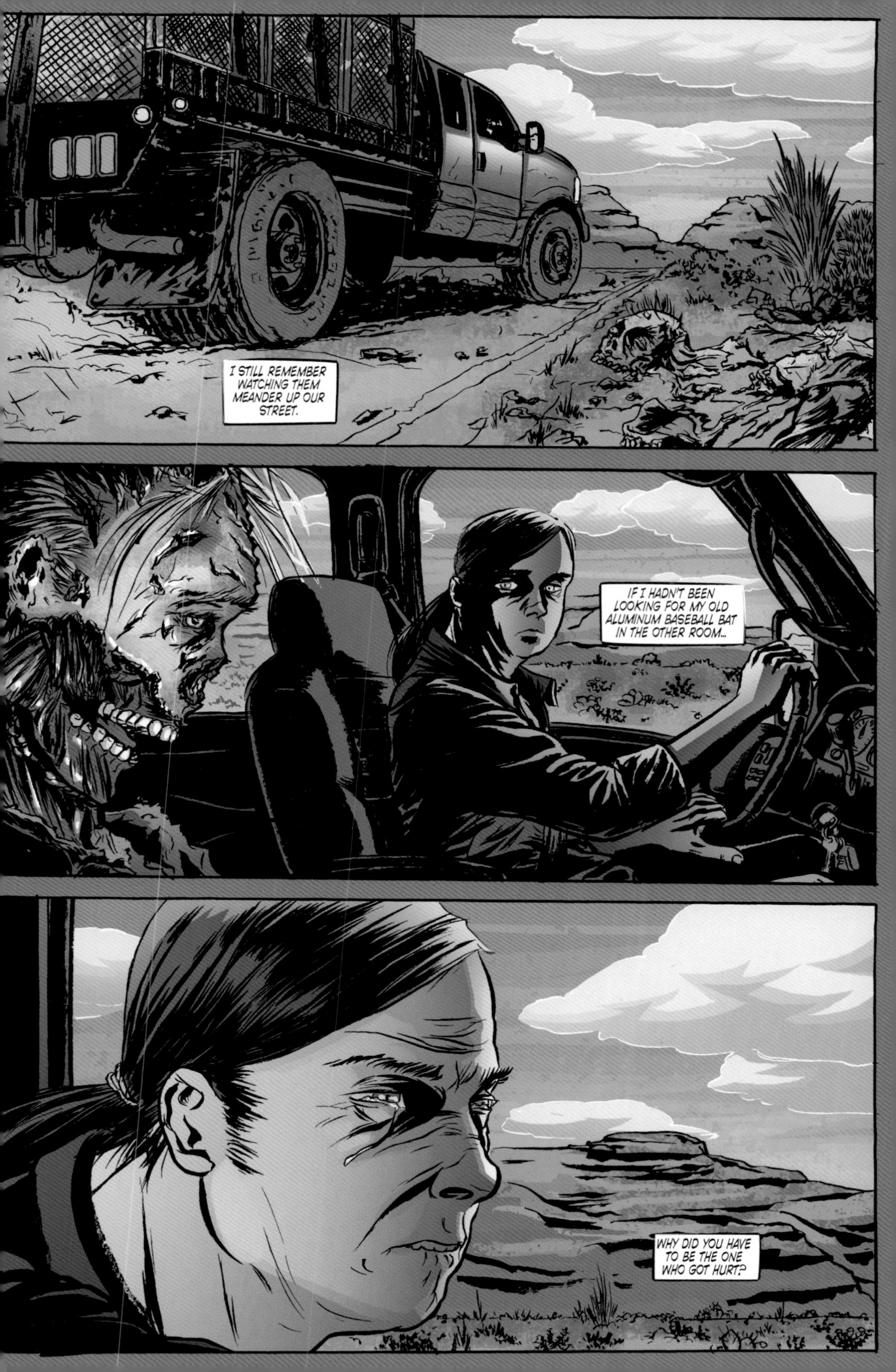
I STILL REMEMBER WATCHING THEM MEANDER UP OUR STREET.
IF I HADN'T BEEN LOOKING FOR MY OLD ALUMINUM BASEBALL BAT IN THE OTHER ROOM...
WHY DID YOU HAVE TO BE THE ONE WHO GOT HURT?

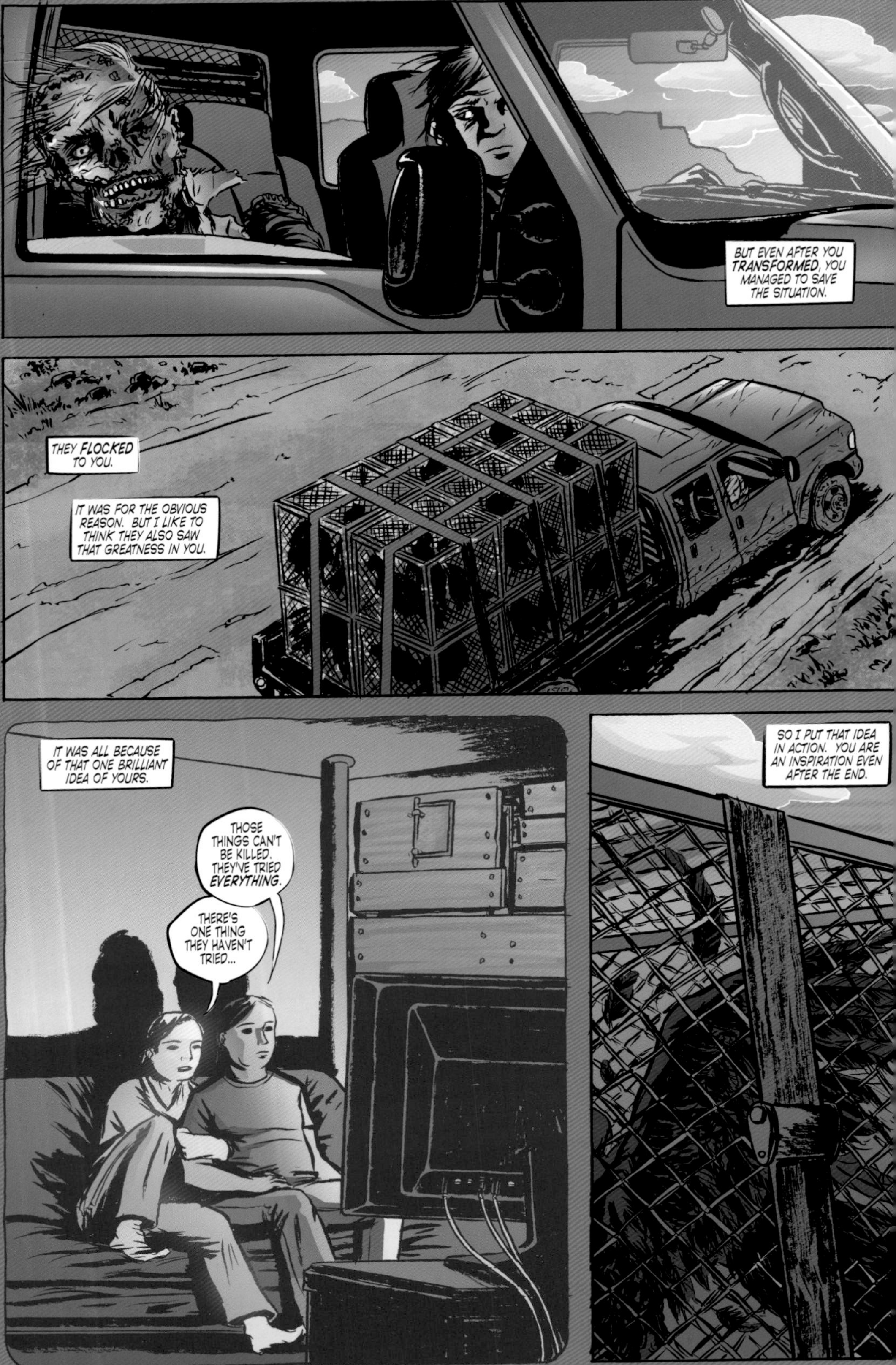
BUT EVEN AFTER YOU TRANSFORMED, YOU MANAGED TO SAVE THE SITUATION.
THEY FLOCKED TO YOU.
IT WAS FOR THE OBVIOUS REASON. BUT I LIKE TO THINK THEY ALSO SAW THAT GREATNESS IN YOU.
IT WAS ALL BECAUSE OF THAT ONE BRILLIANT IDEA OF YOURS.
THOSE THINGS CAN'T BE KILLED. THEY'VE TRIED EVERYTHING.
THERE'S ONE THING THEY HAVEN'T TRIED...
SO I PUT THAT IDEA IN ACTION. YOU ARE AN INSPIRATION EVEN AFTER THE END.

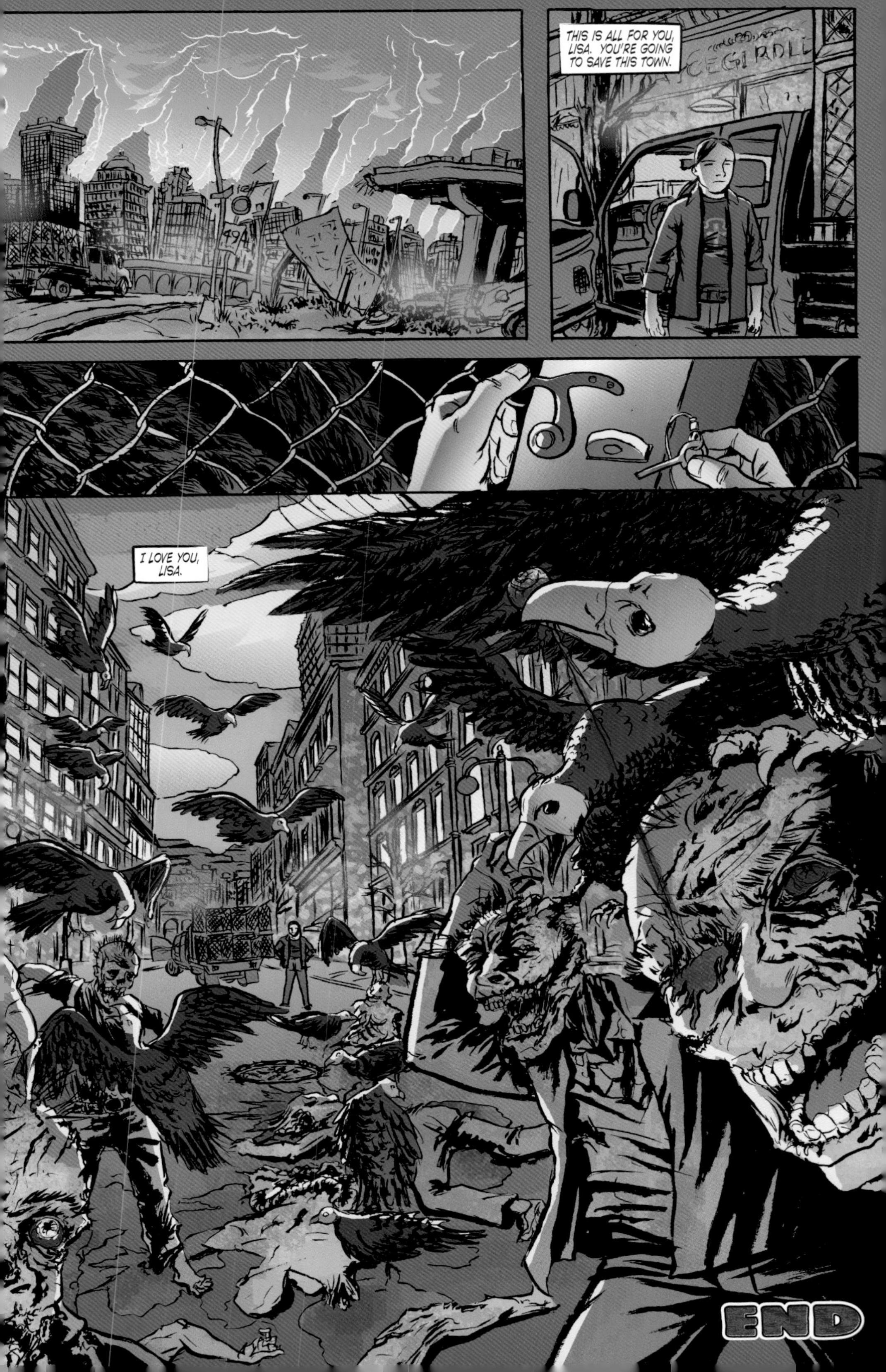
THIS IS ALL FOR YOU, LISA. YOU'RE GOING TO SAVE THIS TOWN.
I LOVE YOU, LISA.
END

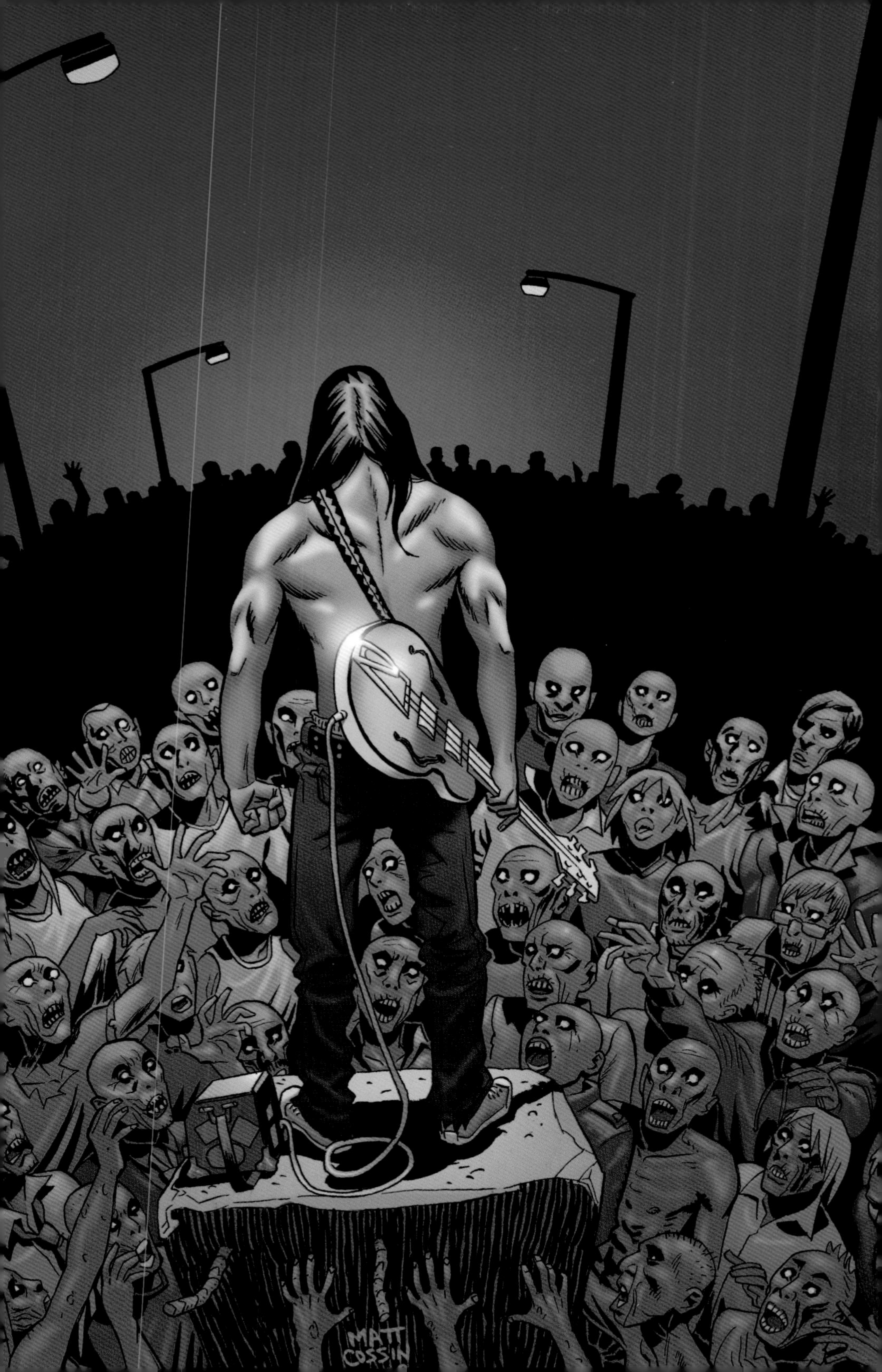
MATT
COSSIN

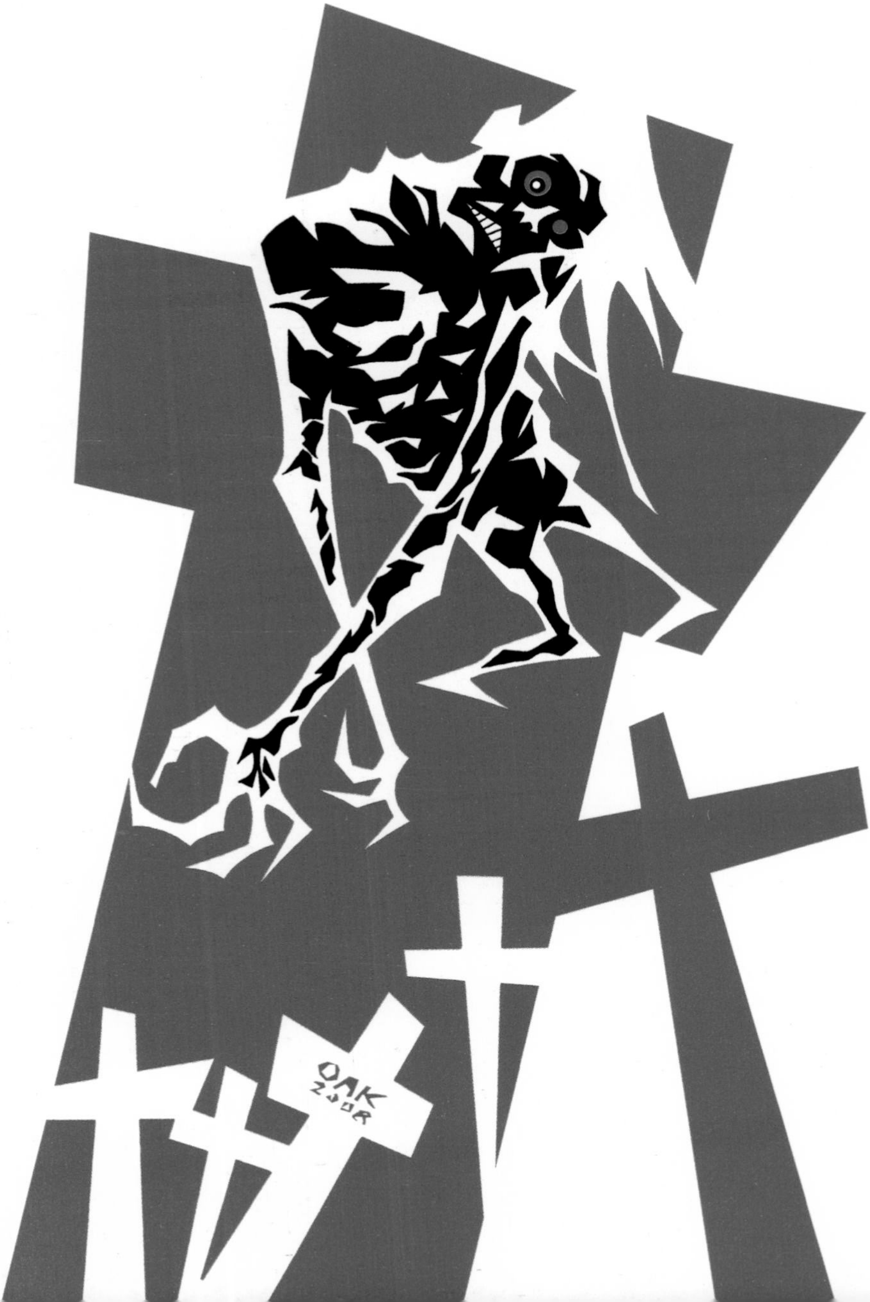
OAK
2008

HEADSHOT

Story: MONTE COOK
Art: JEREMY ROCK

I DON'T LIKE HENRY CARVE

Story: IAN BRILL
Art: TOBY CYPRESS

DEVIL DOGS

Story: PIERLUIGI COTHRAN
Art: TODD HERMAN

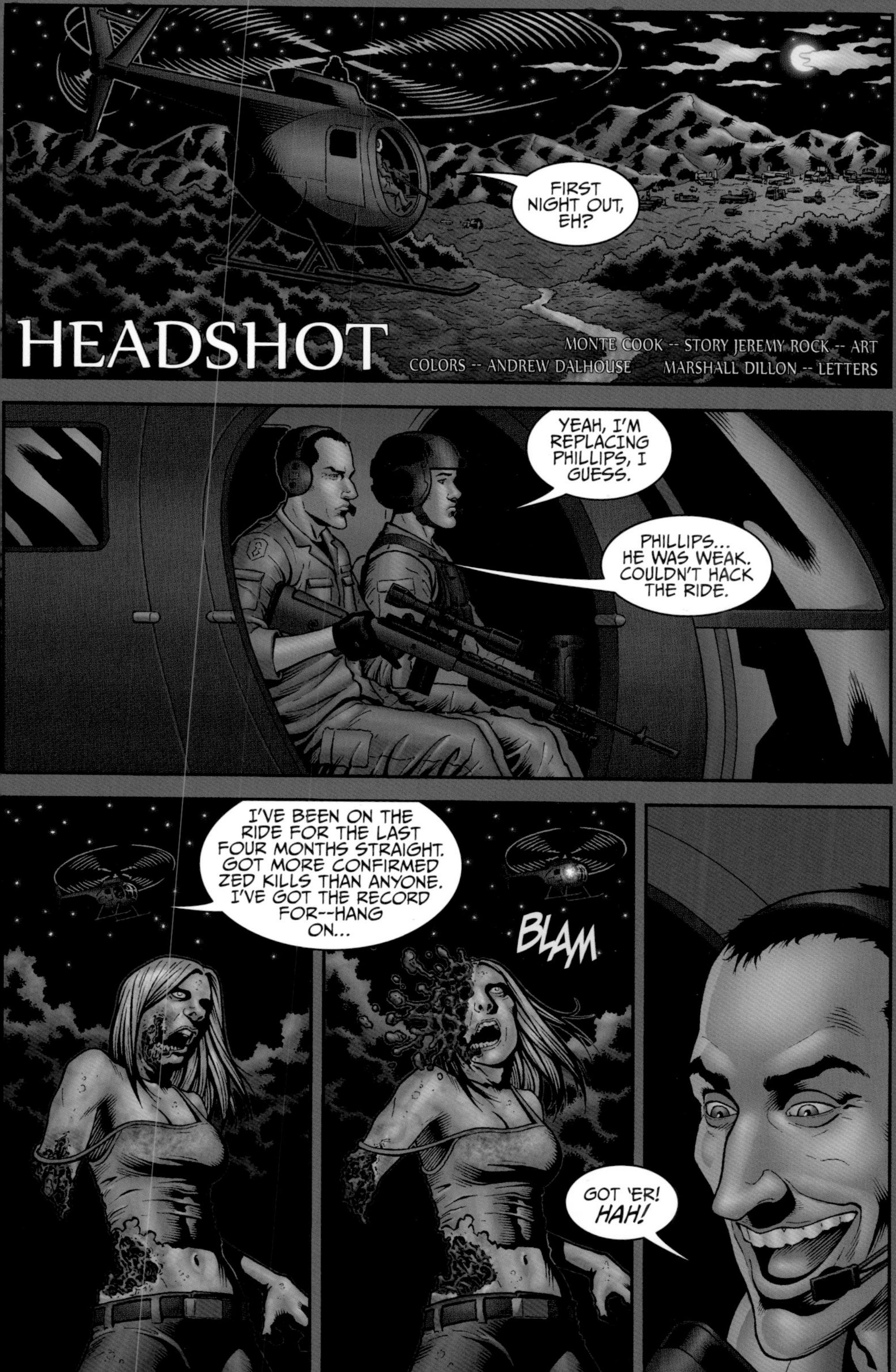
FIRST NIGHT OUT, EH?
HEADSHOT
MONTE COOK -- STORY JEREMY ROCK -- ART
COLORS -- ANDREW DALHOUSE MARSHALL DILLON -- LETTERS
YEAH, I'M REPLACING PHILLIPS, I GUESS.
PHILLIPS... HE WAS WEAK. COULDN'T HACK THE RIDE.
I'VE BEEN ON THE RIDE FOR THE LAST FOUR MONTHS STRAIGHT. GOT MORE CONFIRMED ZED KILLS THAN ANYONE. I'VE GOT THE RECORD FOR--HANG ON...
BLAM
GOT 'ER! HAH!

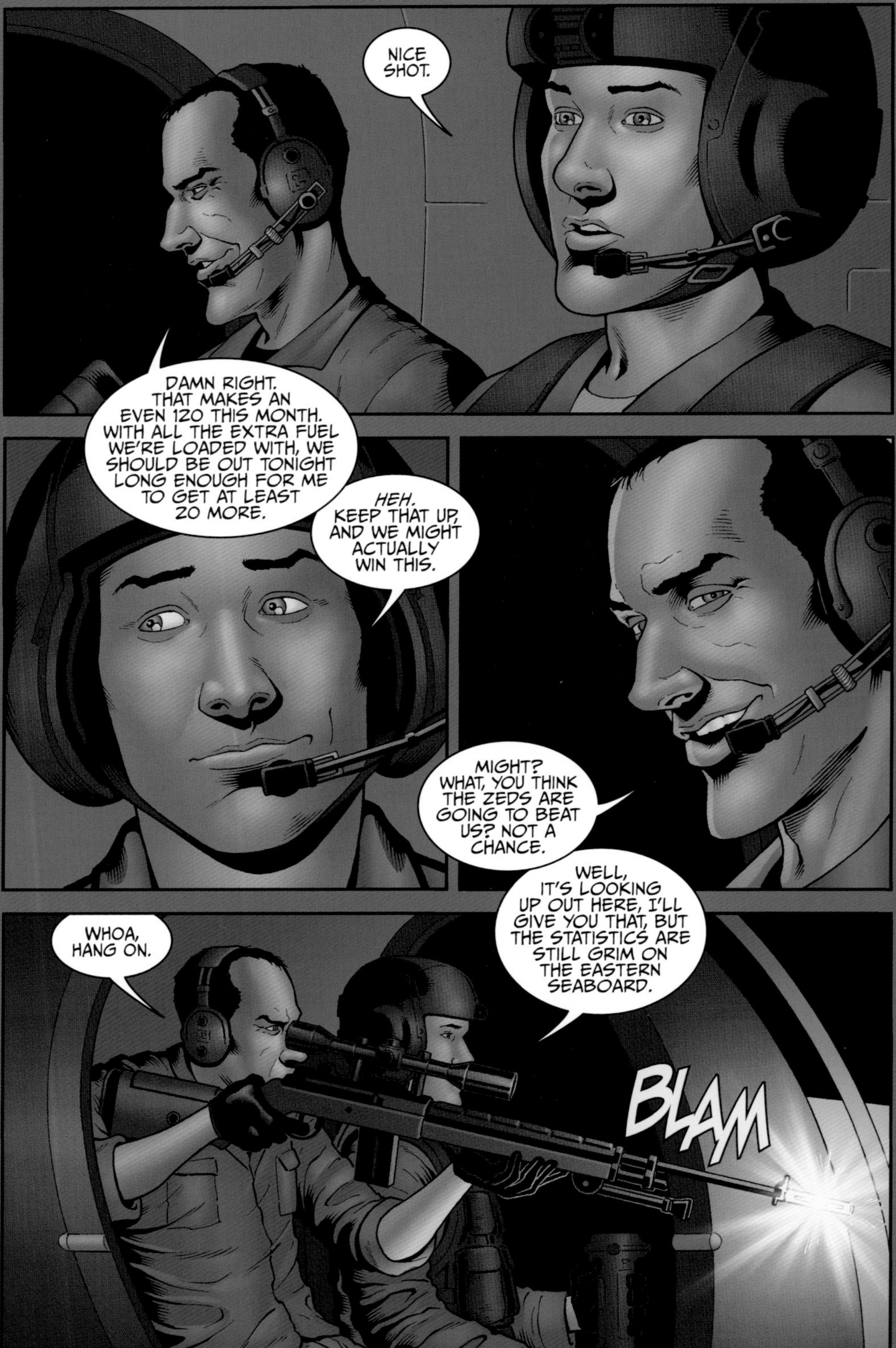

NICE SHOT.
DAMN RIGHT. THAT MAKES AN EVEN 120 THIS MONTH. WITH ALL THE EXTRA FUEL WE'RE LOADED WITH, WE SHOULD BE OUT TONIGHT LONG ENOUGH FOR ME TO GET AT LEAST 20 MORE.
HEH. KEEP THAT UP, AND WE MIGHT ACTUALLY WIN THIS.
MIGHT? WHAT, YOU THINK THE ZEDS ARE GOING TO BEAT US? NOT A CHANCE.
WELL, IT'S LOOKING UP OUT HERE, I'LL GIVE YOU THAT, BUT THE STATISTICS ARE STILL GRIM ON THE EASTERN SEABOARD.
WHOA, HANG ON.
BLAM

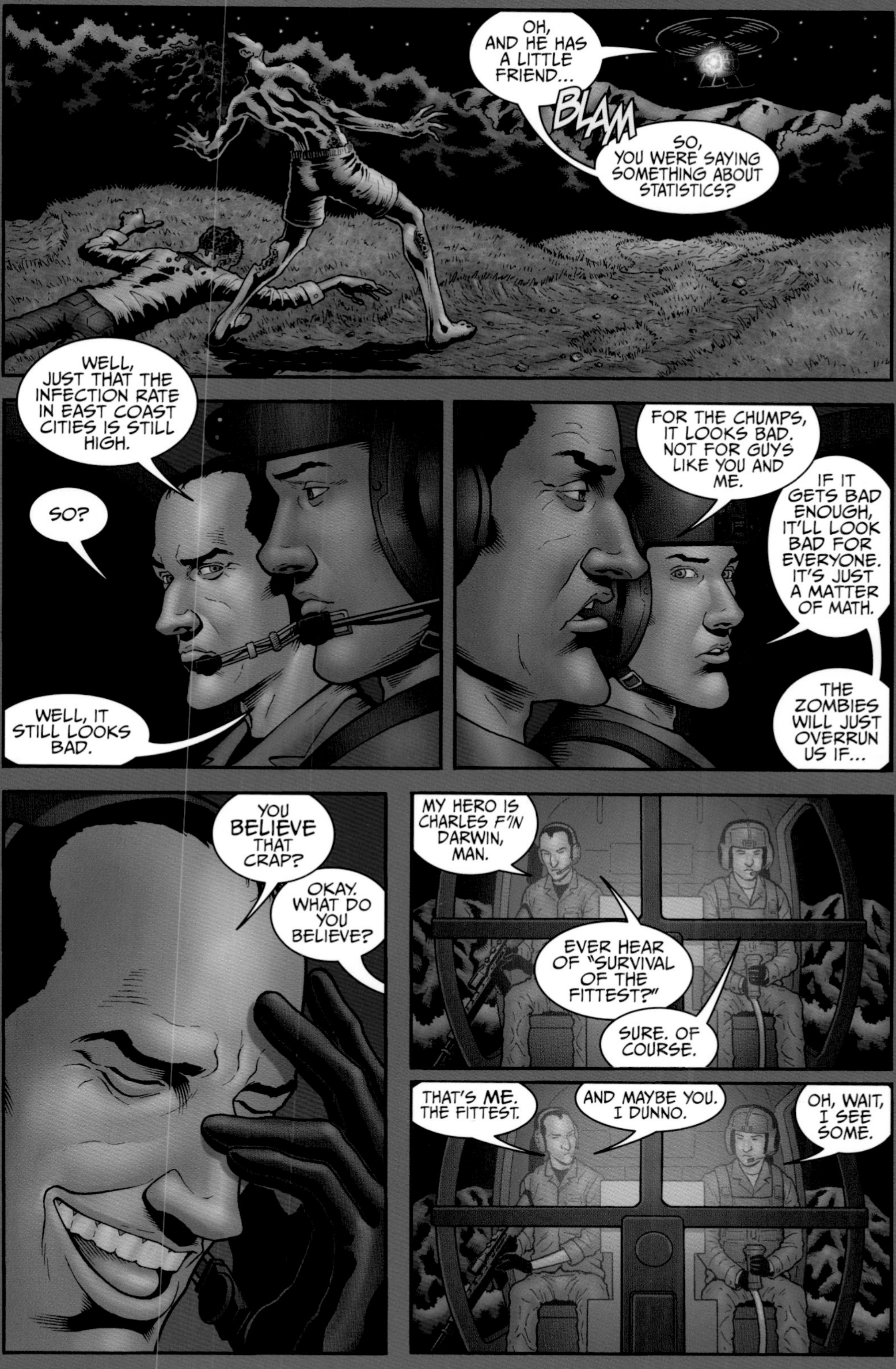
OH, AND HE HAS A LITTLE FRIEND...
BLAM
SO, YOU WERE SAYING SOMETHING ABOUT STATISTICS?
WELL, JUST THAT THE INFECTION RATE IN EAST COAST CITIES IS STILL HIGH.
SO?
WELL, IT STILL LOOKS BAD.
FOR THE CHUMPS, IT LOOKS BAD. NOT FOR GUYS LIKE YOU AND ME.
IF IT GETS BAD ENOUGH, IT'LL LOOK BAD FOR EVERYONE. IT'S JUST A MATTER OF MATH.
THE ZOMBIES WILL JUST OVERRUN US IF...
YOU BELIEVE THAT CRAP?
OKAY. WHAT DO YOU BELIEVE?
MY HERO IS CHARLES F'IN DARWIN, MAN.
EVER HEAR OF "SURVIVAL OF THE FITTEST?"
SURE. OF COURSE.
THAT'S ME. THE FITTEST.
AND MAYBE YOU. I DUNNO.
OH, WAIT, I SEE SOME.

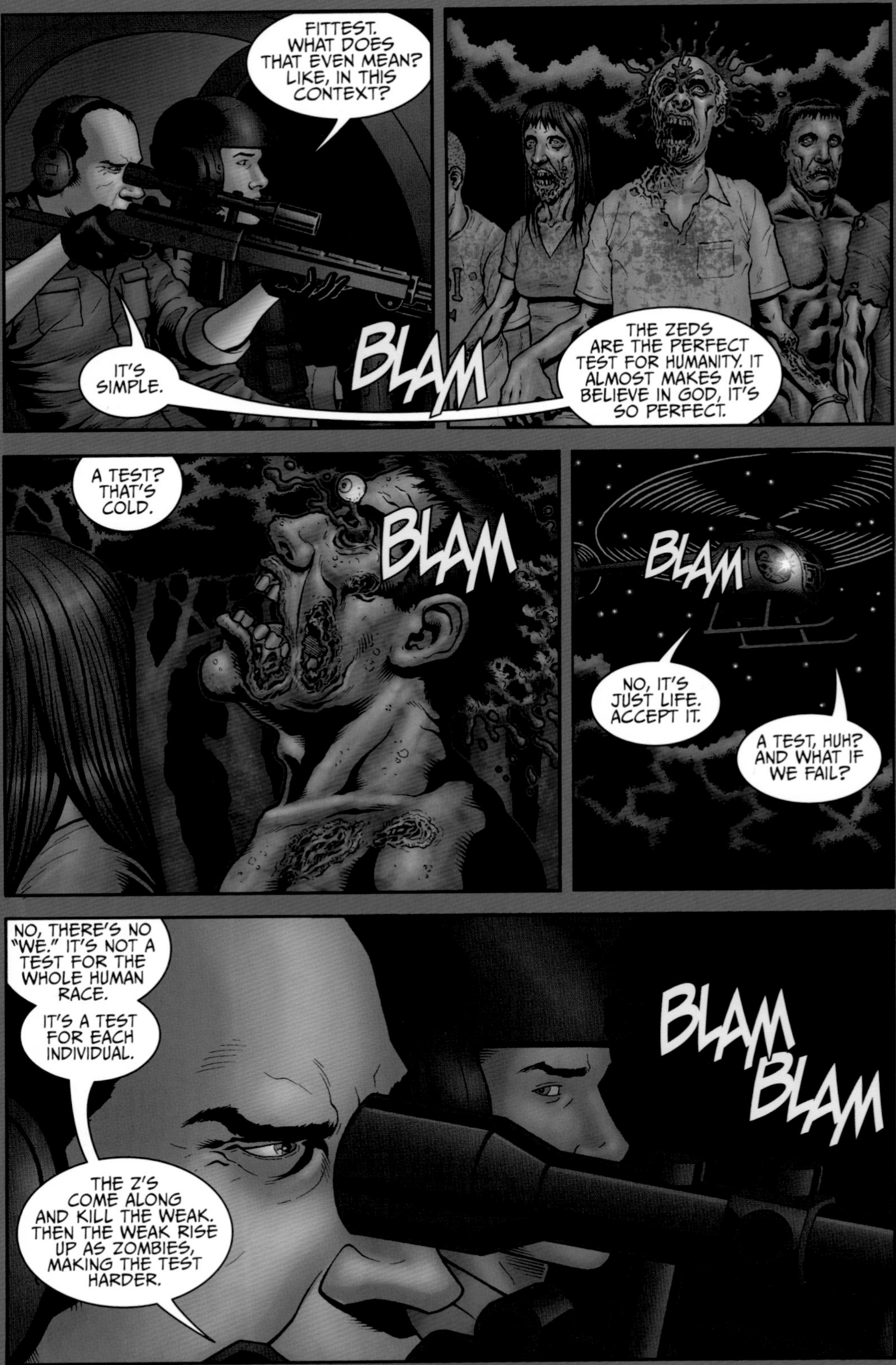
FITTEST. WHAT DOES THAT EVEN MEAN? LIKE, IN THIS CONTEXT?
IT'S SIMPLE.
BLAM
THE ZEDS ARE THE PERFECT TEST FOR HUMANITY. IT ALMOST MAKES ME BELIEVE IN GOD, IT'S SO PERFECT.
A TEST? THAT'S COLD.
BLAM
BLAM
NO, IT'S JUST LIFE. ACCEPT IT.
A TEST, HUH? AND WHAT IF WE FAIL?
NO, THERE'S NO "WE." IT'S NOT A TEST FOR THE WHOLE HUMAN RACE.
IT'S A TEST FOR EACH INDIVIDUAL.
THE Z'S COME ALONG AND KILL THE WEAK. THEN THE WEAK RISE UP AS ZOMBIES, MAKING THE TEST HARDER.
BLAM
BLAM

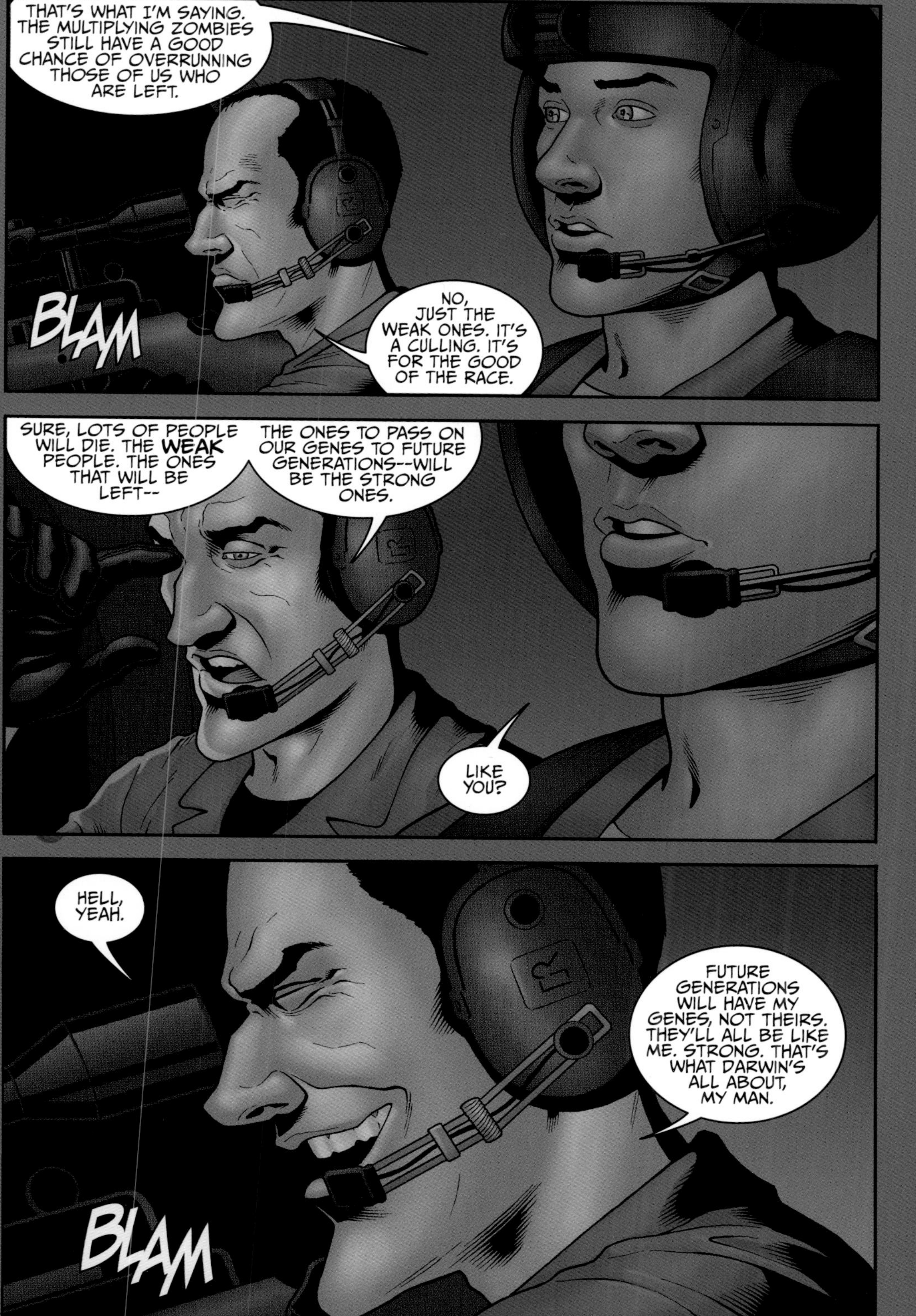
THAT'S WHAT I'M SAYING. THE MULTIPLYING ZOMBIES STILL HAVE A GOOD CHANCE OF OVERRUNNING THOSE OF US WHO ARE LEFT.
BLAM
NO, JUST THE WEAK ONES. IT'S A CULLING. IT'S FOR THE GOOD OF THE RACE.
SURE, LOTS OF PEOPLE WILL DIE. THE WEAK PEOPLE. THE ONES THAT WILL BE LEFT--
THE ONES TO PASS ON OUR GENES TO FUTURE GENERATIONS--WILL BE THE STRONG ONES.
LIKE YOU?
HELL, YEAH.
FUTURE GENERATIONS WILL HAVE MY GENES, NOT THEIRS. THEY'LL ALL BE LIKE ME. STRONG. THAT'S WHAT DARWIN'S ALL ABOUT, MY MAN.
BLAM

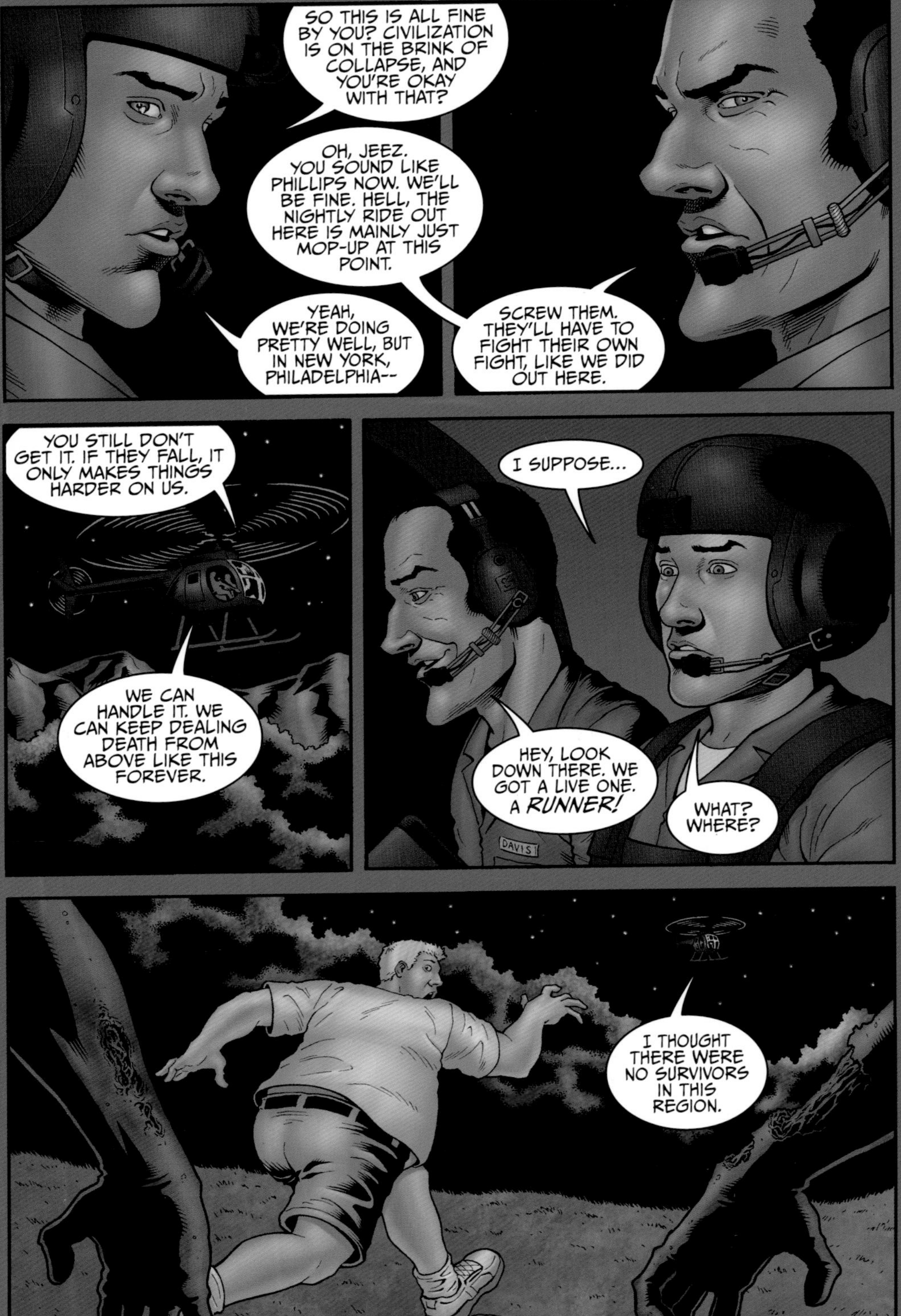

SO THIS IS ALL FINE BY YOU? CIVILIZATION IS ON THE BRINK OF COLLAPSE, AND YOU'RE OKAY WITH THAT?
OH, JEEZ. YOU SOUND LIKE PHILLIPS NOW. WE'LL BE FINE. HELL, THE NIGHTLY RIDE OUT HERE IS MAINLY JUST MOP-UP AT THIS POINT.
YEAH, WE'RE DOING PRETTY WELL, BUT IN NEW YORK, PHILADELPHIA--
SCREW THEM. THEY'LL HAVE TO FIGHT THEIR OWN FIGHT, LIKE WE DID OUT HERE.
YOU STILL DON'T GET IT. IF THEY FALL, IT ONLY MAKES THINGS HARDER ON US.
WE CAN HANDLE IT. WE CAN KEEP DEALING DEATH FROM ABOVE LIKE THIS FOREVER.
I SUPPOSE...
HEY, LOOK DOWN THERE. WE GOT A LIVE ONE. A *RUNNER!*
WHAT? WHERE?
DAVIS
I THOUGHT THERE WERE NO SURVIVORS IN THIS REGION.

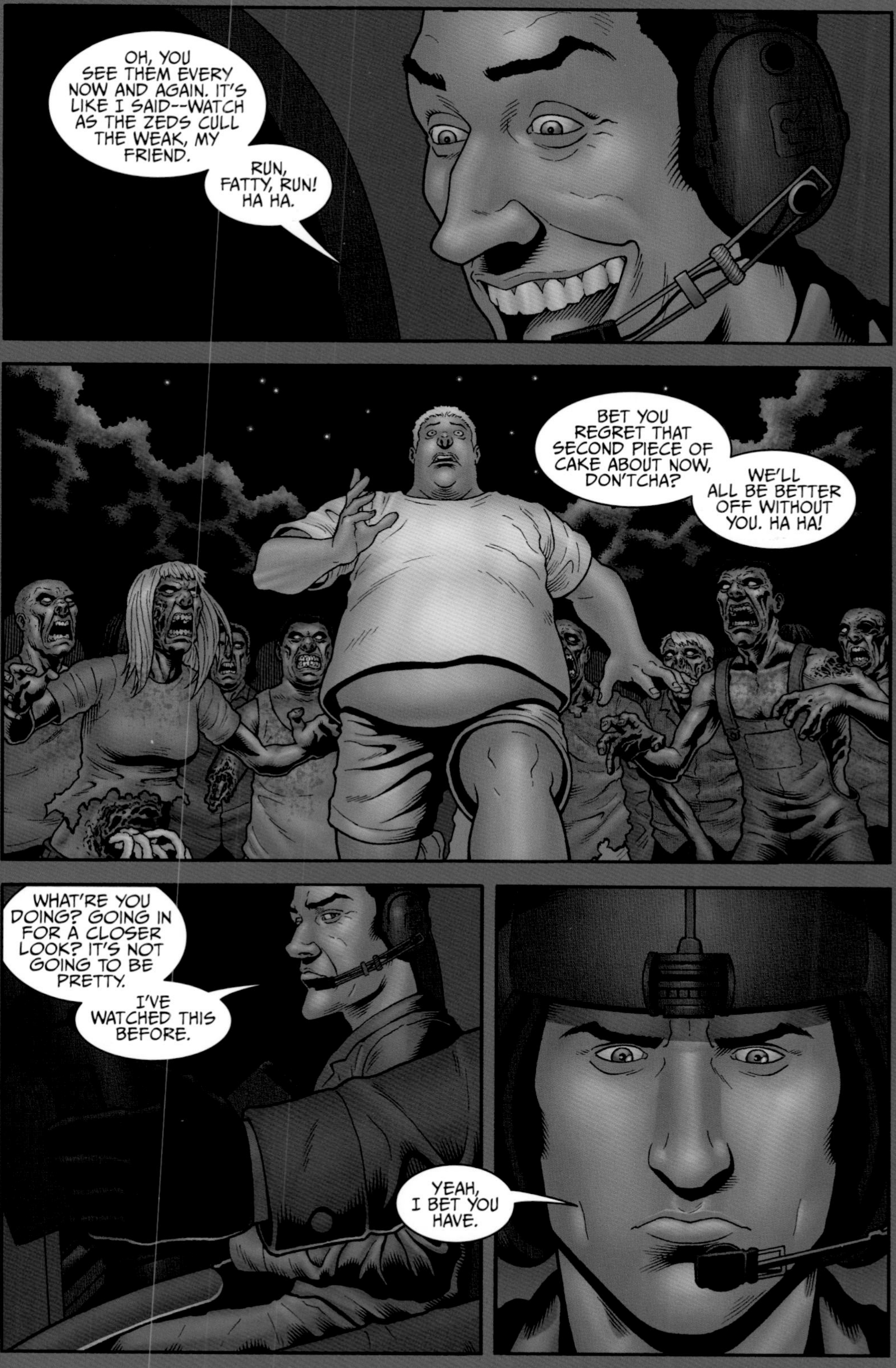
OH, YOU SEE THEM EVERY NOW AND AGAIN. IT'S LIKE I SAID--WATCH AS THE ZEDS CULL THE WEAK, MY FRIEND.
RUN, FATTY, RUN! HA HA.
BET YOU REGRET THAT SECOND PIECE OF CAKE ABOUT NOW, DON'TCHA?
WE'LL ALL BE BETTER OFF WITHOUT YOU. HA HA!
WHAT'RE YOU DOING? GOING IN FOR A CLOSER LOOK? IT'S NOT GOING TO BE PRETTY.
I'VE WATCHED THIS BEFORE.
YEAH, I BET YOU HAVE.

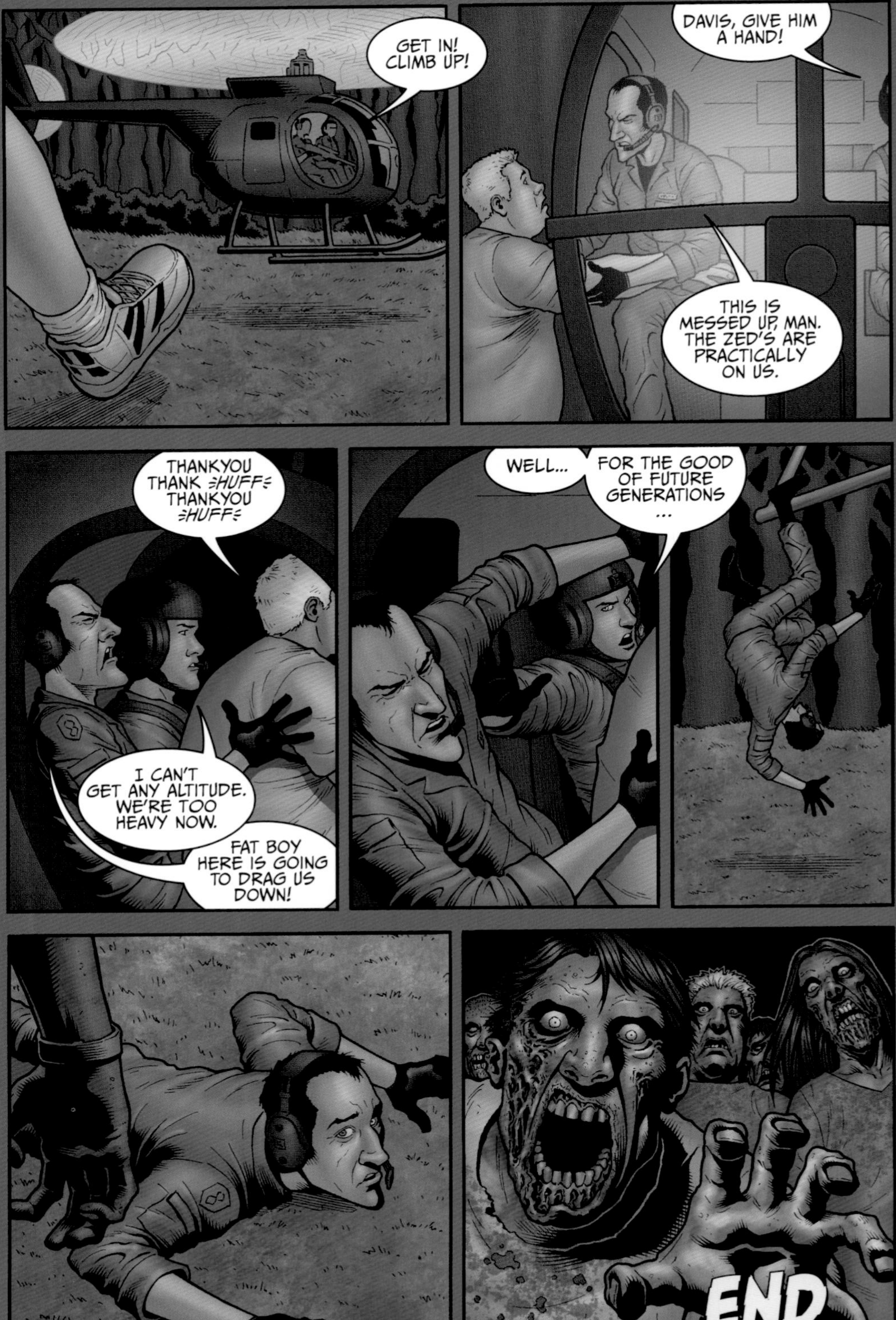
GET IN! CLIMB UP!
DAVIS, GIVE HIM A HAND!
THIS IS MESSED UP, MAN. THE ZED'S ARE PRACTICALLY ON US.
THANKYOU THANK =HUFF= THANKYOU =HUFF=
I CAN'T GET ANY ALTITUDE. WE'RE TOO HEAVY NOW.
FAT BOY HERE IS GOING TO DRAG US DOWN!
WELL...
FOR THE GOOD OF FUTURE GENERATIONS ...
END

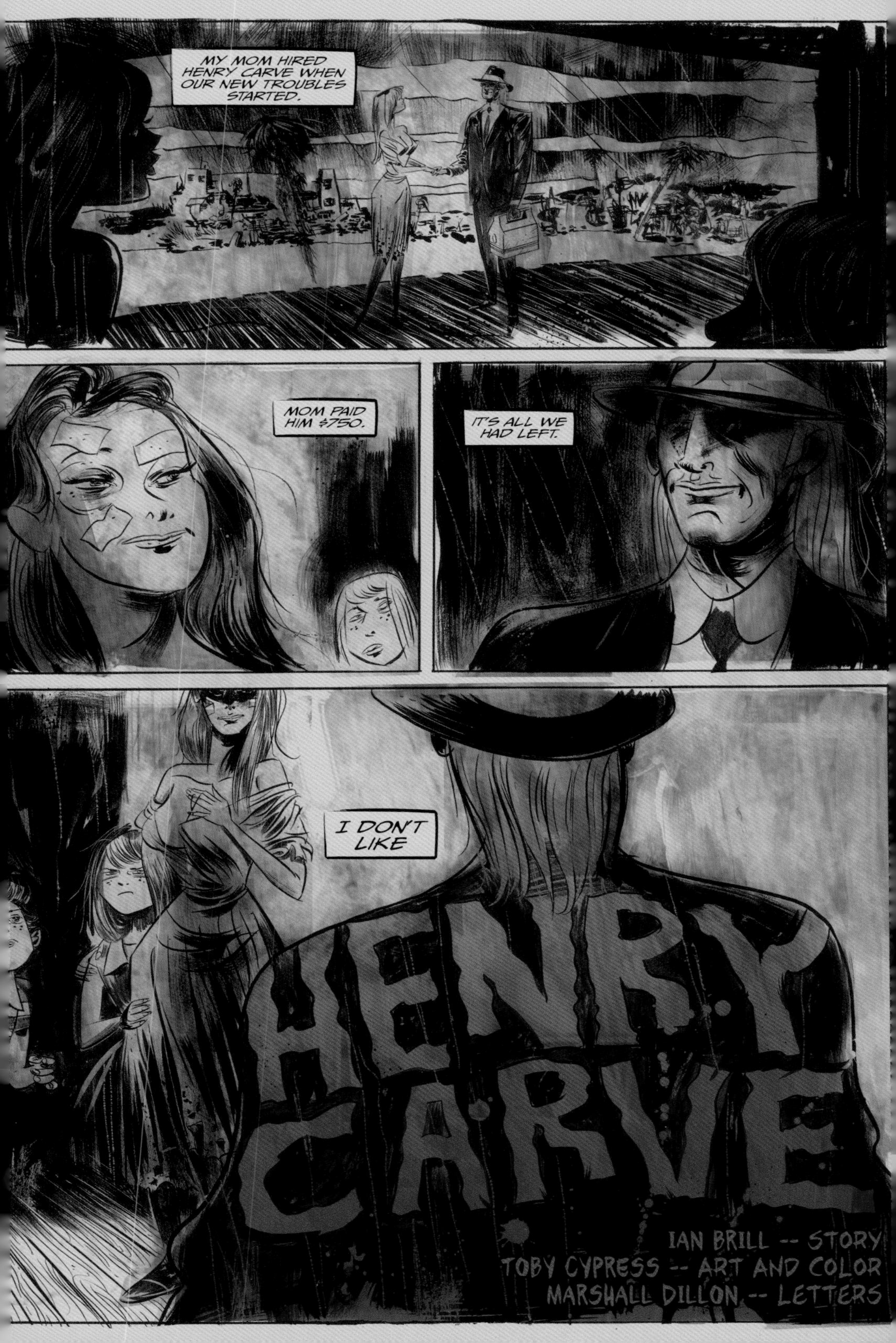
MY MOM HIRED HENRY CARVE WHEN OUR NEW TROUBLES STARTED.
MOM PAID HIM $750.
IT'S ALL WE HAD LEFT.
I DON'T LIKE
HENRY CARVE
IAN BRILL -- STORY
TOBY CYPRESS -- ART AND COLOR
MARSHALL DILLON -- LETTERS

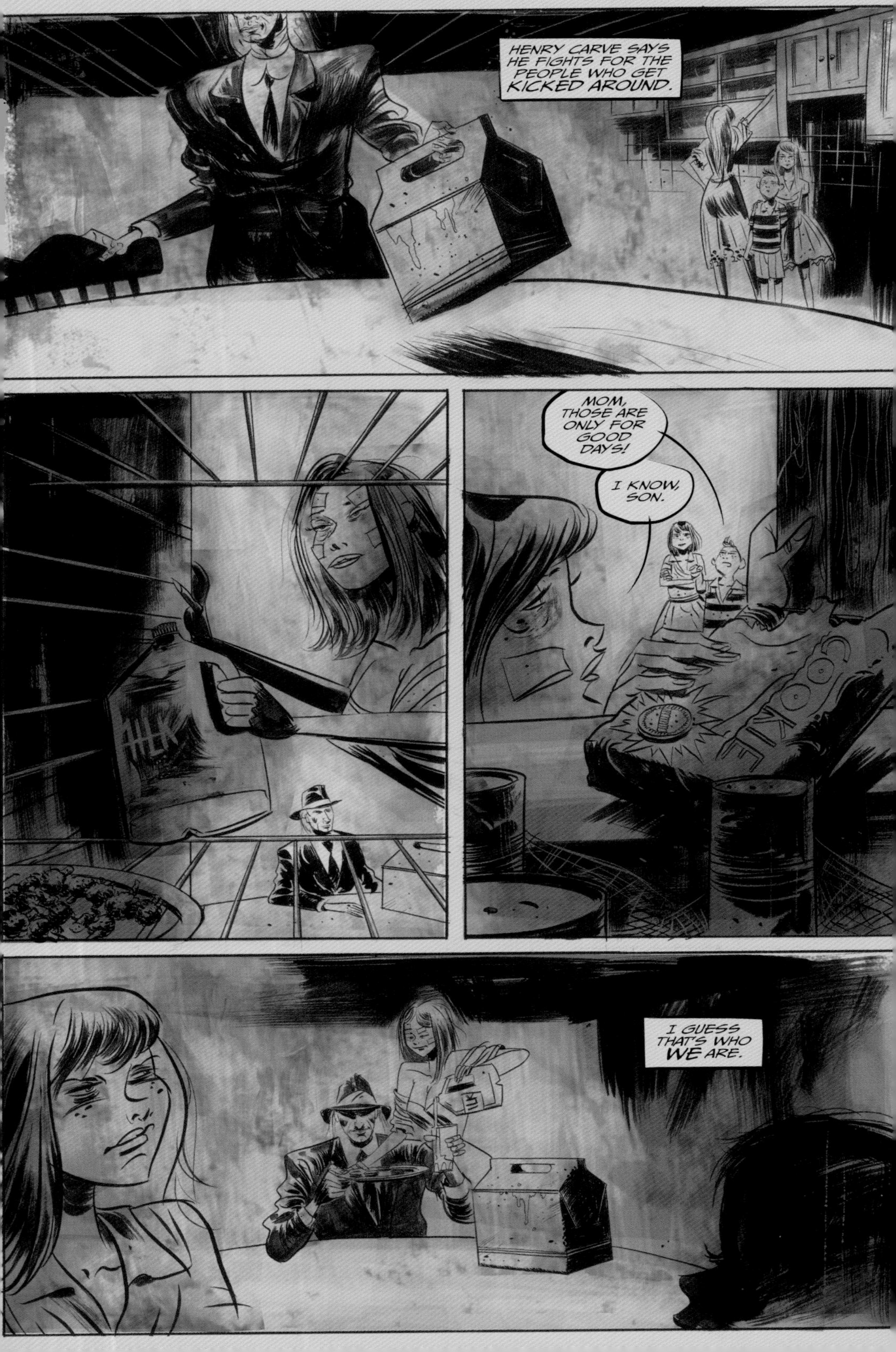
HENRY CARVE SAYS HE FIGHTS FOR THE PEOPLE WHO GET KICKED AROUND.
MILK
MOM, THOSE ARE ONLY FOR GOOD DAYS!
I KNOW, SON.
COOKIE
I GUESS THAT'S WHO WE ARE.

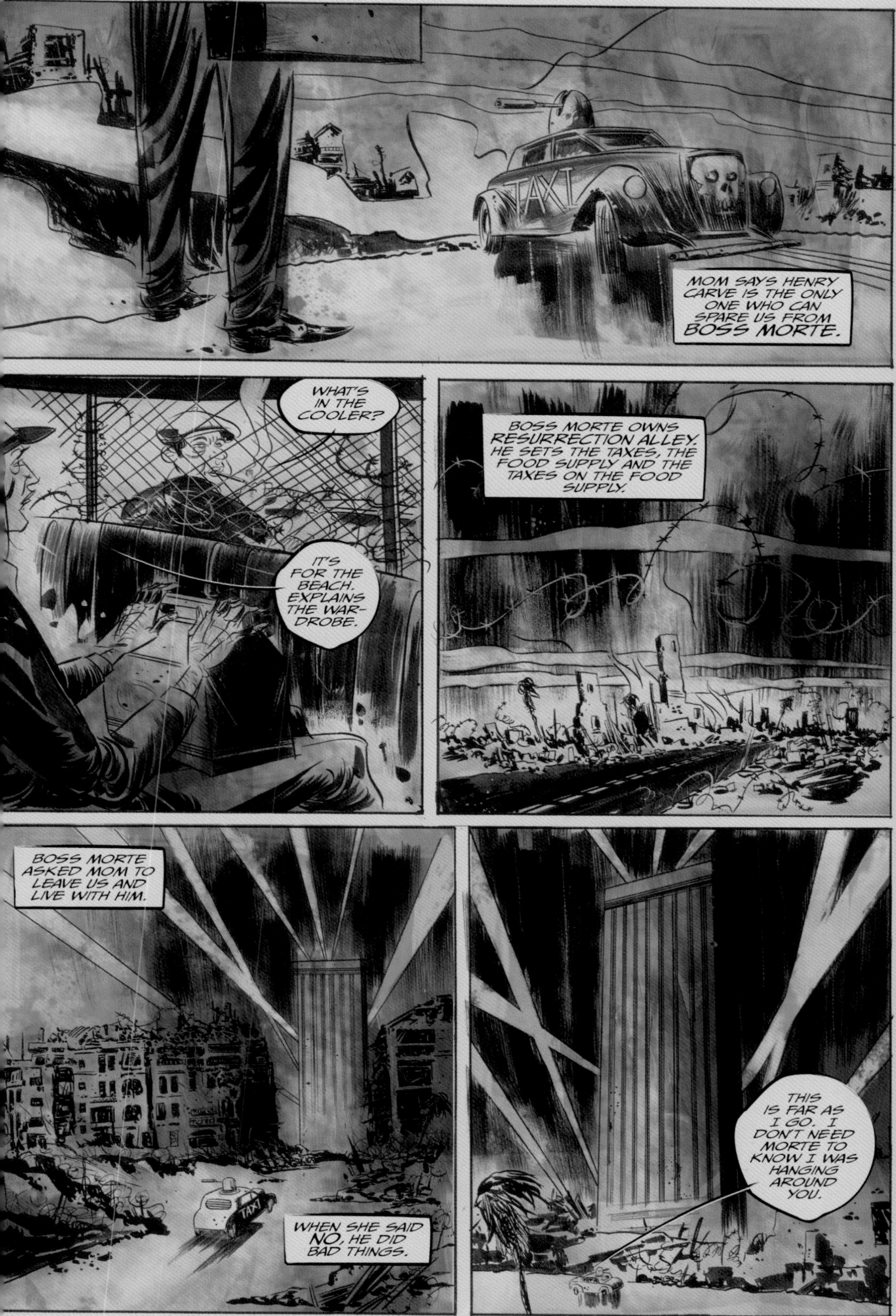
MOM SAYS HENRY CARVE IS THE ONLY ONE WHO CAN SPARE US FROM BOSS MORTE.
WHAT'S IN THE COOLER?
IT'S FOR THE BEACH. EXPLAINS THE WAR-DROBE.
BOSS MORTE OWNS RESURRECTION ALLEY. HE SETS THE TAXES, THE FOOD SUPPLY AND THE TAXES ON THE FOOD SUPPLY.
BOSS MORTE ASKED MOM TO LEAVE US AND LIVE WITH HIM.
WHEN SHE SAID NO, HE DID BAD THINGS.
THIS IS FAR AS I GO. I DON'T NEED MORTE TO KNOW I WAS HANGING AROUND YOU.

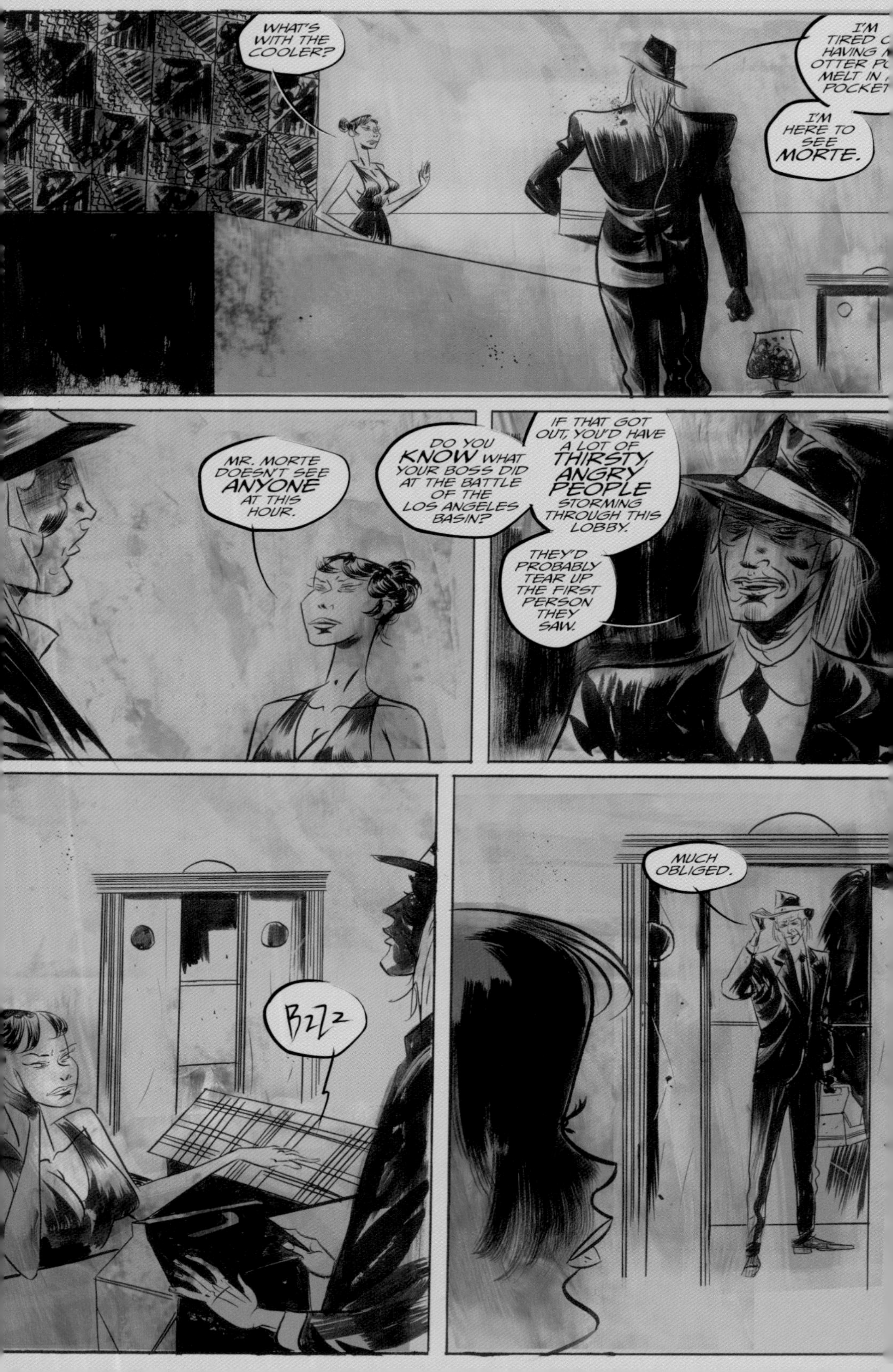
WHAT'S WITH THE COOLER?
I'M TIRED O HAVING OTTER PO MELT IN POCKET
I'M HERE TO SEE MORTE.
MR. MORTE DOESN'T SEE ANYONE AT THIS HOUR.
DO YOU KNOW WHAT YOUR BOSS DID AT THE BATTLE OF THE LOS ANGELES BASIN?
IF THAT GOT OUT, YOU'D HAVE A LOT OF THIRSTY, ANGRY PEOPLE STORMING THROUGH THIS LOBBY.
THEY'D PROBABLY TEAR UP THE FIRST PERSON THEY SAW.
BZZZ
MUCH OBLIGED.

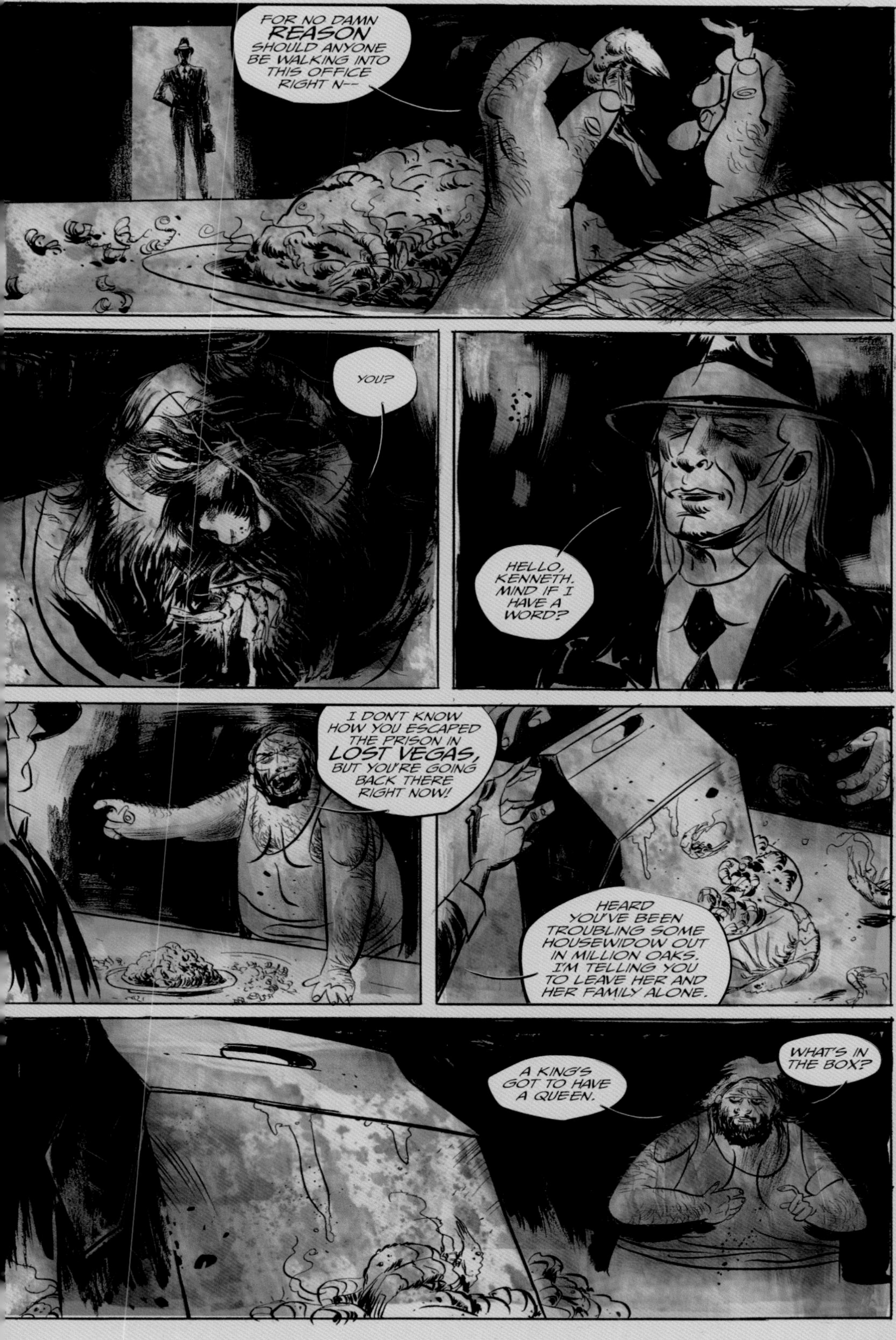
FOR NO DAMN REASON SHOULD ANYONE BE WALKING INTO THIS OFFICE RIGHT N--
YOU?
HELLO, KENNETH. MIND IF I HAVE A WORD?
I DON'T KNOW HOW YOU ESCAPED THE PRISON IN LOST VEGAS, BUT YOU'RE GOING BACK THERE RIGHT NOW!
HEARD YOU'VE BEEN TROUBLING SOME HOUSEWIDOW OUT IN MILLION OAKS. I'M TELLING YOU TO LEAVE HER AND HER FAMILY ALONE.
WHAT'S IN THE BOX?
A KING'S GOT TO HAVE A QUEEN.

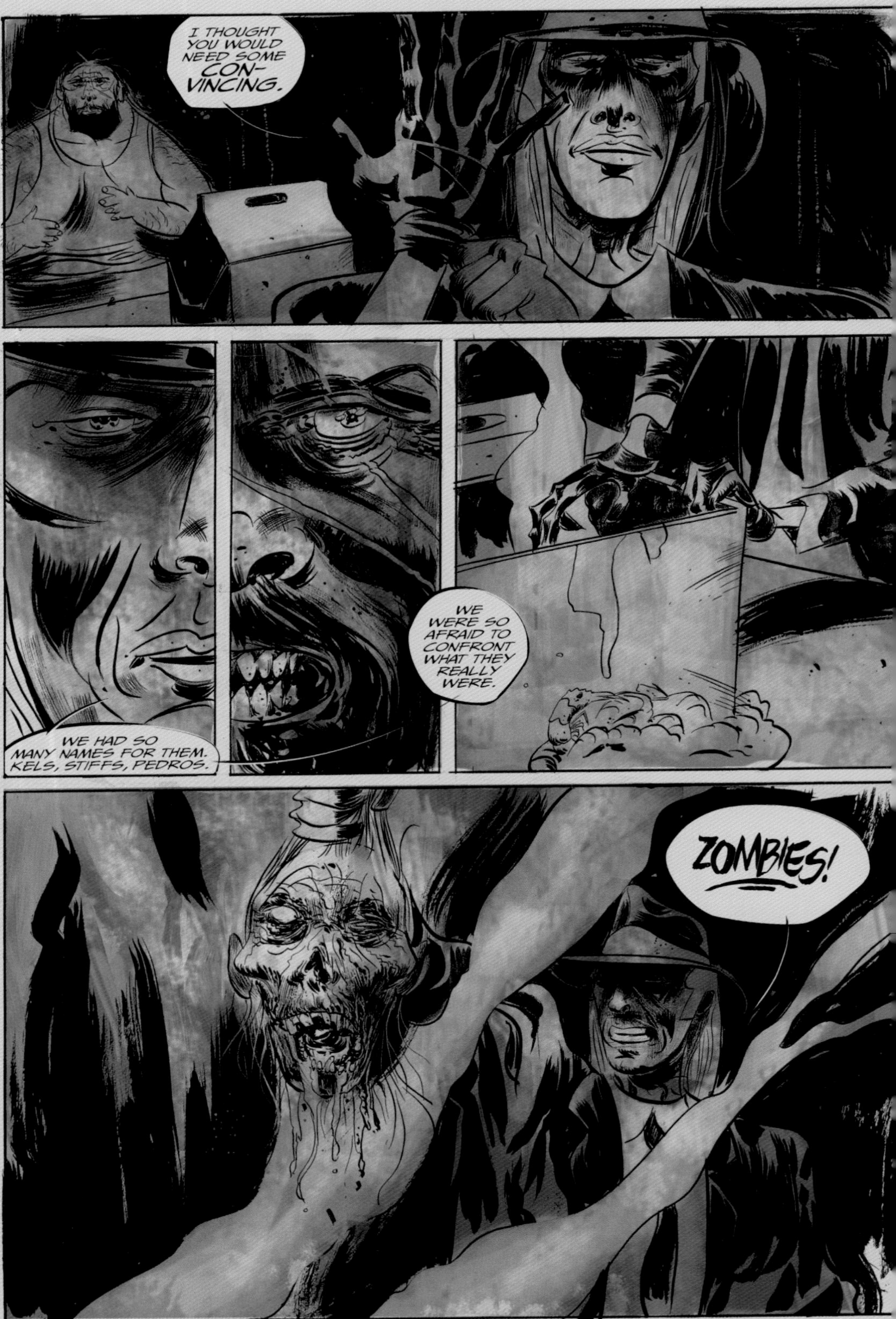
I THOUGHT YOU WOULD NEED SOME CON-VINCING.
WE HAD SO MANY NAMES FOR THEM. KELS, STIFFS, PEDROS.
WE WERE SO AFRAID TO CONFRONT WHAT THEY REALLY WERE.
ZOMBIES!

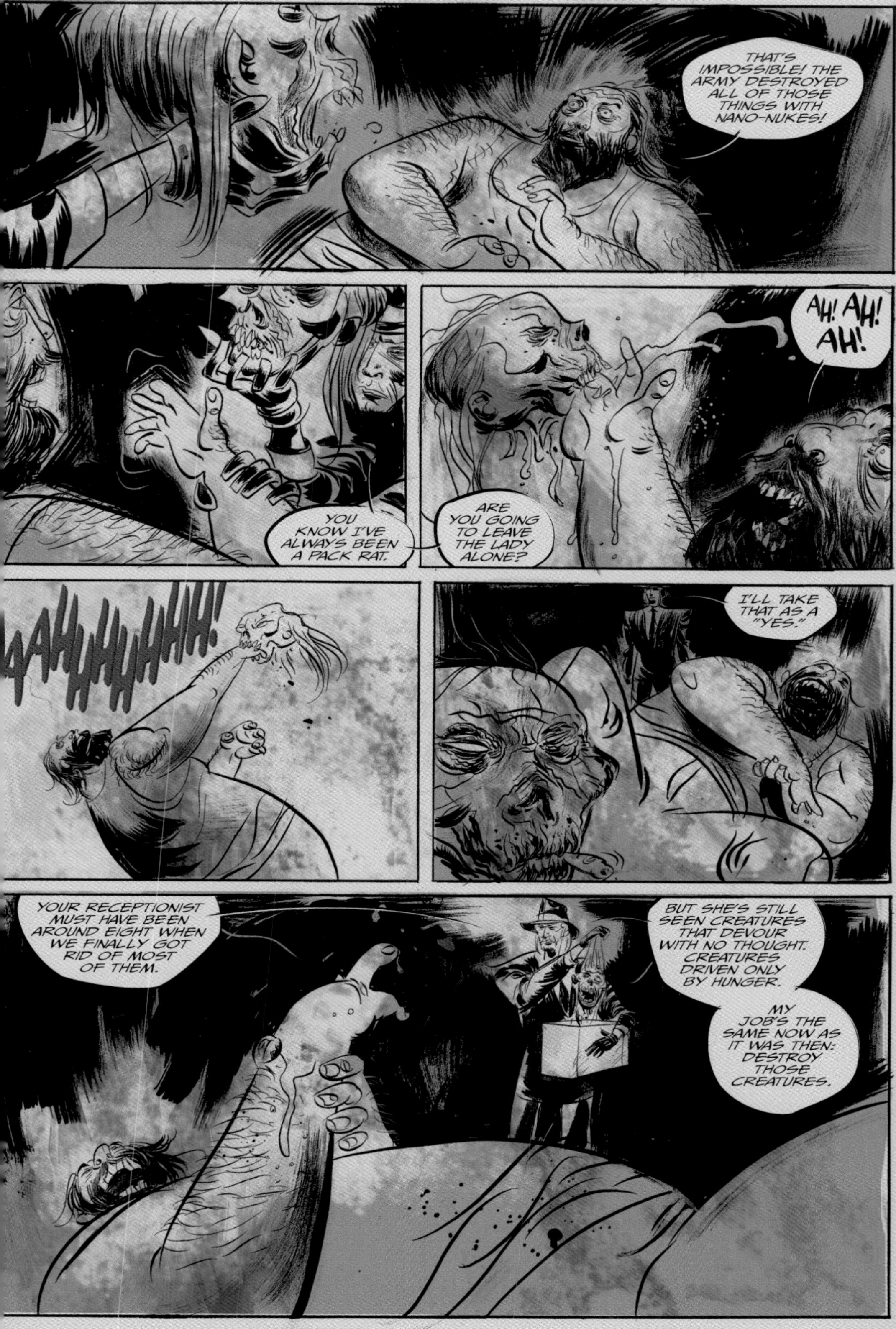
THAT'S IMPOSSIBLE! THE ARMY DESTROYED ALL OF THOSE THINGS WITH NANO-NUKES!
YOU KNOW I'VE ALWAYS BEEN A PACK RAT.
ARE YOU GOING TO LEAVE THE LADY ALONE?
AH! AH! AH!
AAHHHHHHH!
I'LL TAKE THAT AS A "YES."
YOUR RECEPTIONIST MUST HAVE BEEN AROUND EIGHT WHEN WE FINALLY GOT RID OF MOST OF THEM.
BUT SHE'S STILL SEEN CREATURES THAT DEVOUR WITH NO THOUGHT. CREATURES DRIVEN ONLY BY HUNGER.
MY JOB'S THE SAME NOW AS IT WAS THEN: DESTROY THOSE CREATURES.

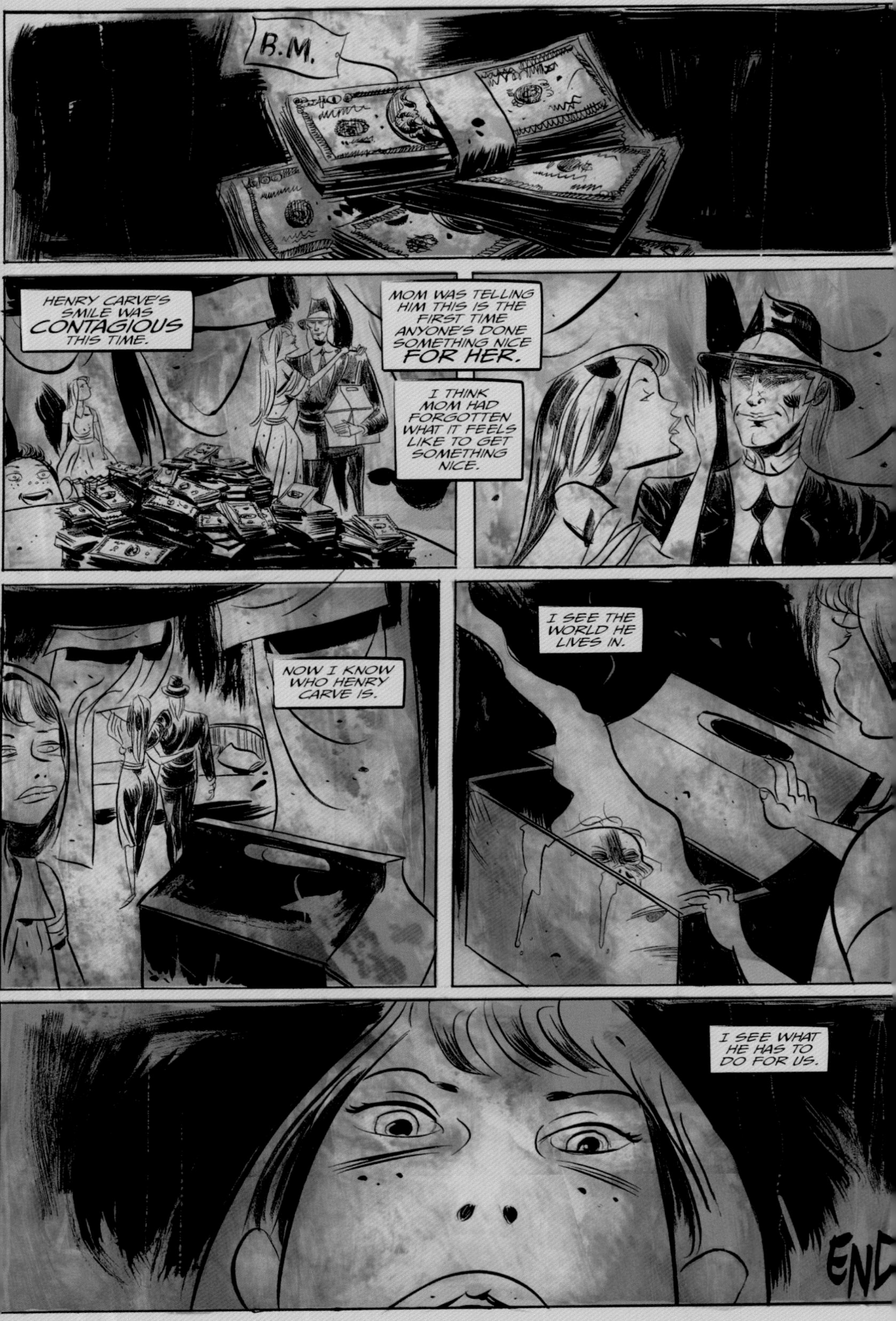
B.M.
HENRY CARVE'S SMILE WAS CONTAGIOUS THIS TIME.
MOM WAS TELLING HIM THIS IS THE FIRST TIME ANYONE'S DONE SOMETHING NICE FOR HER.
I THINK MOM HAD FORGOTTEN WHAT IT FEELS LIKE TO GET SOMETHING NICE.
NOW I KNOW WHO HENRY CARVE IS.
I SEE THE WORLD HE LIVES IN.
I SEE WHAT HE HAS TO DO FOR US.
END

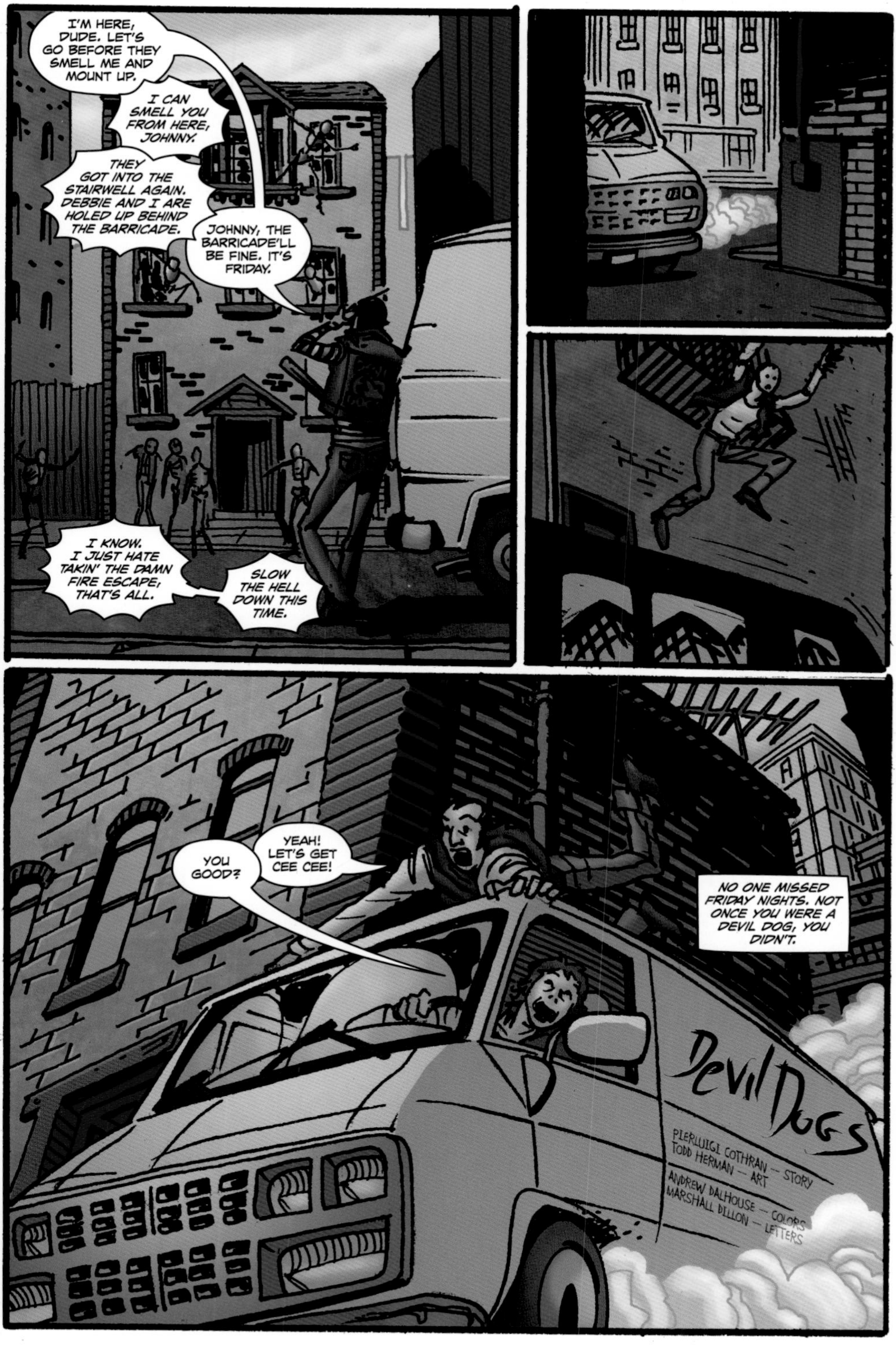
I'M HERE, DUDE. LET'S GO BEFORE THEY SMELL ME AND MOUNT UP.
I CAN SMELL YOU FROM HERE, JOHNNY.
THEY GOT INTO THE STAIRWELL AGAIN. DEBBIE AND I ARE HOLED UP BEHIND THE BARRICADE.
JOHNNY, THE BARRICADE'LL BE FINE. IT'S FRIDAY.
I KNOW. I JUST HATE TAKIN' THE DAMN FIRE ESCAPE, THAT'S ALL.
SLOW THE HELL DOWN THIS TIME.
YOU GOOD?
YEAH! LET'S GET CEE CEE!
NO ONE MISSED FRIDAY NIGHTS. NOT ONCE YOU WERE A DEVIL DOG, YOU DIDN'T.
Devil Dogs
PIERLUIGI COTHRAN — STORY
TODD HERMAN — ART
ANDREW DALHOUSE — COLORS
MARSHALL DILLON — LETTERS

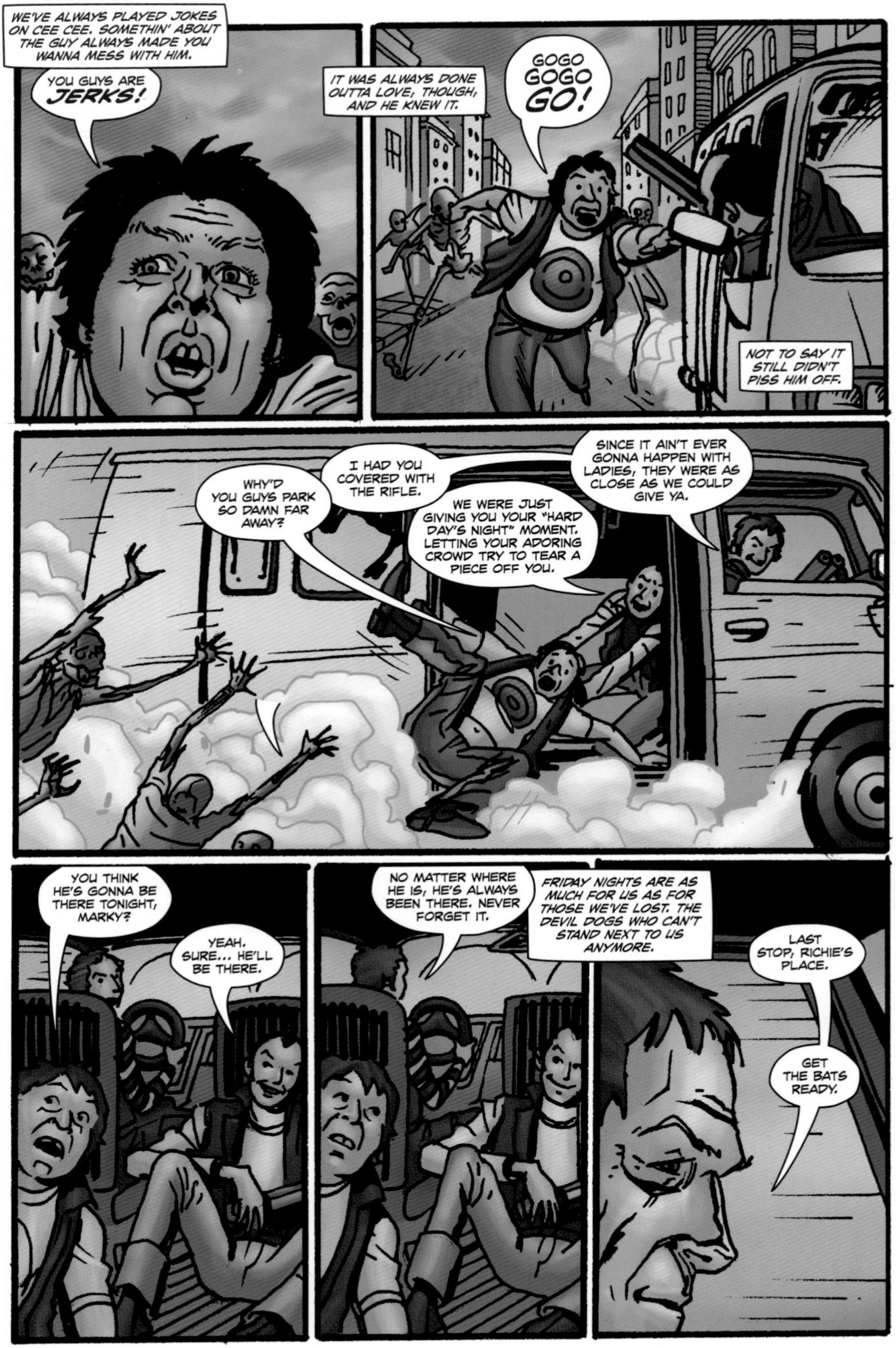

WE'VE ALWAYS PLAYED JOKES ON CEE CEE. SOMETHIN' ABOUT THE GUY ALWAYS MADE YOU WANNA MESS WITH HIM.
YOU GUYS ARE JERKS!
IT WAS ALWAYS DONE OUTTA LOVE, THOUGH, AND HE KNEW IT.
GOGO GOGO GO!
NOT TO SAY IT STILL DIDN'T PISS HIM OFF.
WHY'D YOU GUYS PARK SO DAMN FAR AWAY?
I HAD YOU COVERED WITH THE RIFLE.
WE WERE JUST GIVING YOU YOUR "HARD DAY'S NIGHT" MOMENT. LETTING YOUR ADORING CROWD TRY TO TEAR A PIECE OFF YOU.
SINCE IT AIN'T EVER GONNA HAPPEN WITH LADIES, THEY WERE AS CLOSE AS WE COULD GIVE YA.
YOU THINK HE'S GONNA BE THERE TONIGHT, MARKY?
YEAH. SURE... HE'LL BE THERE.
NO MATTER WHERE HE IS, HE'S ALWAYS BEEN THERE. NEVER FORGET IT.
FRIDAY NIGHTS ARE AS MUCH FOR US AS FOR THOSE WE'VE LOST. THE DEVIL DOGS WHO CAN'T STAND NEXT TO US ANYMORE.
LAST STOP, RICHIE'S PLACE.
GET THE BATS READY.

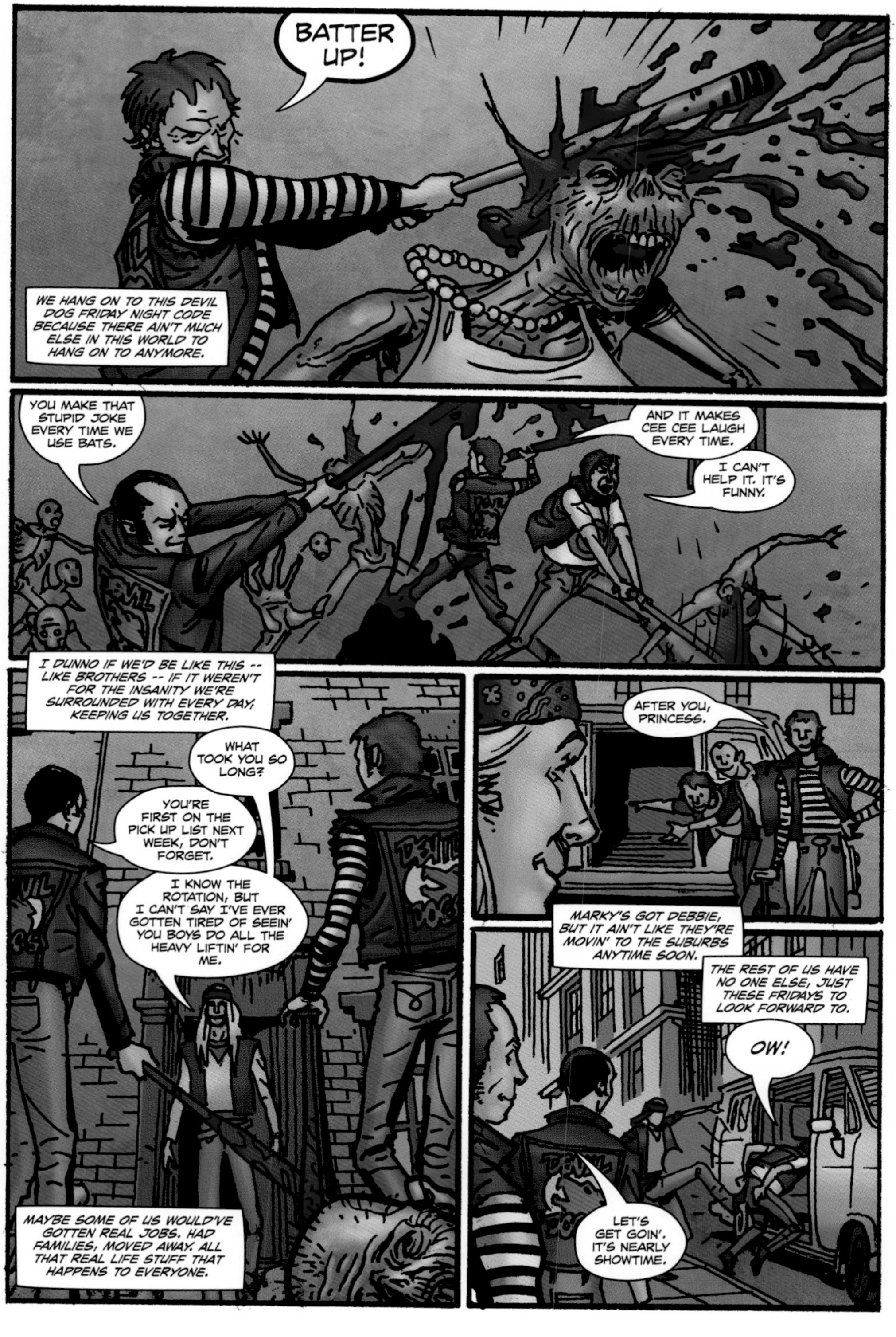
BATTER UP!
WE HANG ON TO THIS DEVIL DOG FRIDAY NIGHT CODE BECAUSE THERE AIN'T MUCH ELSE IN THIS WORLD TO HANG ON TO ANYMORE.
YOU MAKE THAT STUPID JOKE EVERY TIME WE USE BATS.
AND IT MAKES CEE CEE LAUGH EVERY TIME.
I CAN'T HELP IT. IT'S FUNNY.
I DUNNO IF WE'D BE LIKE THIS -- LIKE BROTHERS -- IF IT WEREN'T FOR THE INSANITY WE'RE SURROUNDED WITH EVERY DAY, KEEPING US TOGETHER.
WHAT TOOK YOU SO LONG?
YOU'RE FIRST ON THE PICK UP LIST NEXT WEEK, DON'T FORGET.
I KNOW THE ROTATION, BUT I CAN'T SAY I'VE EVER GOTTEN TIRED OF SEEIN' YOU BOYS DO ALL THE HEAVY LIFTIN' FOR ME.
MAYBE SOME OF US WOULD'VE GOTTEN REAL JOBS. HAD FAMILIES, MOVED AWAY. ALL THAT REAL LIFE STUFF THAT HAPPENS TO EVERYONE.
AFTER YOU, PRINCESS.
MARKY'S GOT DEBBIE, BUT IT AIN'T LIKE THEY'RE MOVIN' TO THE SUBURBS ANYTIME SOON.
THE REST OF US HAVE NO ONE ELSE, JUST THESE FRIDAYS TO LOOK FORWARD TO.
OW!
LET'S GET GOIN'. IT'S NEARLY SHOWTIME.

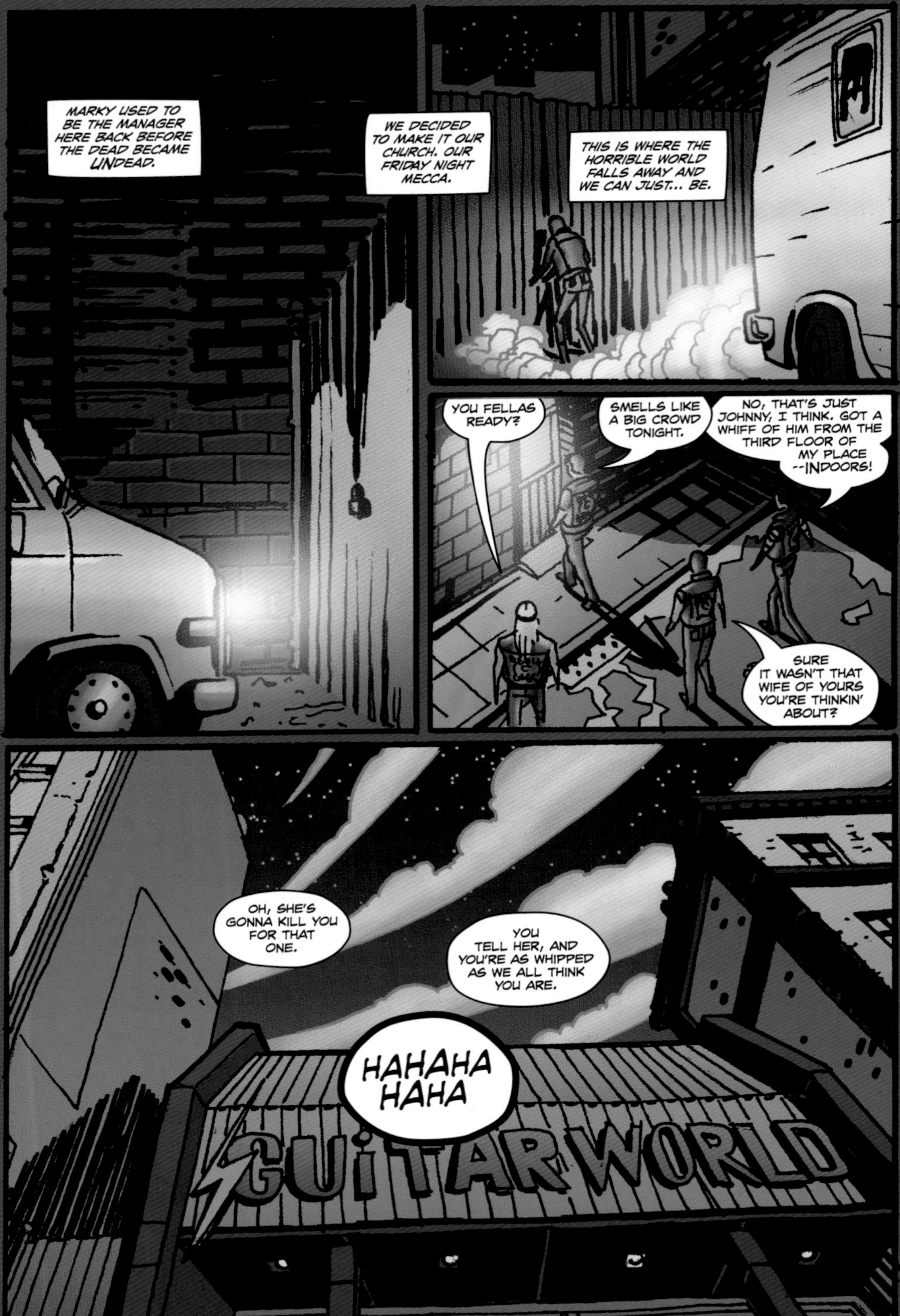
MARKY USED TO BE THE MANAGER HERE BACK BEFORE THE DEAD BECAME UNDEAD.
WE DECIDED TO MAKE IT OUR CHURCH. OUR FRIDAY NIGHT MECCA.
THIS IS WHERE THE HORRIBLE WORLD FALLS AWAY AND WE CAN JUST... BE.
YOU FELLAS READY?
SMELLS LIKE A BIG CROWD TONIGHT.
NO, THAT'S JUST JOHNNY, I THINK. GOT A WHIFF OF HIM FROM THE THIRD FLOOR OF MY PLACE --INDOORS!
SURE IT WASN'T THAT WIFE OF YOURS YOU'RE THINKIN' ABOUT?
OH, SHE'S GONNA KILL YOU FOR THAT ONE.
YOU TELL HER, AND YOU'RE AS WHIPPED AS WE ALL THINK YOU ARE.
HAHAHA HAHA
GUITAR WORLD

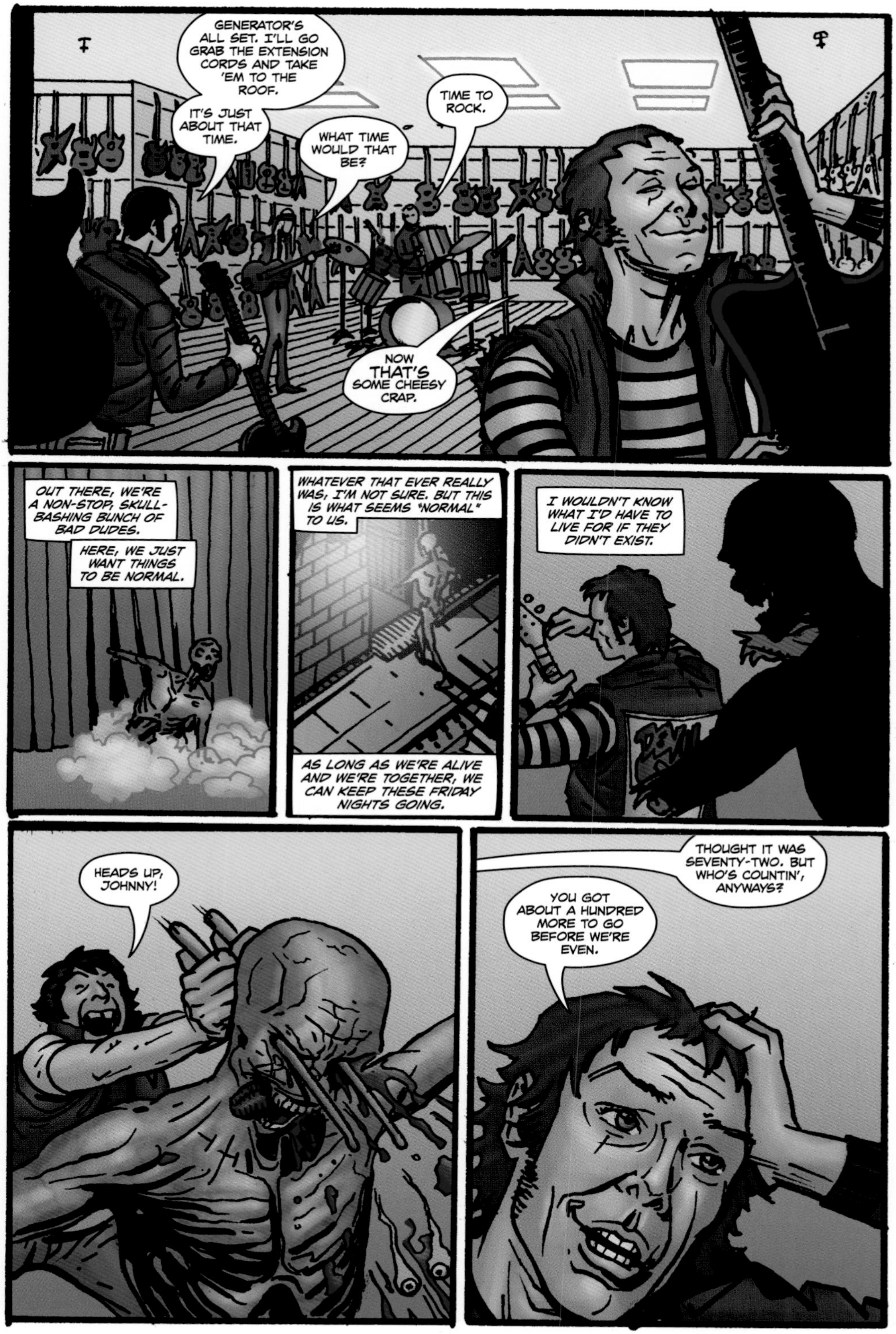
GENERATOR'S ALL SET. I'LL GO GRAB THE EXTENSION CORDS AND TAKE 'EM TO THE ROOF.
IT'S JUST ABOUT THAT TIME.
WHAT TIME WOULD THAT BE?
TIME TO ROCK.
NOW THAT'S SOME CHEESY CRAP.
OUT THERE, WE'RE A NON-STOP, SKULL-BASHING BUNCH OF BAD DUDES.
HERE, WE JUST WANT THINGS TO BE NORMAL.
WHATEVER THAT EVER REALLY WAS, I'M NOT SURE. BUT THIS IS WHAT SEEMS "NORMAL" TO US.
AS LONG AS WE'RE ALIVE AND WE'RE TOGETHER, WE CAN KEEP THESE FRIDAY NIGHTS GOING.
I WOULDN'T KNOW WHAT I'D HAVE TO LIVE FOR IF THEY DIDN'T EXIST.
HEADS UP, JOHNNY!
THOUGHT IT WAS SEVENTY-TWO. BUT WHO'S COUNTIN', ANYWAYS?
YOU GOT ABOUT A HUNDRED MORE TO GO BEFORE WE'RE EVEN.

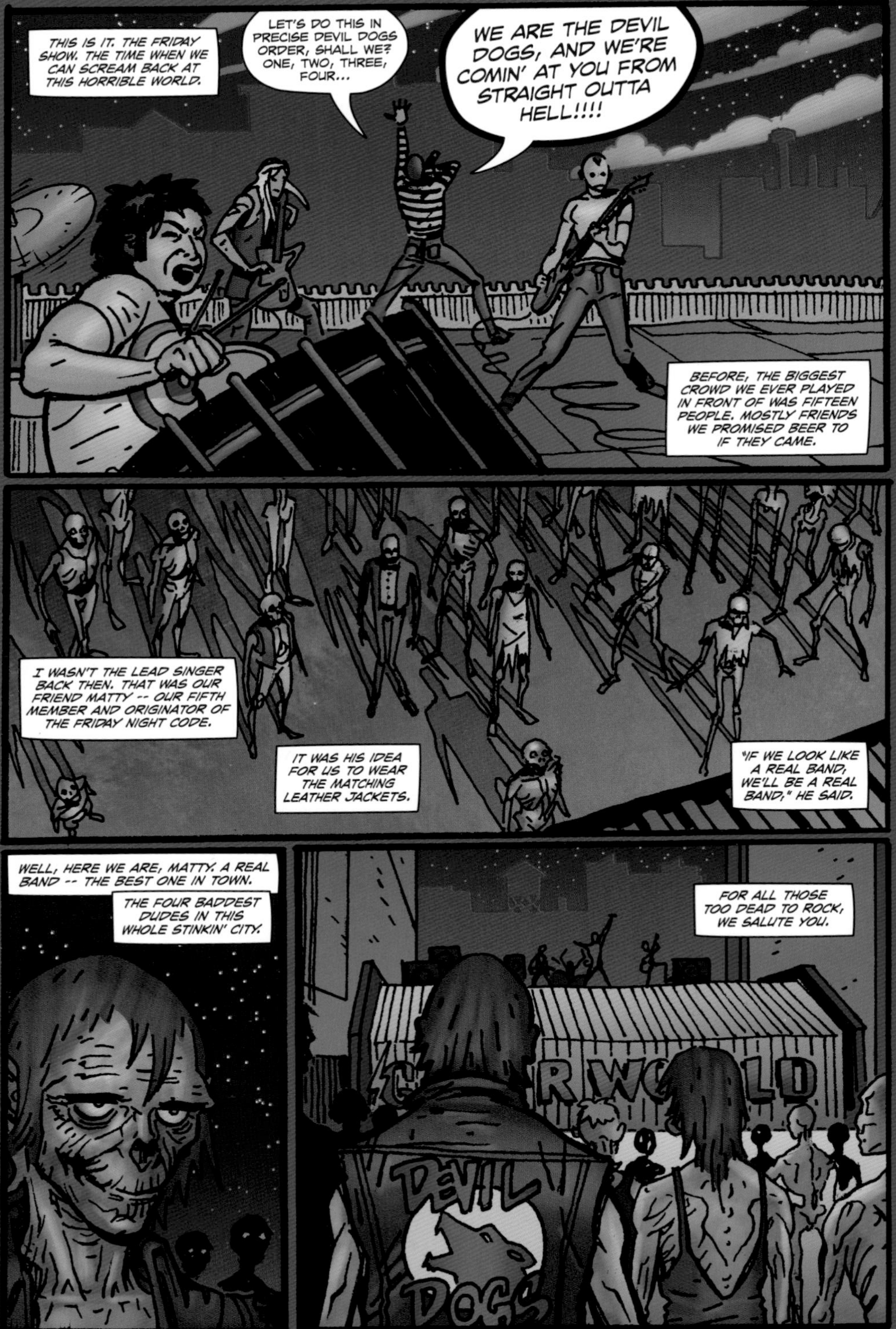
THIS IS IT. THE FRIDAY SHOW. THE TIME WHEN WE CAN SCREAM BACK AT THIS HORRIBLE WORLD.
LET'S DO THIS IN PRECISE DEVIL DOGS ORDER, SHALL WE? ONE, TWO, THREE, FOUR...
WE ARE THE DEVIL DOGS, AND WE'RE COMIN' AT YOU FROM STRAIGHT OUTTA HELL!!!!
BEFORE, THE BIGGEST CROWD WE EVER PLAYED IN FRONT OF WAS FIFTEEN PEOPLE. MOSTLY FRIENDS WE PROMISED BEER TO IF THEY CAME.
I WASN'T THE LEAD SINGER BACK THEN. THAT WAS OUR FRIEND MATTY -- OUR FIFTH MEMBER AND ORIGINATOR OF THE FRIDAY NIGHT CODE.
IT WAS HIS IDEA FOR US TO WEAR THE MATCHING LEATHER JACKETS.
"IF WE LOOK LIKE A REAL BAND, WE'LL BE A REAL BAND," HE SAID.
WELL, HERE WE ARE, MATTY. A REAL BAND -- THE BEST ONE IN TOWN.
THE FOUR BADDEST DUDES IN THIS WHOLE STINKIN' CITY.
FOR ALL THOSE TOO DEAD TO ROCK, WE SALUTE YOU.
DEVIL
DOGS

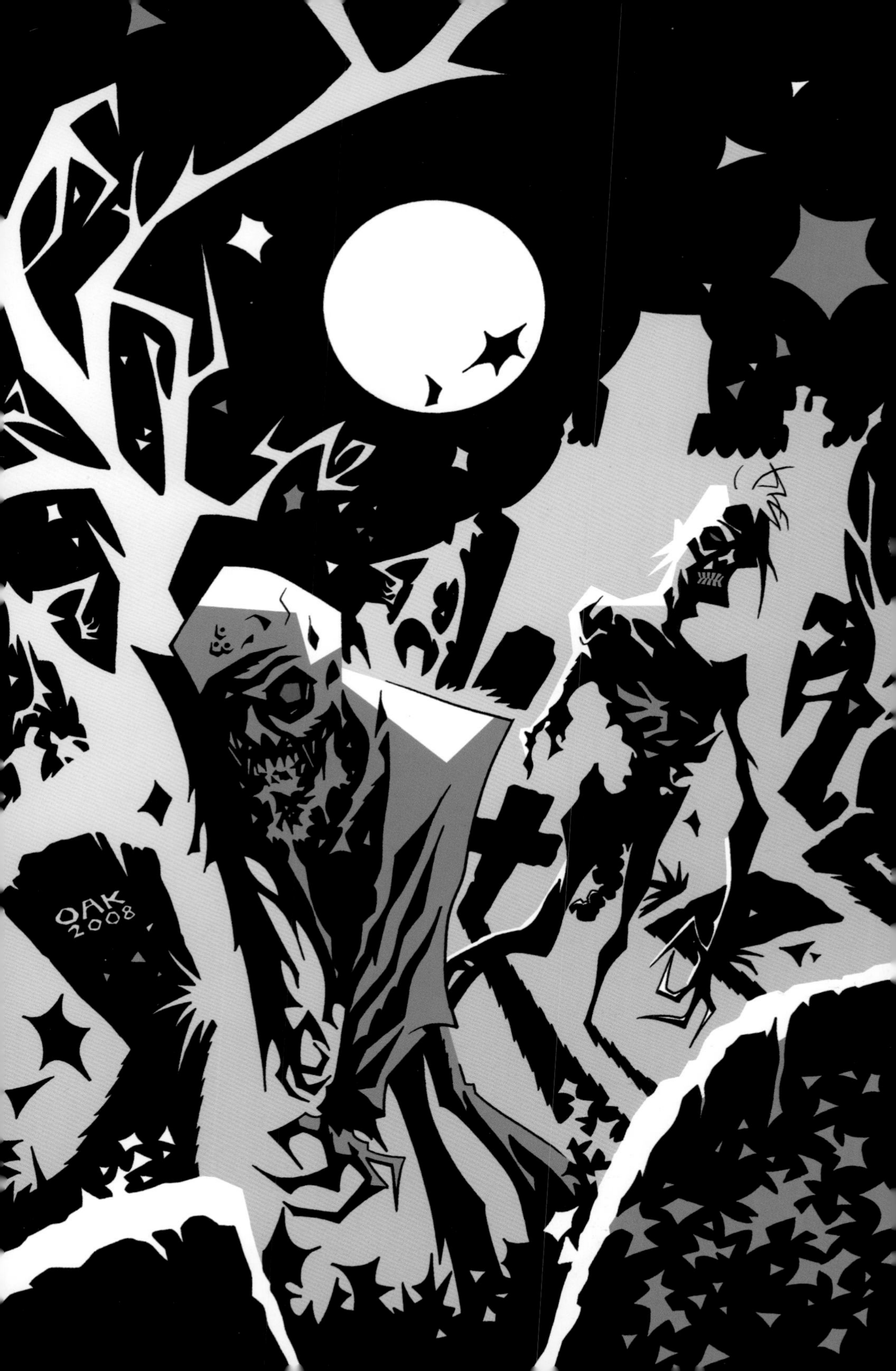
OAK
2008

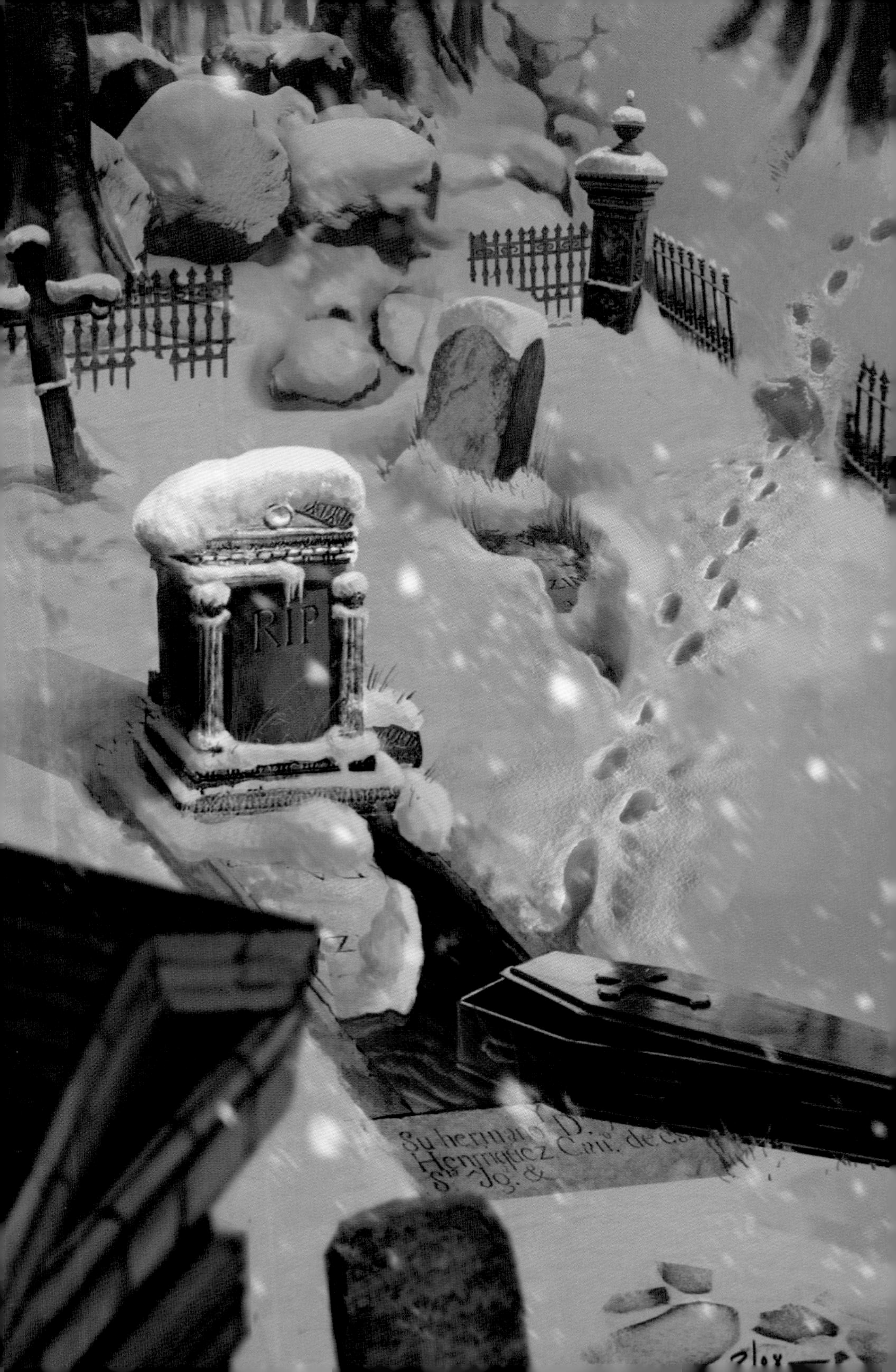
RIP

LUCKY DOG
Story: KARL KESEL
Art: JESSE HAMM

ETC.
Story: SHANE OAKLEY
Art: PAUL HARRISON-DAVIES

NAILS
Story/Art: JON SCHNEPP

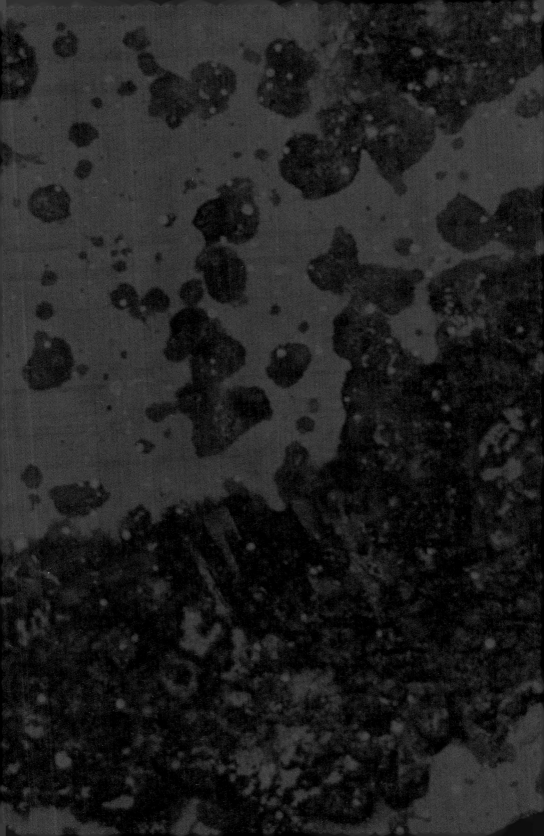

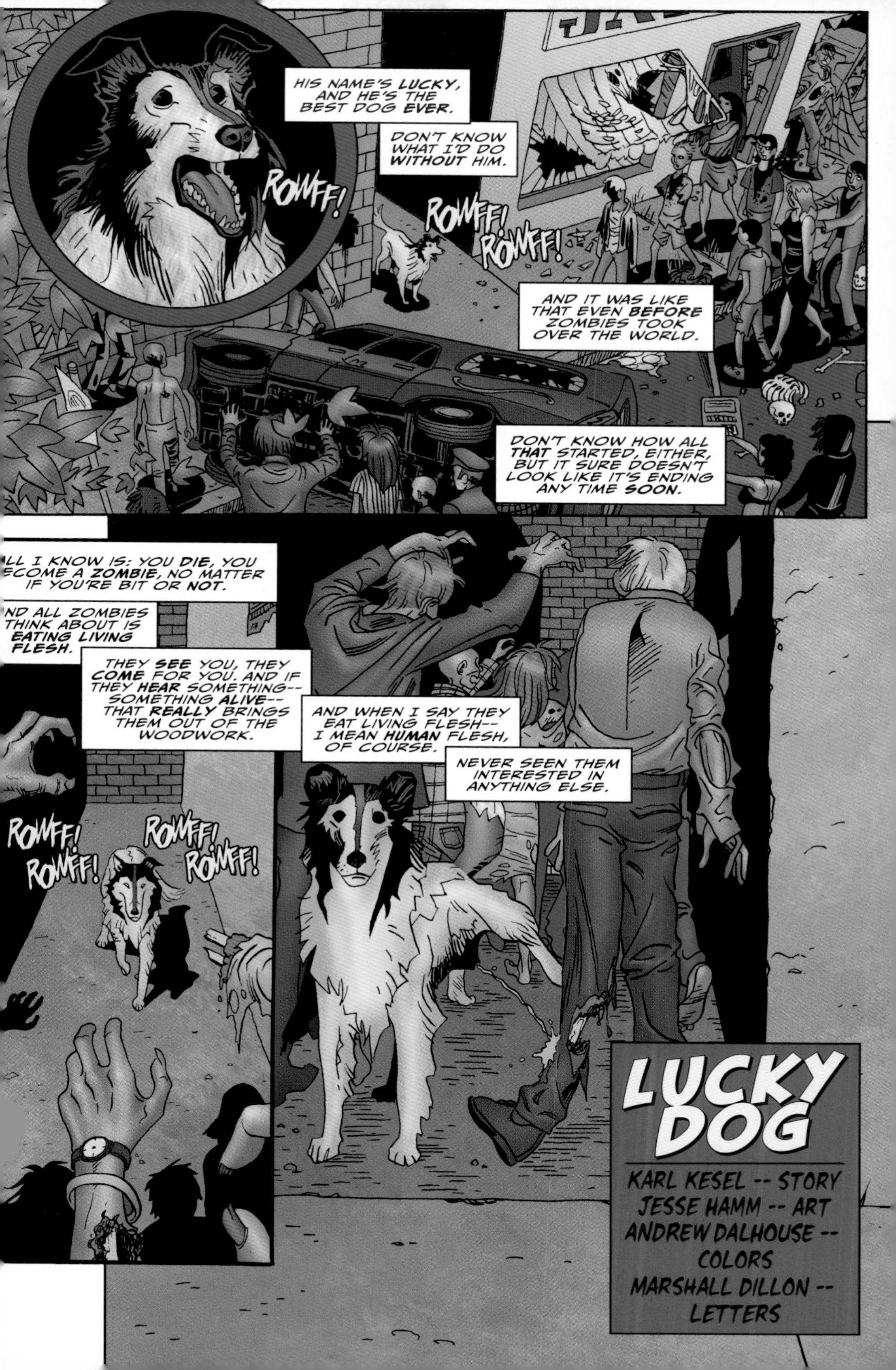

HIS NAME'S LUCKY, AND HE'S THE BEST DOG EVER.
DON'T KNOW WHAT I'D DO WITHOUT HIM.
ROWFF!
ROWFF! ROWFF!
AND IT WAS LIKE THAT EVEN BEFORE ZOMBIES TOOK OVER THE WORLD.
DON'T KNOW HOW ALL THAT STARTED, EITHER, BUT IT SURE DOESN'T LOOK LIKE IT'S ENDING ANY TIME SOON.
LL I KNOW IS: YOU DIE, YOU ECOME A ZOMBIE, NO MATTER IF YOU'RE BIT OR NOT.
ND ALL ZOMBIES THINK ABOUT IS EATING LIVING FLESH.
THEY SEE YOU, THEY COME FOR YOU. AND IF THEY HEAR SOMETHING-- SOMETHING ALIVE-- THAT REALLY BRINGS THEM OUT OF THE WOODWORK.
AND WHEN I SAY THEY EAT LIVING FLESH-- I MEAN HUMAN FLESH, OF COURSE.
NEVER SEEN THEM INTERESTED IN ANYTHING ELSE.
ROWFF! ROWFF!
ROWFF! ROWFF!
LUCKY DOG
KARL KESEL -- STORY
JESSE HAMM -- ART
ANDREW DALHOUSE -- COLORS
MARSHALL DILLON -- LETTERS

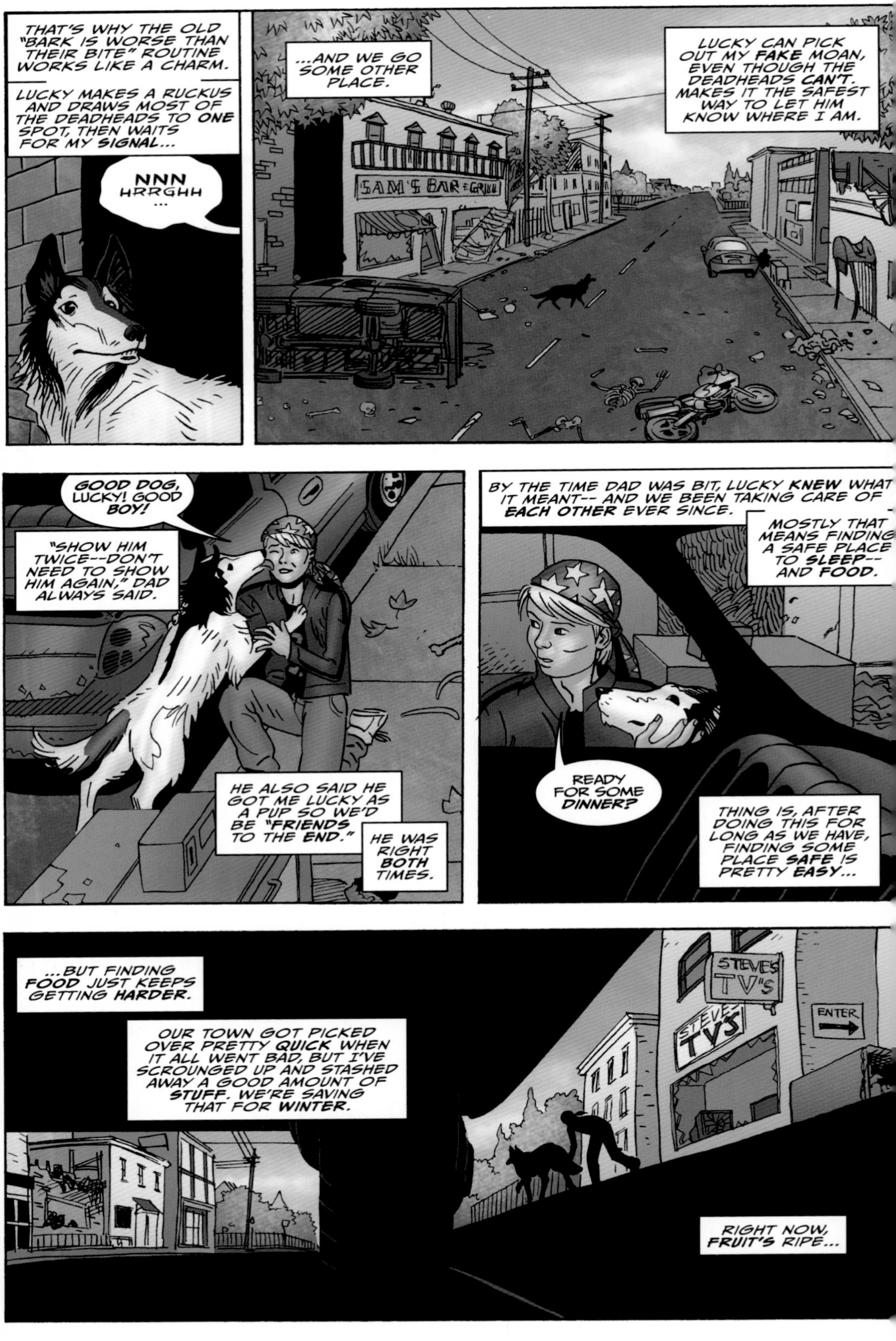
THAT'S WHY THE OLD "BARK IS WORSE THAN THEIR BITE" ROUTINE WORKS LIKE A CHARM.
LUCKY MAKES A RUCKUS AND DRAWS MOST OF THE DEADHEADS TO ONE SPOT, THEN WAITS FOR MY SIGNAL...
NNN HRRGHH ...
...AND WE GO SOME OTHER PLACE.
LUCKY CAN PICK OUT MY FAKE MOAN, EVEN THOUGH THE DEADHEADS CAN'T. MAKES IT THE SAFEST WAY TO LET HIM KNOW WHERE I AM.
SAM'S BAR & GRILL
GOOD DOG, LUCKY! GOOD BOY!
"SHOW HIM TWICE--DON'T NEED TO SHOW HIM AGAIN," DAD ALWAYS SAID.
HE ALSO SAID HE GOT ME LUCKY AS A PUP SO WE'D BE "FRIENDS TO THE END."
HE WAS RIGHT BOTH TIMES.
BY THE TIME DAD WAS BIT, LUCKY KNEW WHAT IT MEANT-- AND WE BEEN TAKING CARE OF EACH OTHER EVER SINCE.
MOSTLY THAT MEANS FINDING A SAFE PLACE TO SLEEP-- AND FOOD.
READY FOR SOME DINNER?
THING IS, AFTER DOING THIS FOR LONG AS WE HAVE, FINDING SOME PLACE SAFE IS PRETTY EASY...
...BUT FINDING FOOD JUST KEEPS GETTING HARDER.
OUR TOWN GOT PICKED OVER PRETTY QUICK WHEN IT ALL WENT BAD, BUT I'VE SCROUNGED UP AND STASHED AWAY A GOOD AMOUNT OF STUFF. WE'RE SAVING THAT FOR WINTER.
STEVE'S TV'S
STEVE'S TV'S
ENTER
RIGHT NOW, FRUIT'S RIPE...

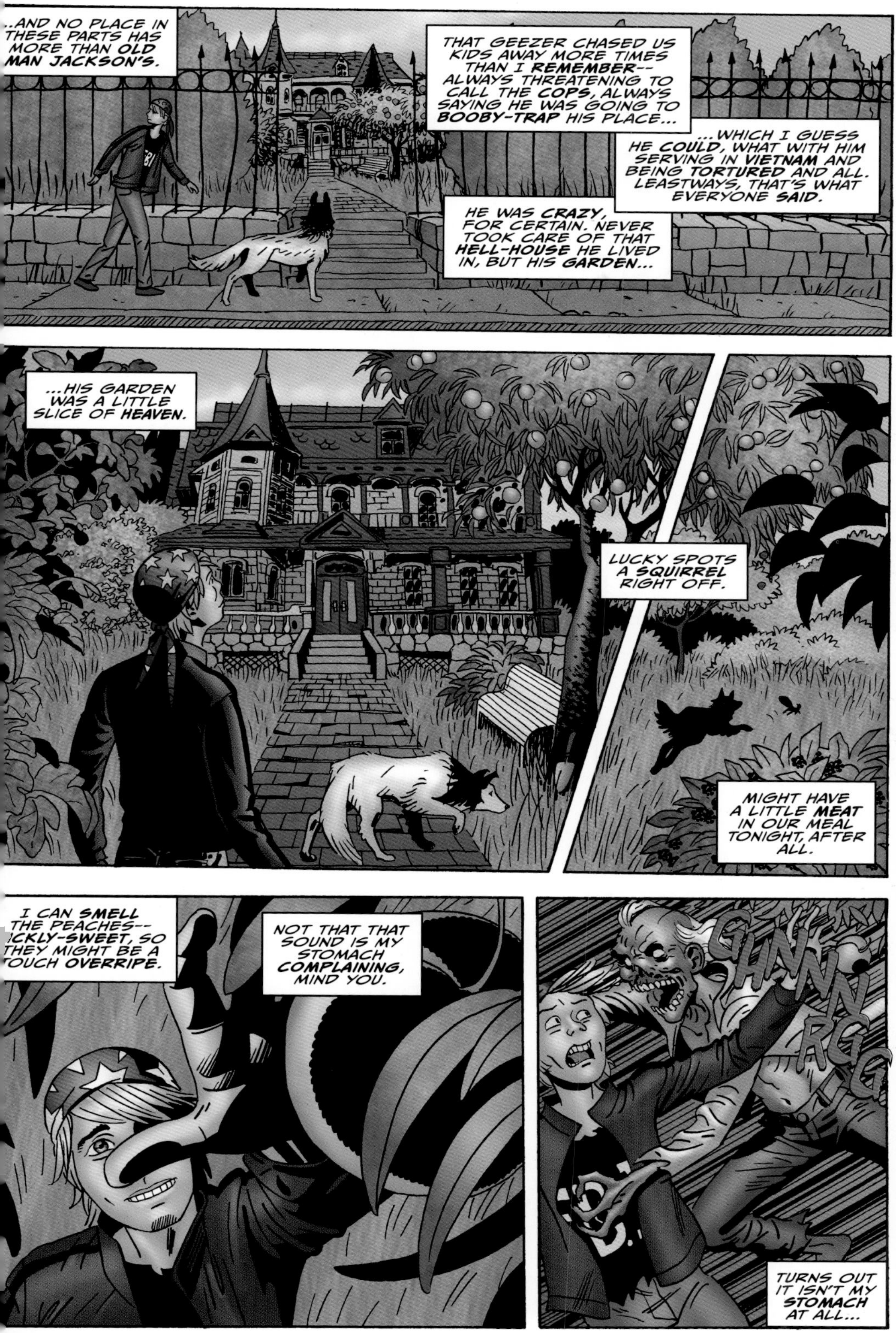
..AND NO PLACE IN THESE PARTS HAS MORE THAN OLD MAN JACKSON'S.
THAT GEEZER CHASED US KIDS AWAY MORE TIMES THAN I REMEMBER-- ALWAYS THREATENING TO CALL THE COPS, ALWAYS SAYING HE WAS GOING TO BOOBY-TRAP HIS PLACE...
...WHICH I GUESS HE COULD, WHAT WITH HIM SERVING IN VIETNAM AND BEING TORTURED AND ALL. LEASTWAYS, THAT'S WHAT EVERYONE SAID.
HE WAS CRAZY, FOR CERTAIN. NEVER TOOK CARE OF THAT HELL-HOUSE HE LIVED IN, BUT HIS GARDEN...
...HIS GARDEN WAS A LITTLE SLICE OF HEAVEN.
LUCKY SPOTS A SQUIRREL RIGHT OFF.
MIGHT HAVE A LITTLE MEAT IN OUR MEAL TONIGHT, AFTER ALL.
I CAN SMELL THE PEACHES-- ICKLY-SWEET, SO THEY MIGHT BE A TOUCH OVERRIPE.
NOT THAT THAT SOUND IS MY STOMACH COMPLAINING, MIND YOU.
GHNNN RGG
TURNS OUT IT ISN'T MY STOMACH AT ALL...

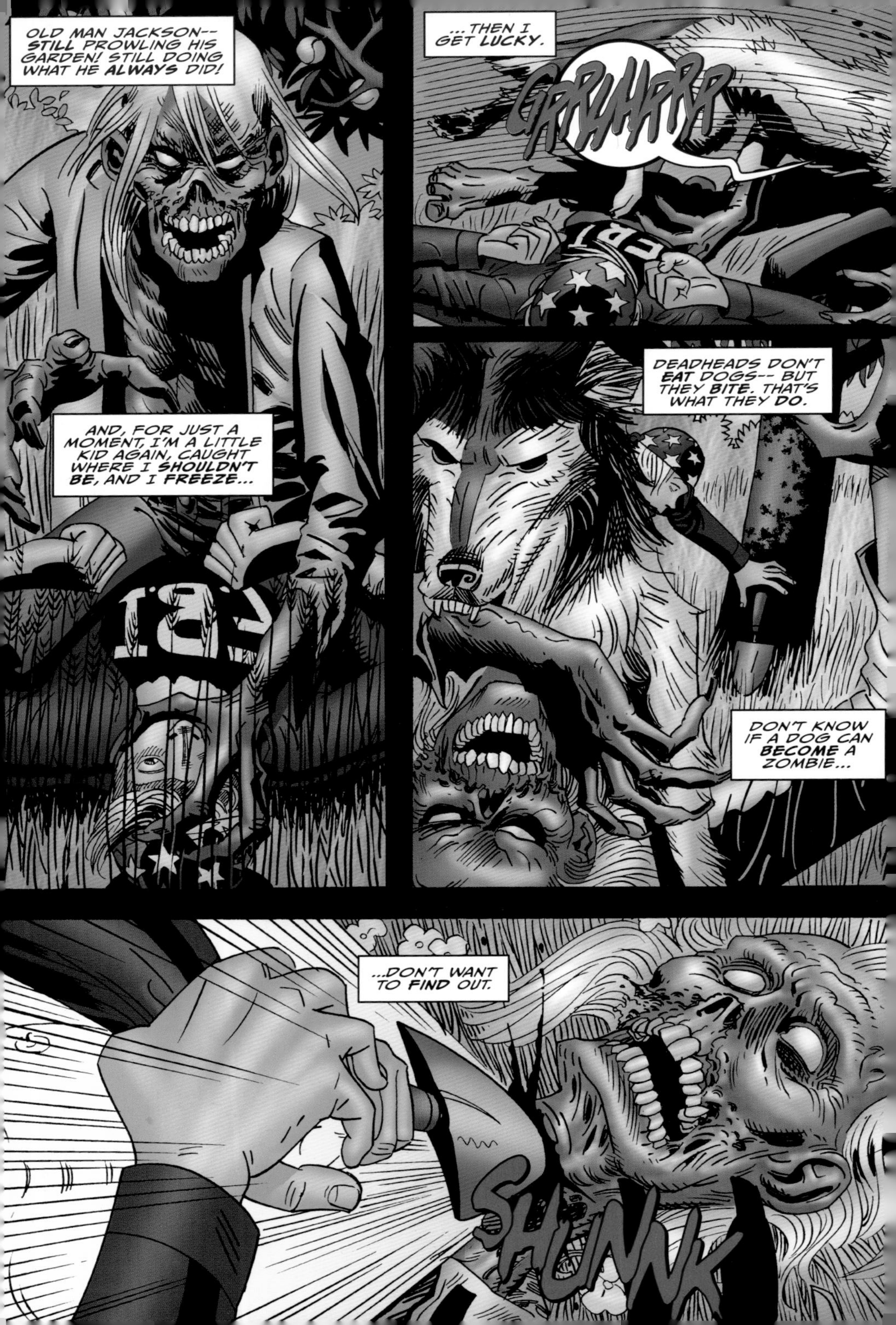
OLD MAN JACKSON-- STILL PROWLING HIS GARDEN! STILL DOING WHAT HE ALWAYS DID!
AND, FOR JUST A MOMENT, I'M A LITTLE KID AGAIN, CAUGHT WHERE I SHOULDN'T BE, AND I FREEZE...
...THEN I GET LUCKY.
GRRAAHRRR
DEADHEADS DON'T EAT DOGS-- BUT THEY BITE. THAT'S WHAT THEY DO.
DON'T KNOW IF A DOG CAN BECOME A ZOMBIE...
...DON'T WANT TO FIND OUT.
SHUNK

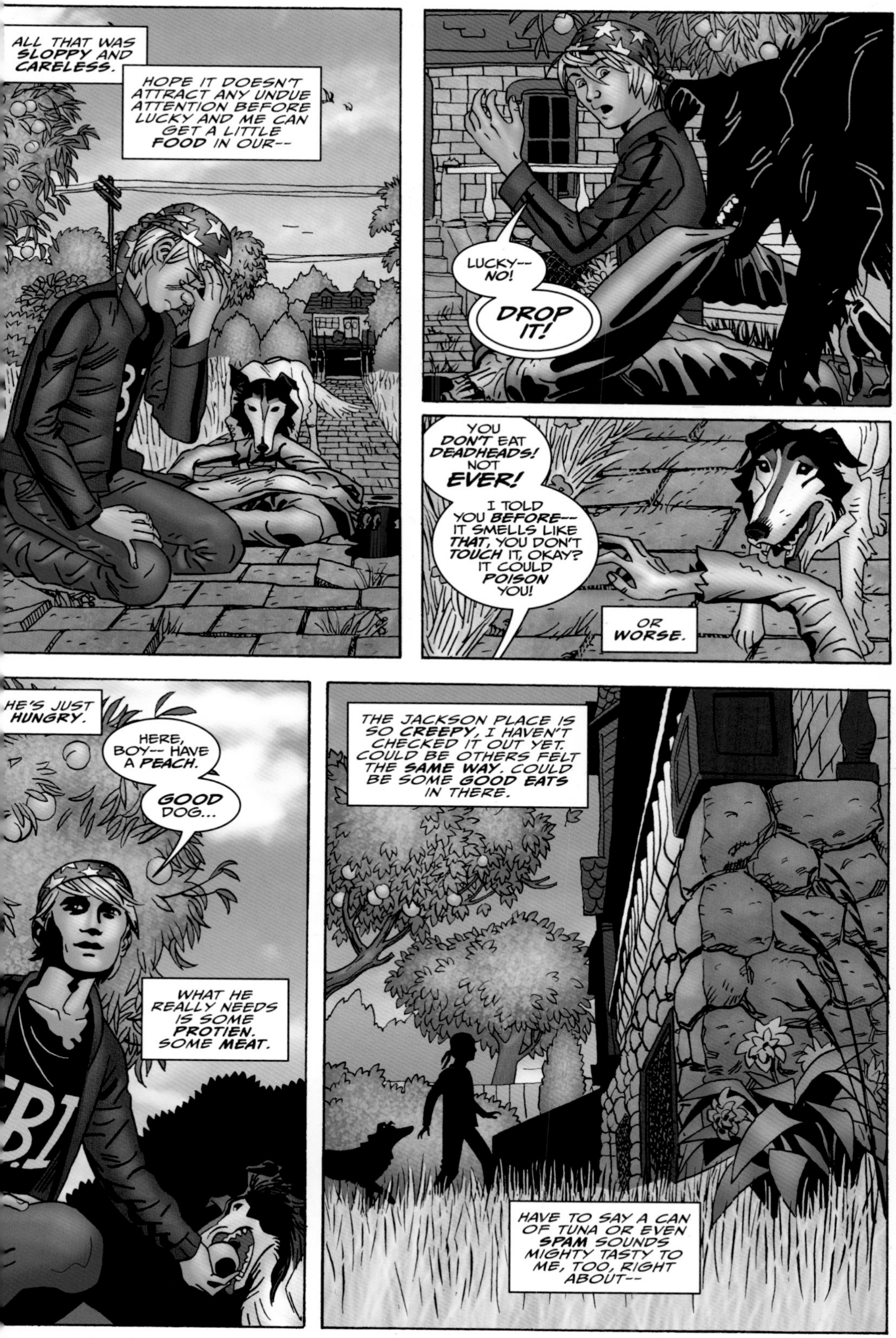
ALL THAT WAS SLOPPY AND CARELESS.
HOPE IT DOESN'T ATTRACT ANY UNDUE ATTENTION BEFORE LUCKY AND ME CAN GET A LITTLE FOOD IN OUR--
LUCKY-- NO!
DROP IT!
YOU DON'T EAT DEADHEADS! NOT EVER!
I TOLD YOU BEFORE-- IT SMELLS LIKE THAT, YOU DON'T TOUCH IT, OKAY? IT COULD POISON YOU!
OR WORSE.
HE'S JUST HUNGRY.
HERE, BOY-- HAVE A PEACH.
GOOD DOG...
WHAT HE REALLY NEEDS IS SOME PROTIEN. SOME MEAT.
THE JACKSON PLACE IS SO CREEPY, I HAVEN'T CHECKED IT OUT YET. COULD BE OTHERS FELT THE SAME WAY. COULD BE SOME GOOD EATS IN THERE.
HAVE TO SAY A CAN OF TUNA OR EVEN SPAM SOUNDS MIGHTY TASTY TO ME, TOO, RIGHT ABOUT--

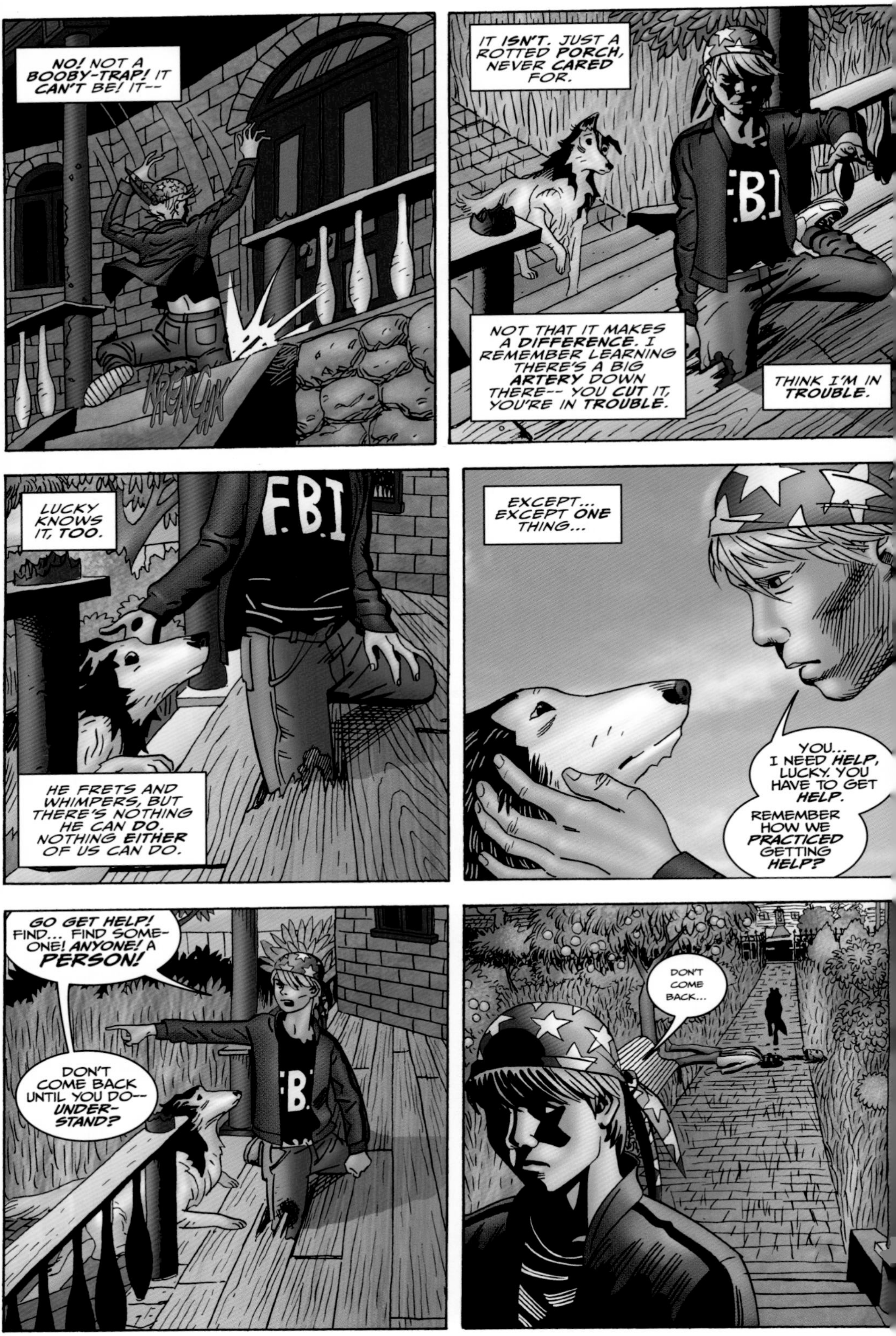
NO! NOT A BOOBY-TRAP! IT CAN'T BE! IT--
KRENCHK
IT ISN'T. JUST A ROTTED PORCH, NEVER CARED FOR.
NOT THAT IT MAKES A DIFFERENCE. I REMEMBER LEARNING THERE'S A BIG ARTERY DOWN THERE-- YOU CUT IT, YOU'RE IN TROUBLE.
THINK I'M IN TROUBLE.
LUCKY KNOWS IT, TOO.
HE FRETS AND WHIMPERS, BUT THERE'S NOTHING HE CAN DO. NOTHING EITHER OF US CAN DO.
EXCEPT... EXCEPT ONE THING...
YOU... I NEED HELP, LUCKY. YOU HAVE TO GET HELP.
REMEMBER HOW WE PRACTICED GETTING HELP?
GO GET HELP! FIND... FIND SOME-ONE! ANYONE! A PERSON!
DON'T COME BACK UNTIL YOU DO-- UNDER-STAND?
DON'T COME BACK...

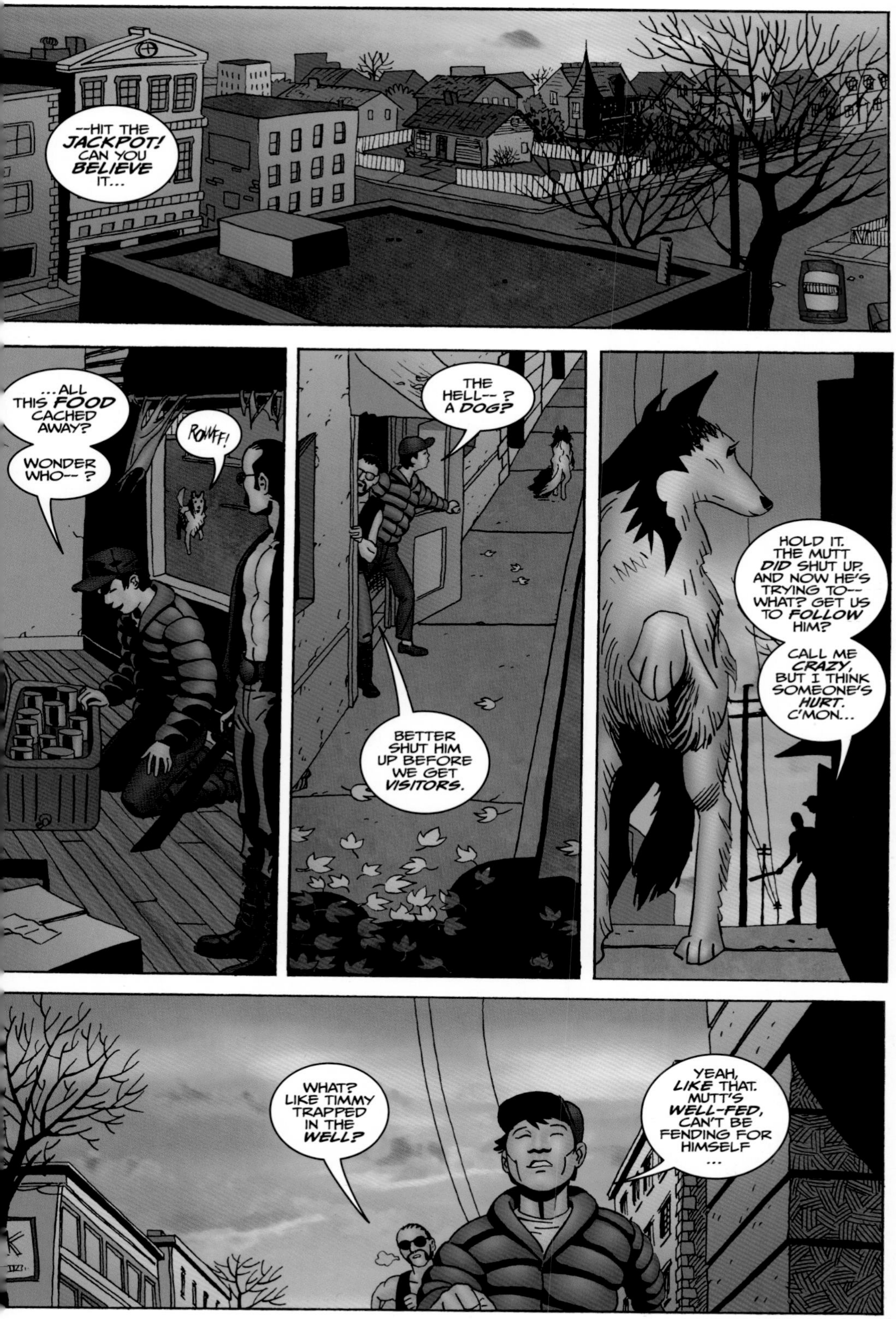
--HIT THE JACKPOT! CAN YOU BELIEVE IT...
...ALL THIS FOOD CACHED AWAY?
WONDER WHO-- ?
ROWFF!
THE HELL-- ? A DOG?
BETTER SHUT HIM UP BEFORE WE GET VISITORS.
HOLD IT. THE MUTT DID SHUT UP. AND NOW HE'S TRYING TO-- WHAT? GET US TO FOLLOW HIM?
CALL ME CRAZY, BUT I THINK SOMEONE'S HURT. C'MON...
WHAT? LIKE TIMMY TRAPPED IN THE WELL?
YEAH, LIKE THAT. MUTT'S WELL-FED, CAN'T BE FENDING FOR HIMSELF ...

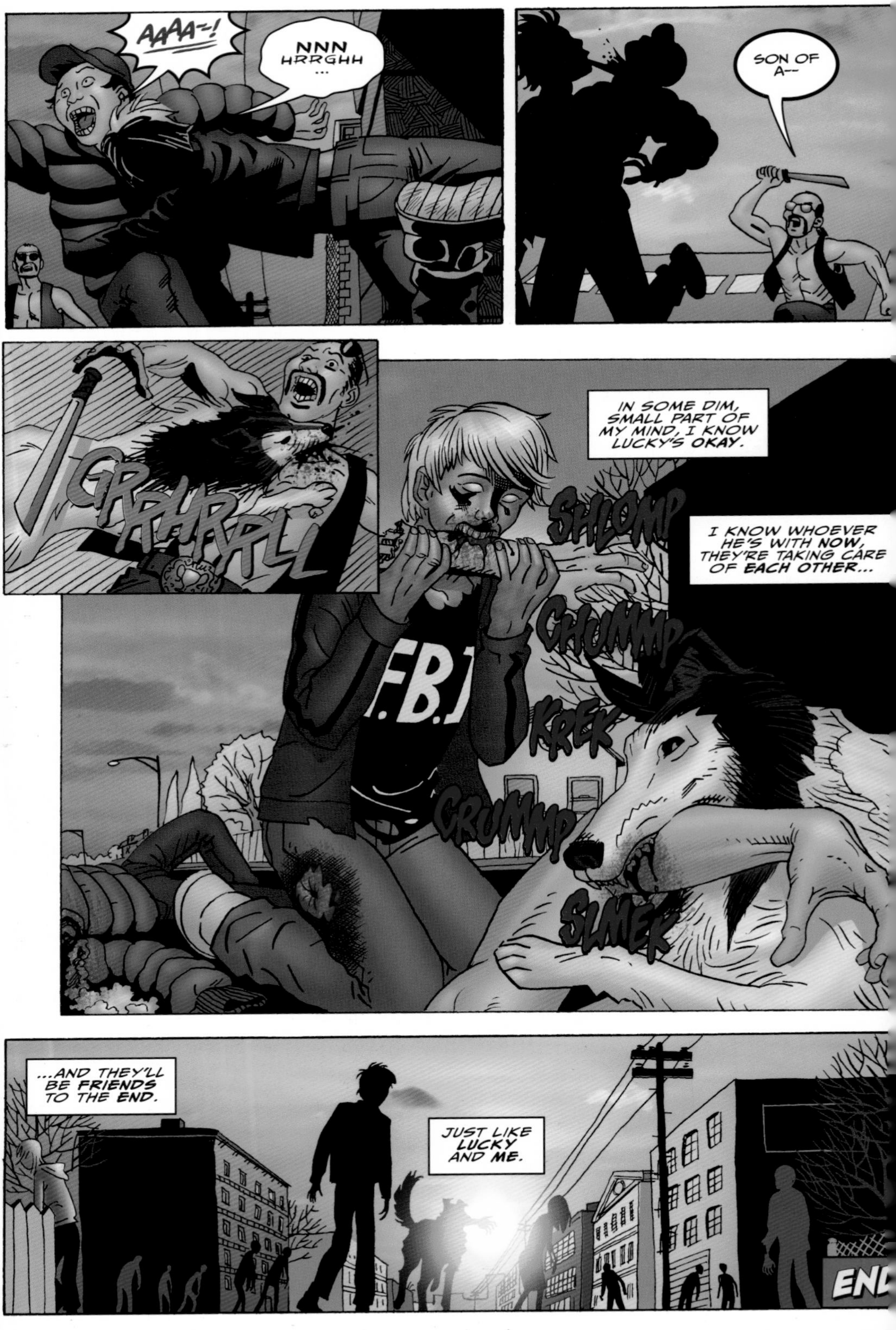
AAAA--!
NNN HRRGHH ...
SON OF A--
GRRHRRLL
IN SOME DIM, SMALL PART OF MY MIND, I KNOW LUCKY'S OKAY.
SHLOMP
I KNOW WHOEVER HE'S WITH NOW, THEY'RE TAKING CARE OF EACH OTHER...
CHUMMP
F.B.I
KREK
CRUMMP
SLMEK
...AND THEY'LL BE FRIENDS TO THE END.
JUST LIKE LUCKY AND ME.
END

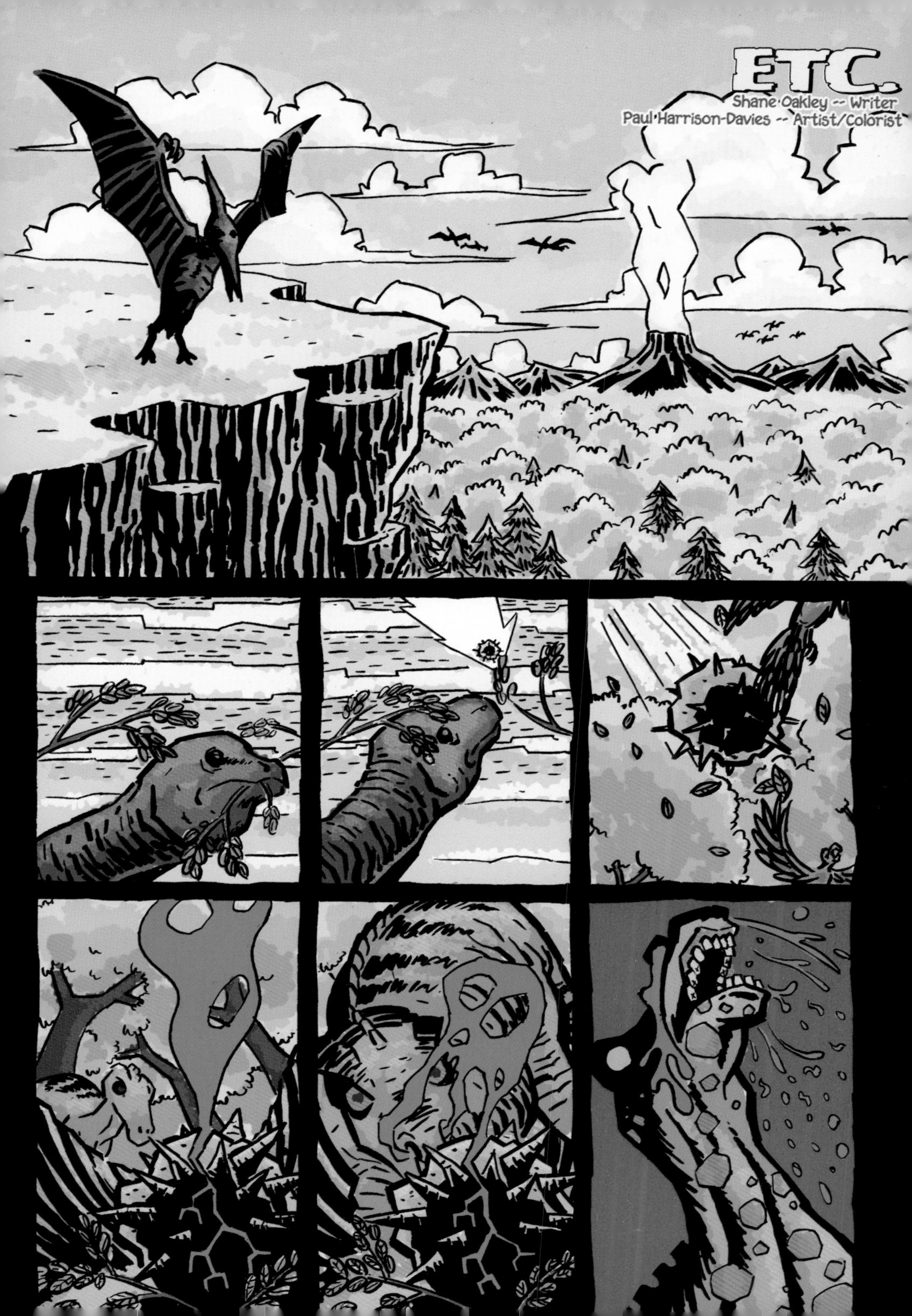

ETC.
Shane Oakley -- Writer
Paul Harrison-Davies -- Artist/Colorist

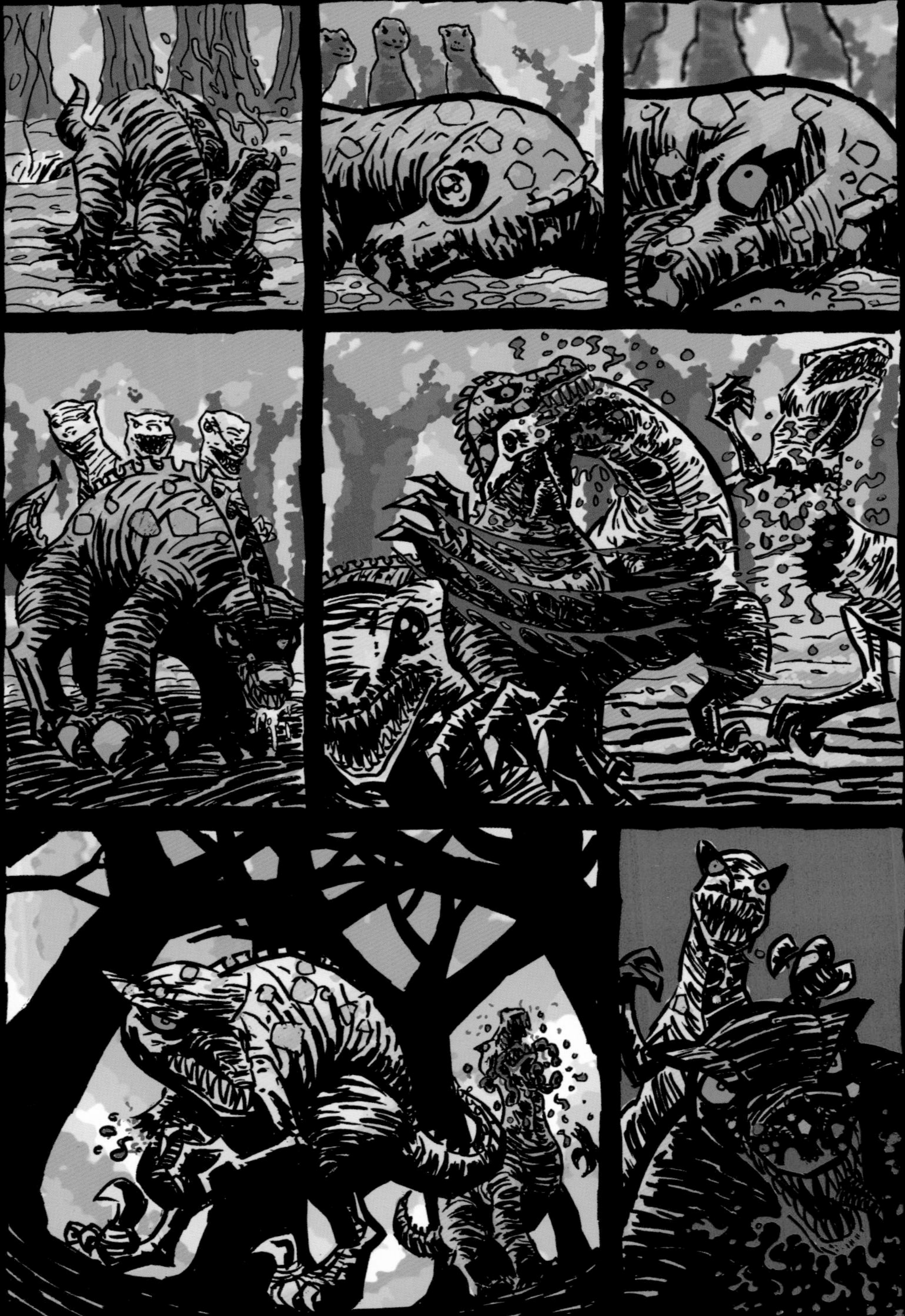

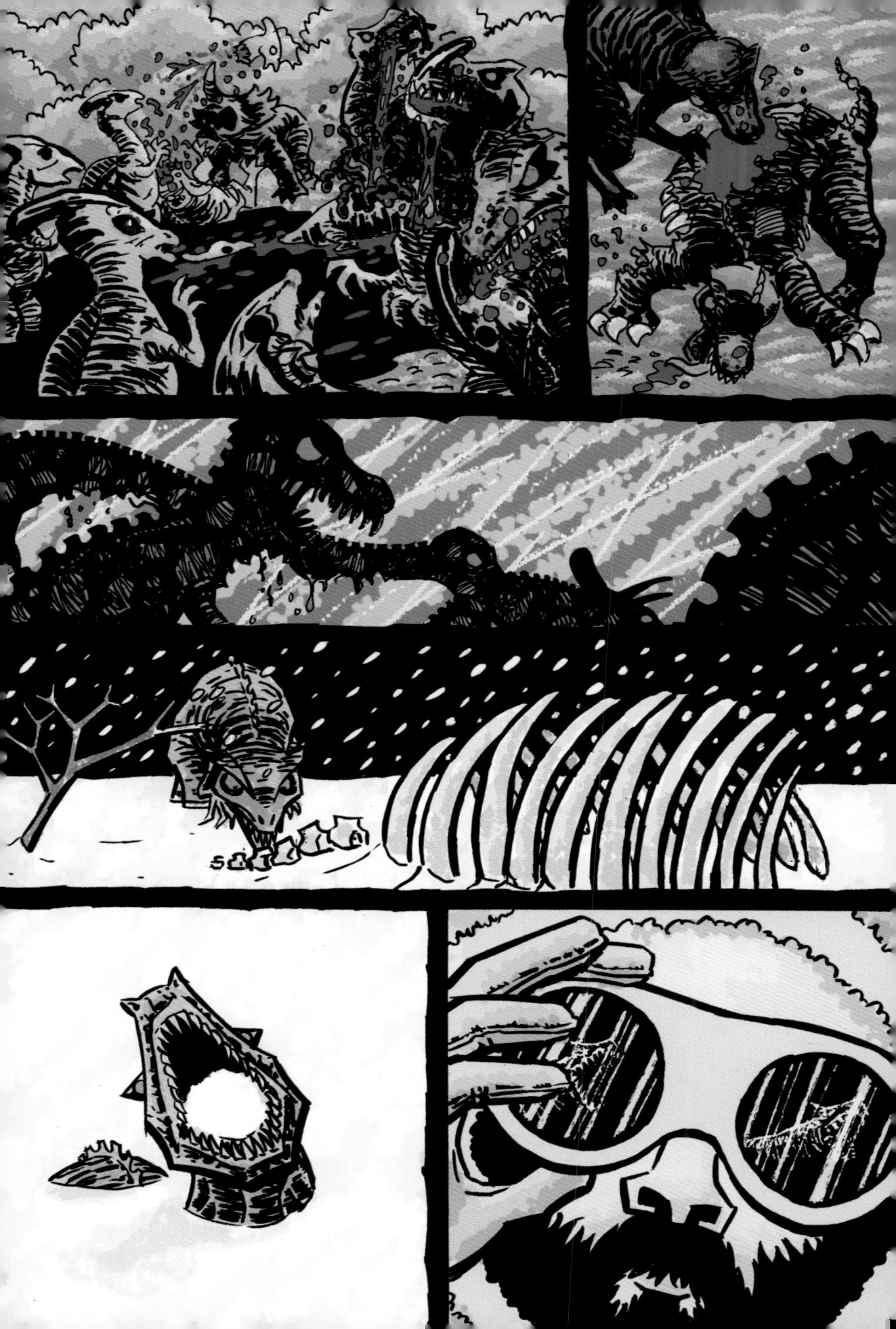

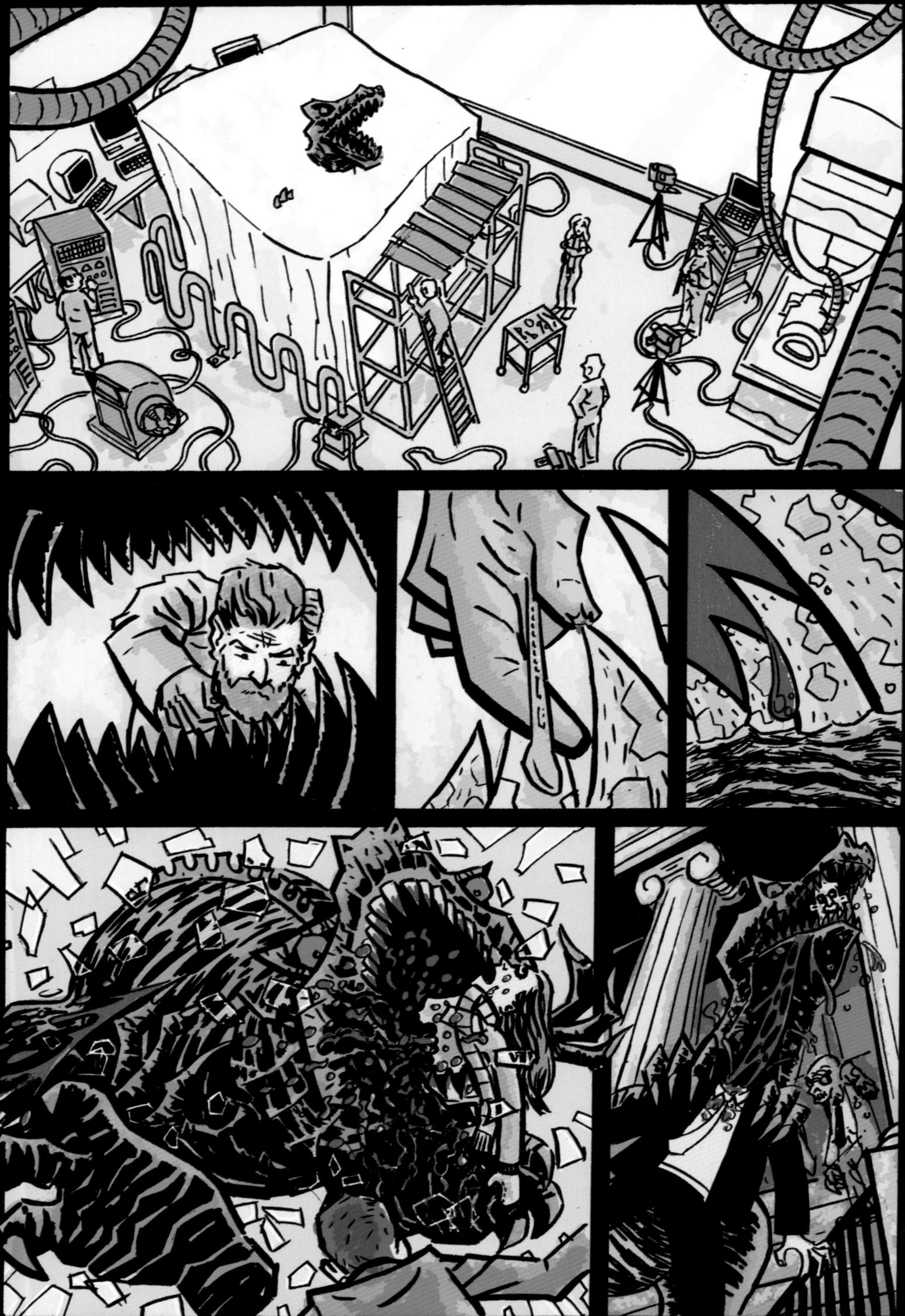

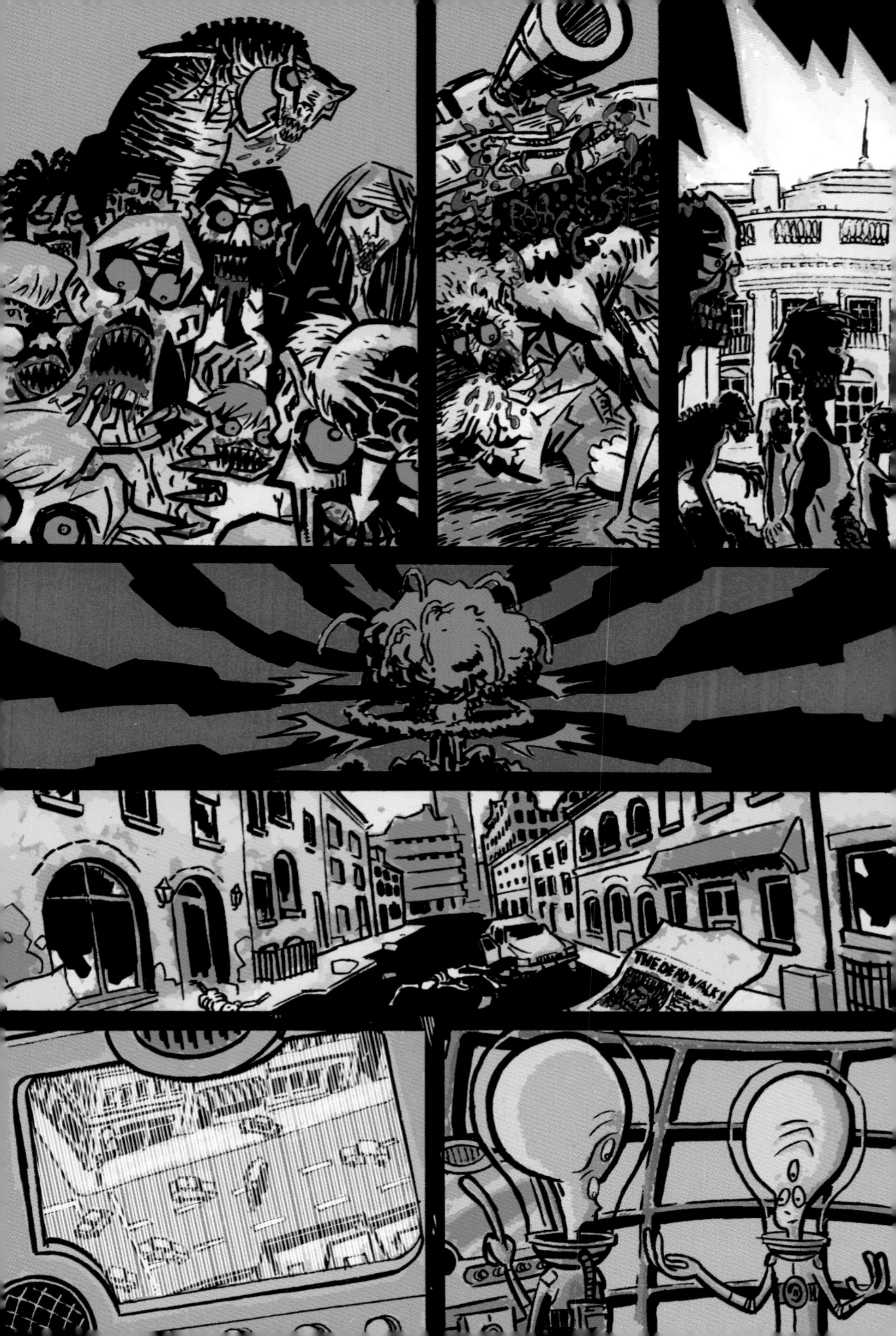
THE DEAD WALK!

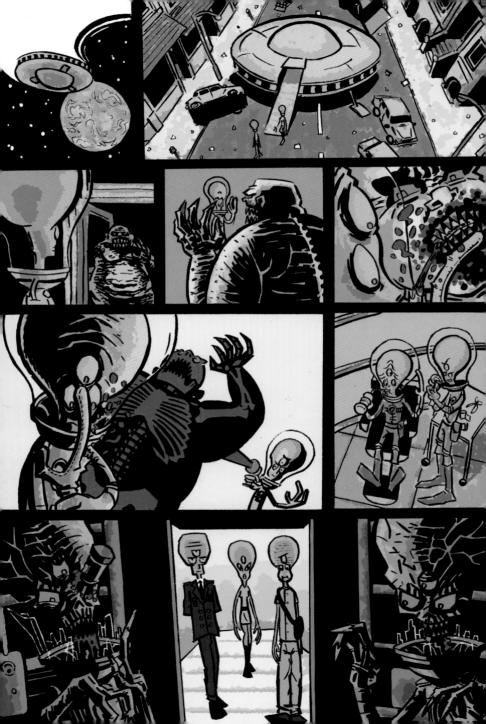

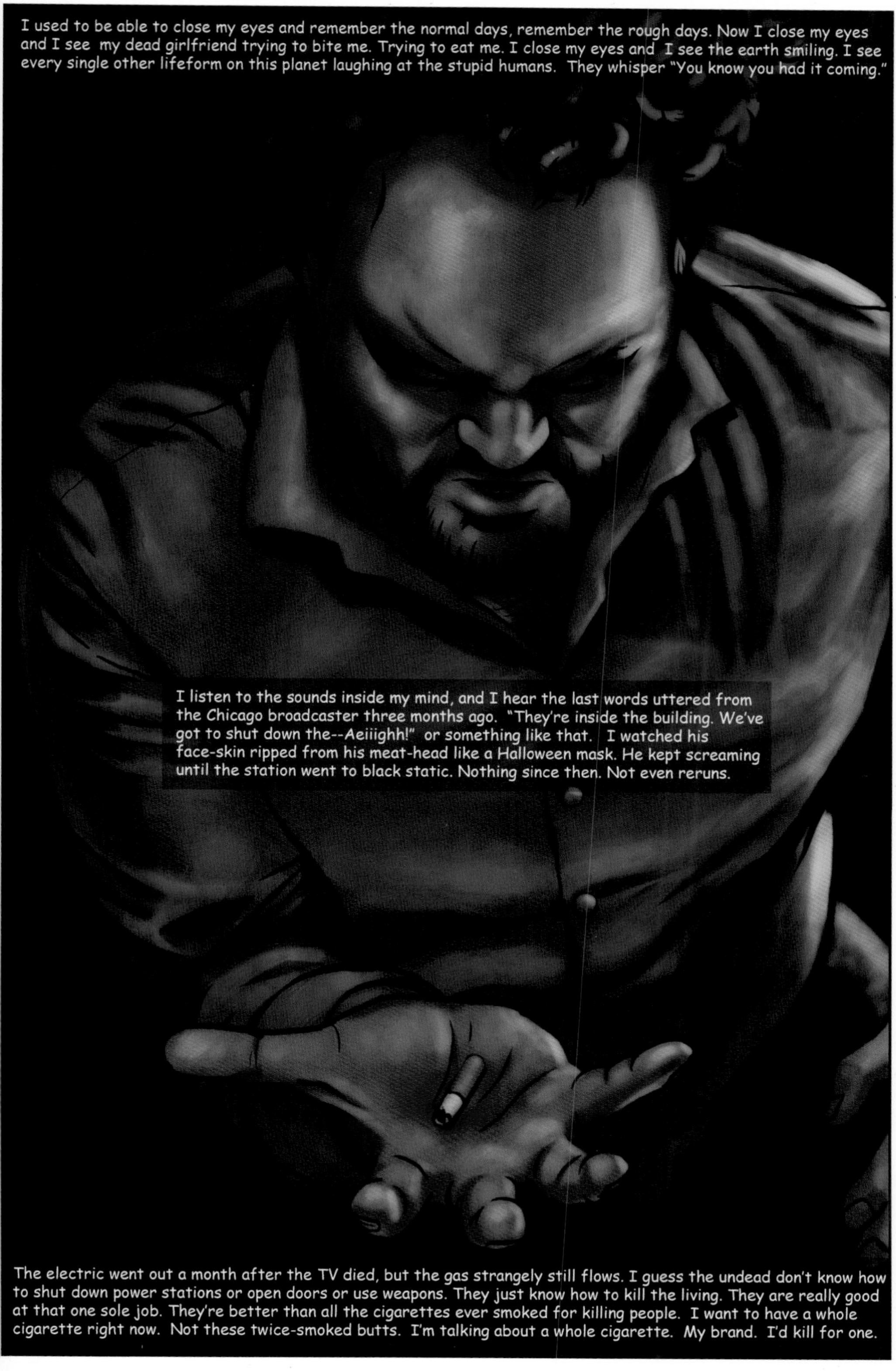
I used to be able to close my eyes and remember the normal days, remember the rough days. Now I close my eyes and I see my dead girlfriend trying to bite me. Trying to eat me. I close my eyes and I see the earth smiling. I see every single other lifeform on this planet laughing at the stupid humans. They whisper "You know you had it coming."
I listen to the sounds inside my mind, and I hear the last words uttered from the Chicago broadcaster three months ago. "They're inside the building. We've got to shut down the--Aeiiighh!" or something like that. I watched his face-skin ripped from his meat-head like a Halloween mask. He kept screaming until the station went to black static. Nothing since then. Not even reruns.
The electric went out a month after the TV died, but the gas strangely still flows. I guess the undead don't know how to shut down power stations or open doors or use weapons. They just know how to kill the living. They are really good at that one sole job. They're better than all the cigarettes ever smoked for killing people. I want to have a whole cigarette right now. Not these twice-smoked butts. I'm talking about a whole cigarette. My brand. I'd kill for one.

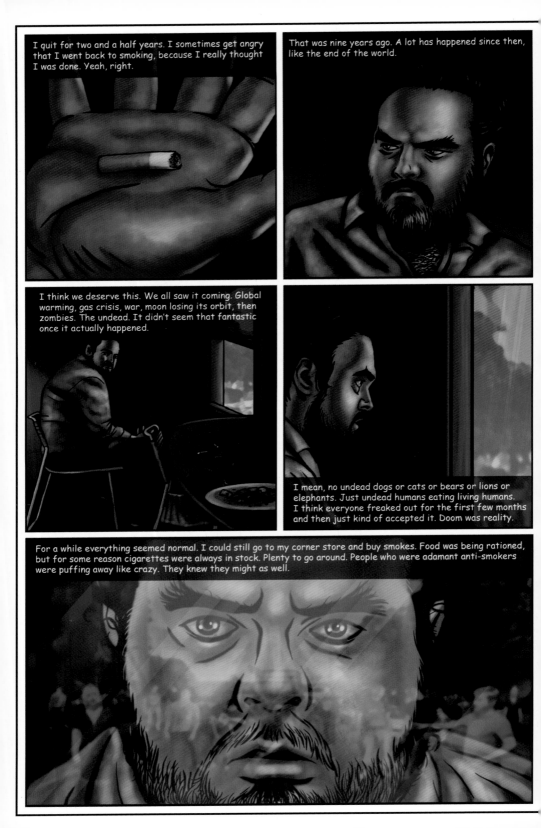

I quit for two and a half years. I sometimes get angry that I went back to smoking, because I really thought I was done. Yeah, right.

That was nine years ago. A lot has happened since then, like the end of the world.

I think we deserve this. We all saw it coming. Global warming, gas crisis, war, moon losing its orbit, then zombies. The undead. It didn't seem that fantastic once it actually happened.

I mean, no undead dogs or cats or bears or lions or elephants. Just undead humans eating living humans. I think everyone freaked out for the first few months and then just kind of accepted it. Doom was reality.

For a while everything seemed normal. I could still go to my corner store and buy smokes. Food was being rationed, but for some reason cigarettes were always in stock. Plenty to go around. People who were adamant anti-smokers were puffing away like crazy. They knew they might as well.

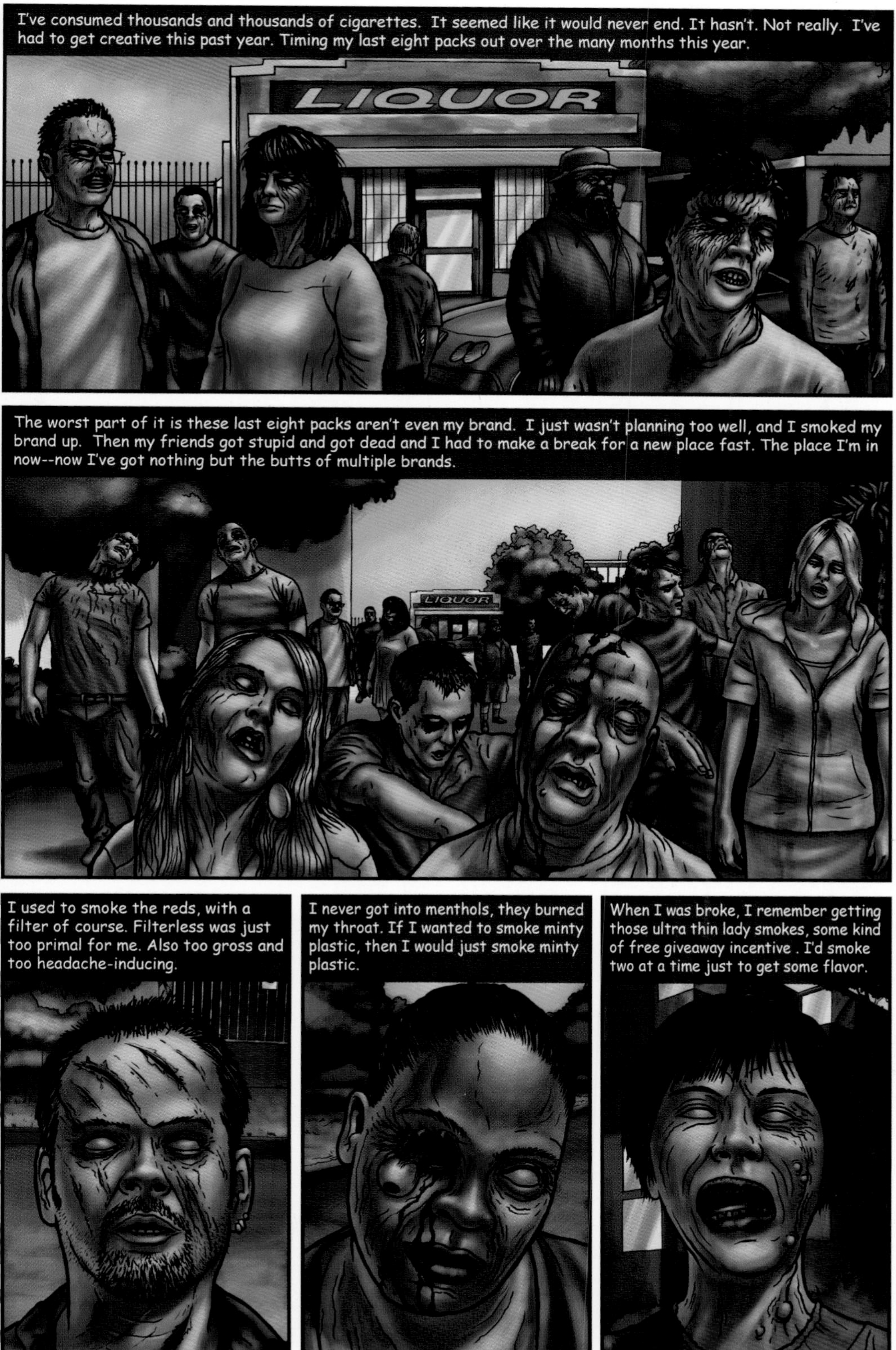
I've consumed thousands and thousands of cigarettes. It seemed like it would never end. It hasn't. Not really. I've had to get creative this past year. Timing my last eight packs out over the many months this year.
LIQUOR
The worst part of it is these last eight packs aren't even my brand. I just wasn't planning too well, and I smoked my brand up. Then my friends got stupid and got dead and I had to make a break for a new place fast. The place I'm in now--now I've got nothing but the butts of multiple brands.
LIQUOR
I used to smoke the reds, with a filter of course. Filterless was just too primal for me. Also too gross and too headache-inducing.
I never got into menthols, they burned my throat. If I wanted to smoke minty plastic, then I would just smoke minty plastic.
When I was broke, I remember getting those ultra thin lady smokes, some kind of free giveaway incentive . I'd smoke two at a time just to get some flavor.

I switched to the all-naturals with no chemicals or additives a few years before the outbreak. Before the end of everything normal.

I remember thinking these were a safer cigarette, so I didn't have to think about tumors and cancer and death quite as much. Before the dead came back.

I quit for two and a half years. That was over nine years ago.

I think I saw my sister on TV, a year after she got taken with most of the East Coast.

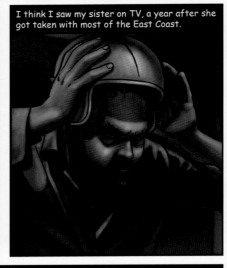

She never smoked. Neither did my parents. Man, the lectures I'd get from all of them.

Those leaf and twig smokes, the ones with no tobacco, no nicotine. They made it really easy to finally quit.

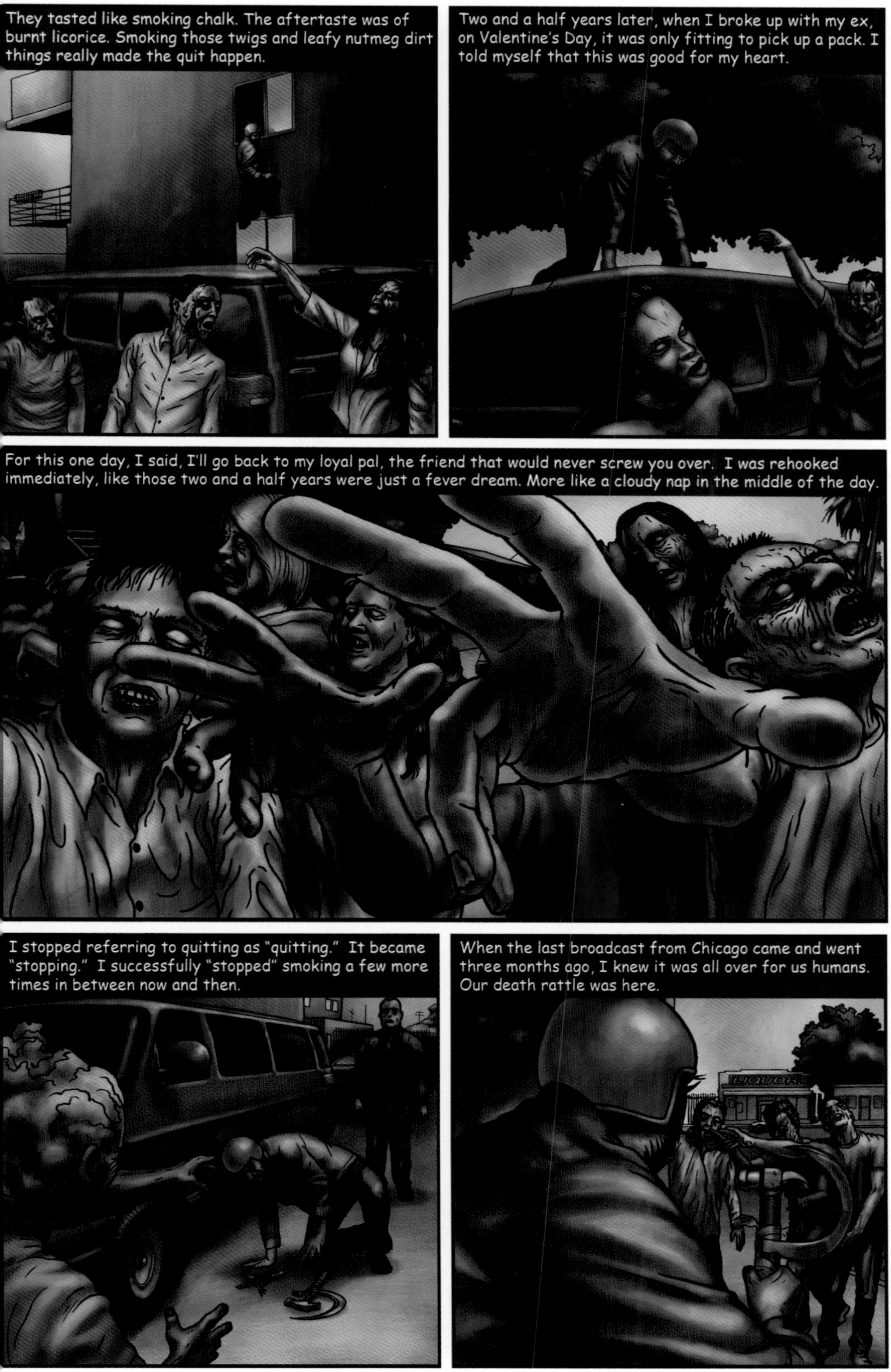
They tasted like smoking chalk. The aftertaste was of burnt licorice. Smoking those twigs and leafy nutmeg dirt things really made the quit happen.
Two and a half years later, when I broke up with my ex, on Valentine's Day, it was only fitting to pick up a pack. I told myself that this was good for my heart.
For this one day, I said, I'll go back to my loyal pal, the friend that would never screw you over. I was rehooked immediately, like those two and a half years were just a fever dream. More like a cloudy nap in the middle of the day.
I stopped referring to quitting as "quitting." It became "stopping." I successfully "stopped" smoking a few more times in between now and then.
When the last broadcast from Chicago came and went three months ago, I knew it was all over for us humans. Our death rattle was here.
LIQUOR

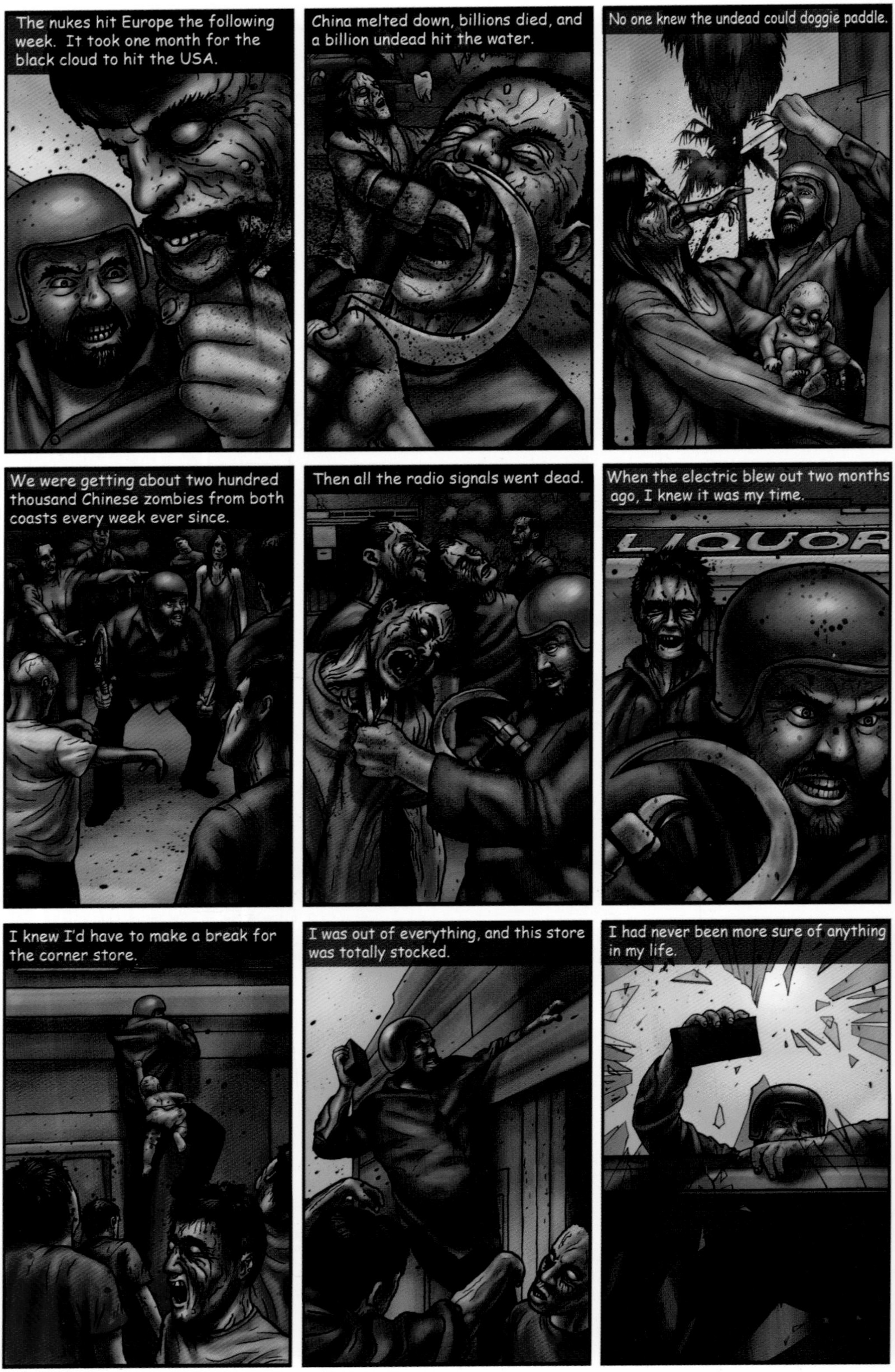
The nukes hit Europe the following week. It took one month for the black cloud to hit the USA.
China melted down, billions died, and a billion undead hit the water.
No one knew the undead could doggie paddle.
We were getting about two hundred thousand Chinese zombies from both coasts every week ever since.
Then all the radio signals went dead.
When the electric blew out two months ago, I knew it was my time.
LIQUOR
I knew I'd have to make a break for the corner store.
I was out of everything, and this store was totally stocked.
I had never been more sure of anything in my life.

I could see all the fresh supplies for these past two years, pure and untouched.

I could see the cans, the cereal, the soup.

I know this is going to be my little slice of heaven.

They have to have smokes. I'm sure of it...

I've been ready for this day for the last eight months.

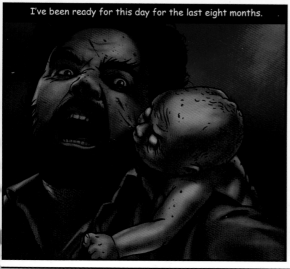

I hope they still have my brand.

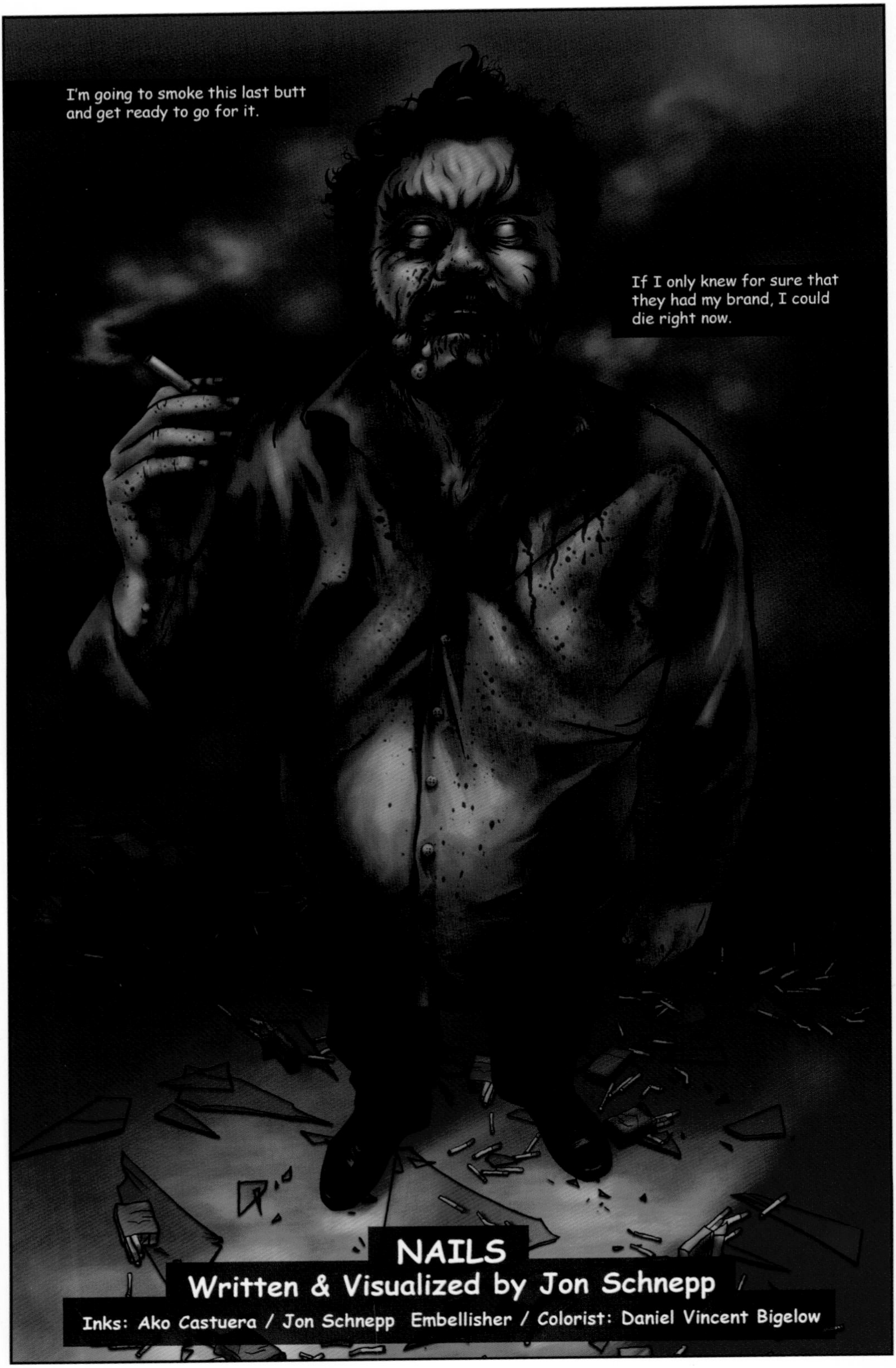
I'm going to smoke this last butt and get ready to go for it.
If I only knew for sure that they had my brand, I could die right now.
NAILS
Written & Visualized by Jon Schnepp
Inks: Ako Castuera / Jon Schnepp Embellisher / Colorist: Daniel Vincent Bigelow

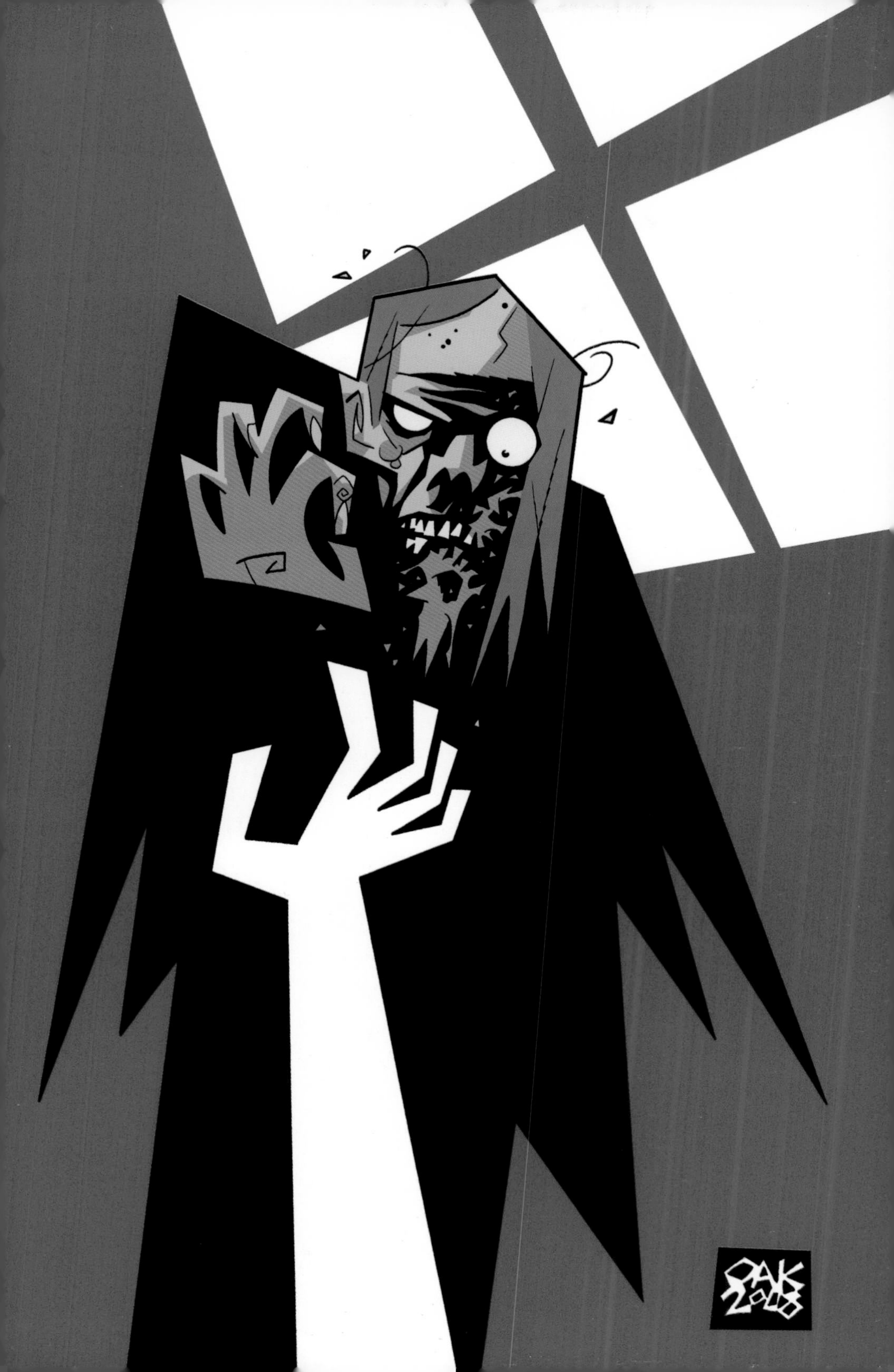

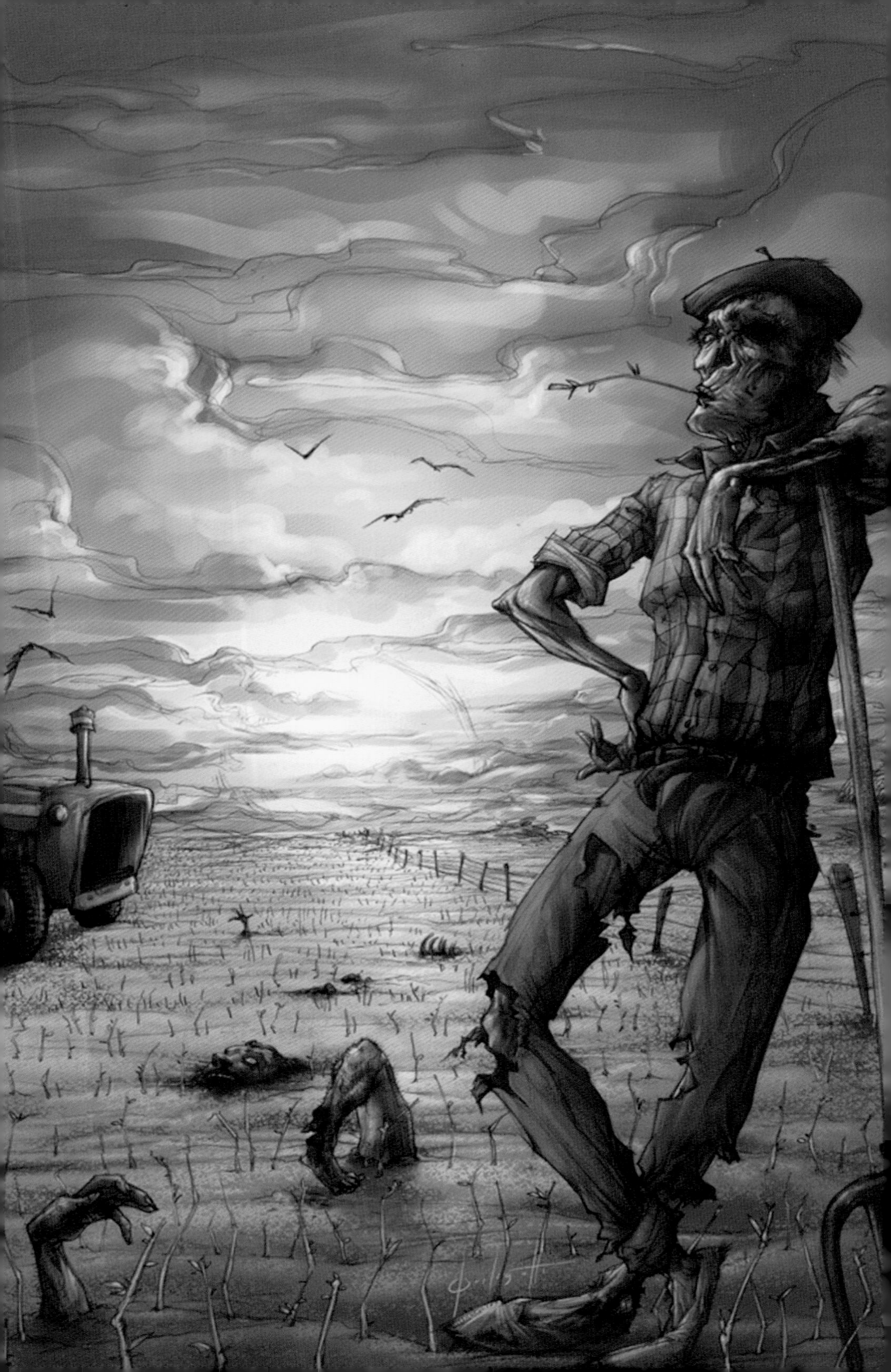

BACKBITER
Story: MICHAEL ALAN NELSON
Art: MATT COSSIN

LIGHTS OUT
Story: ERIC CALDERON
Art: MING DOYLE

INK STAINS
Story: TODD LEPRE
Art: DREW RAUSCH

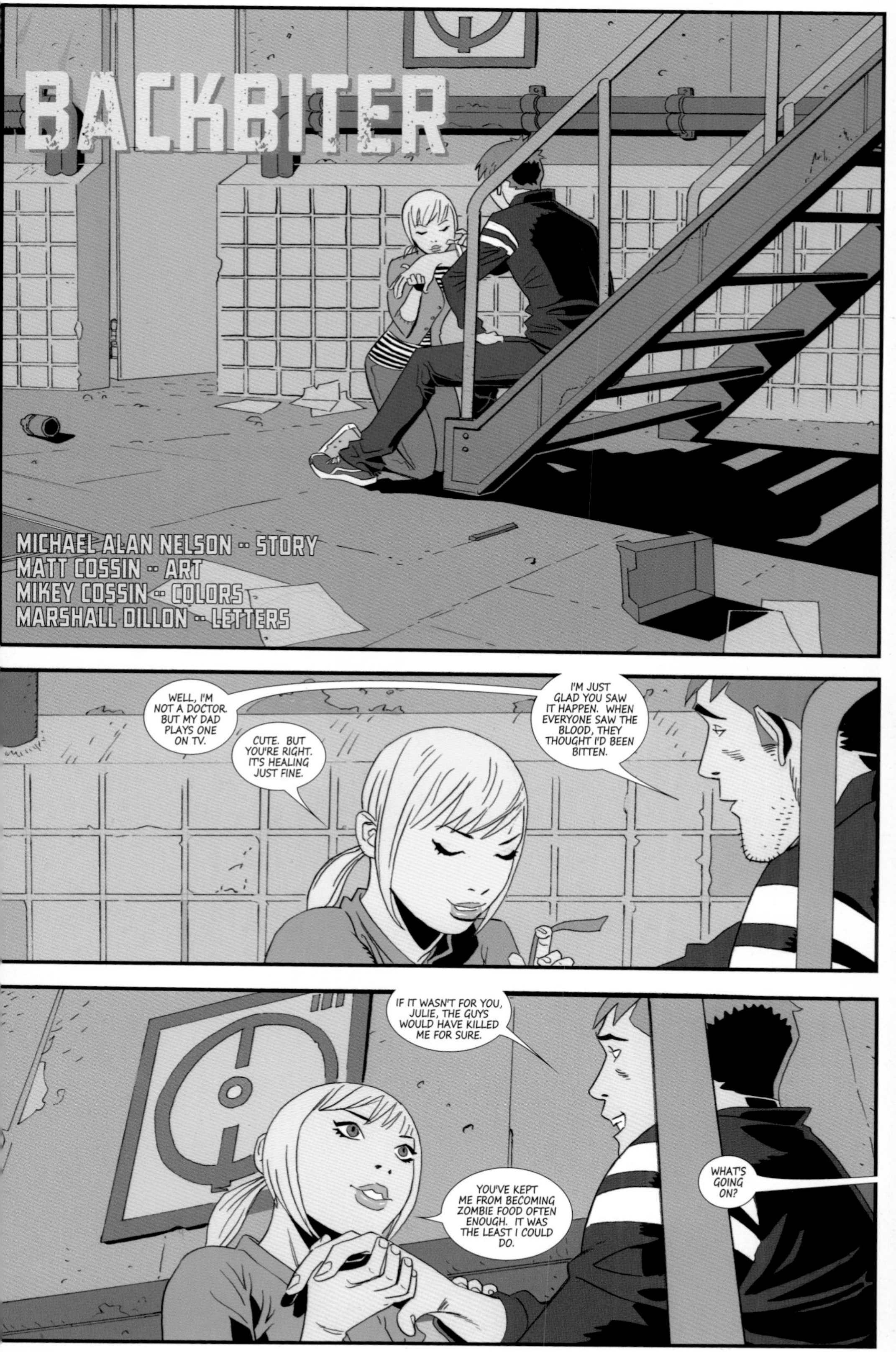
BACKBITER
MICHAEL ALAN NELSON -- STORY
MATT COSSIN -- ART
MIKEY COSSIN -- COLORS
MARSHALL DILLON -- LETTERS
WELL, I'M NOT A DOCTOR. BUT MY DAD PLAYS ONE ON TV.
CUTE. BUT YOU'RE RIGHT. IT'S HEALING JUST FINE.
I'M JUST GLAD YOU SAW IT HAPPEN. WHEN EVERYONE SAW THE BLOOD, THEY THOUGHT I'D BEEN BITTEN.
IF IT WASN'T FOR YOU, JULIE, THE GUYS WOULD HAVE KILLED ME FOR SURE.
YOU'VE KEPT ME FROM BECOMING ZOMBIE FOOD OFTEN ENOUGH. IT WAS THE LEAST I COULD DO.
WHAT'S GOING ON?

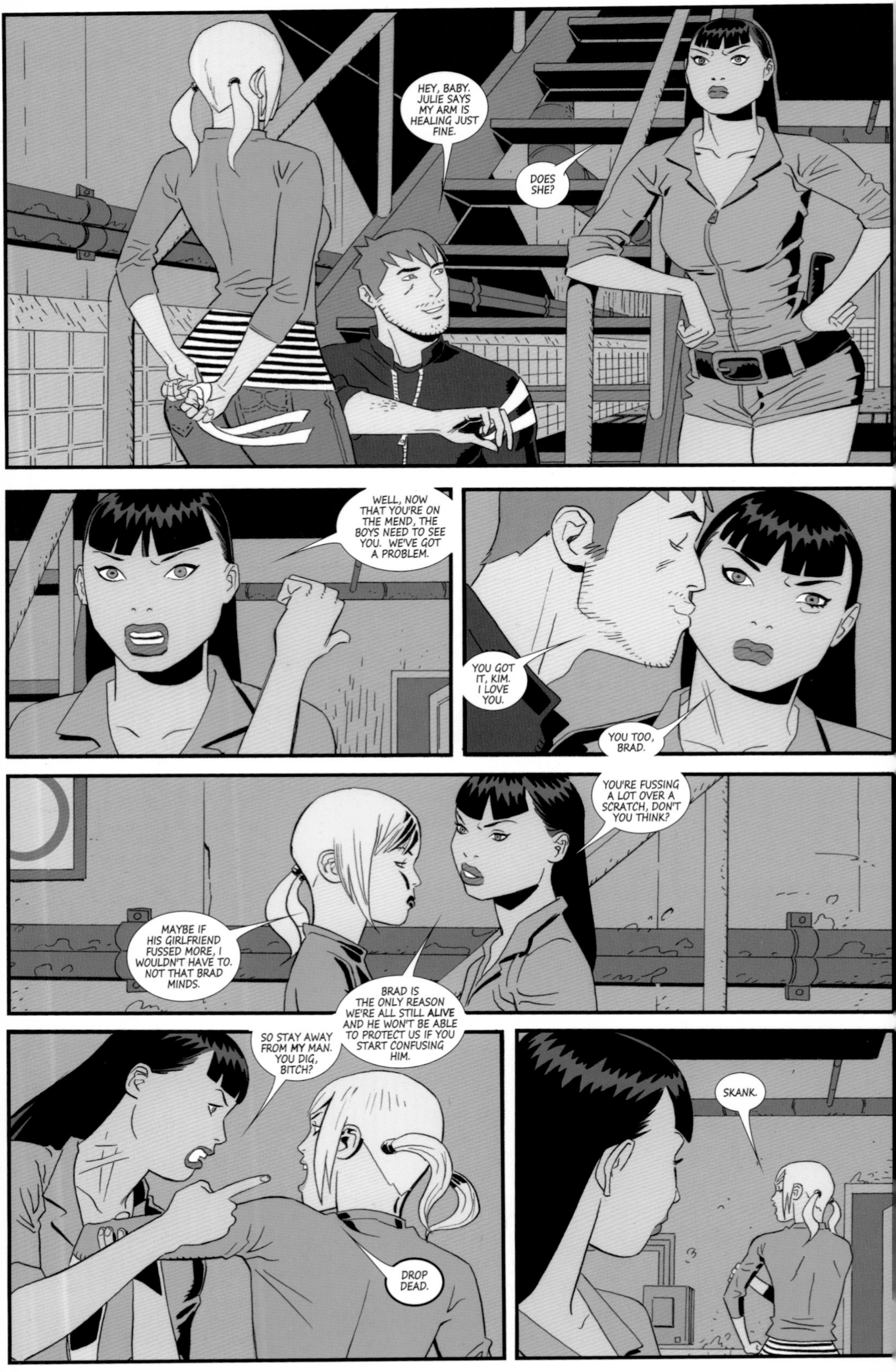
HEY, BABY. JULIE SAYS MY ARM IS HEALING JUST FINE.
DOES SHE?
WELL, NOW THAT YOU'RE ON THE MEND, THE BOYS NEED TO SEE YOU. WE'VE GOT A PROBLEM.
YOU GOT IT, KIM. I LOVE YOU.
YOU TOO, BRAD.
YOU'RE FUSSING A LOT OVER A SCRATCH, DON'T YOU THINK?
MAYBE IF HIS GIRLFRIEND FUSSED MORE, I WOULDN'T HAVE TO. NOT THAT BRAD MINDS.
BRAD IS THE ONLY REASON WE'RE ALL STILL ALIVE AND HE WON'T BE ABLE TO PROTECT US IF YOU START CONFUSING HIM.
SO STAY AWAY FROM MY MAN. YOU DIG, BITCH?
DROP DEAD.
SKANK.

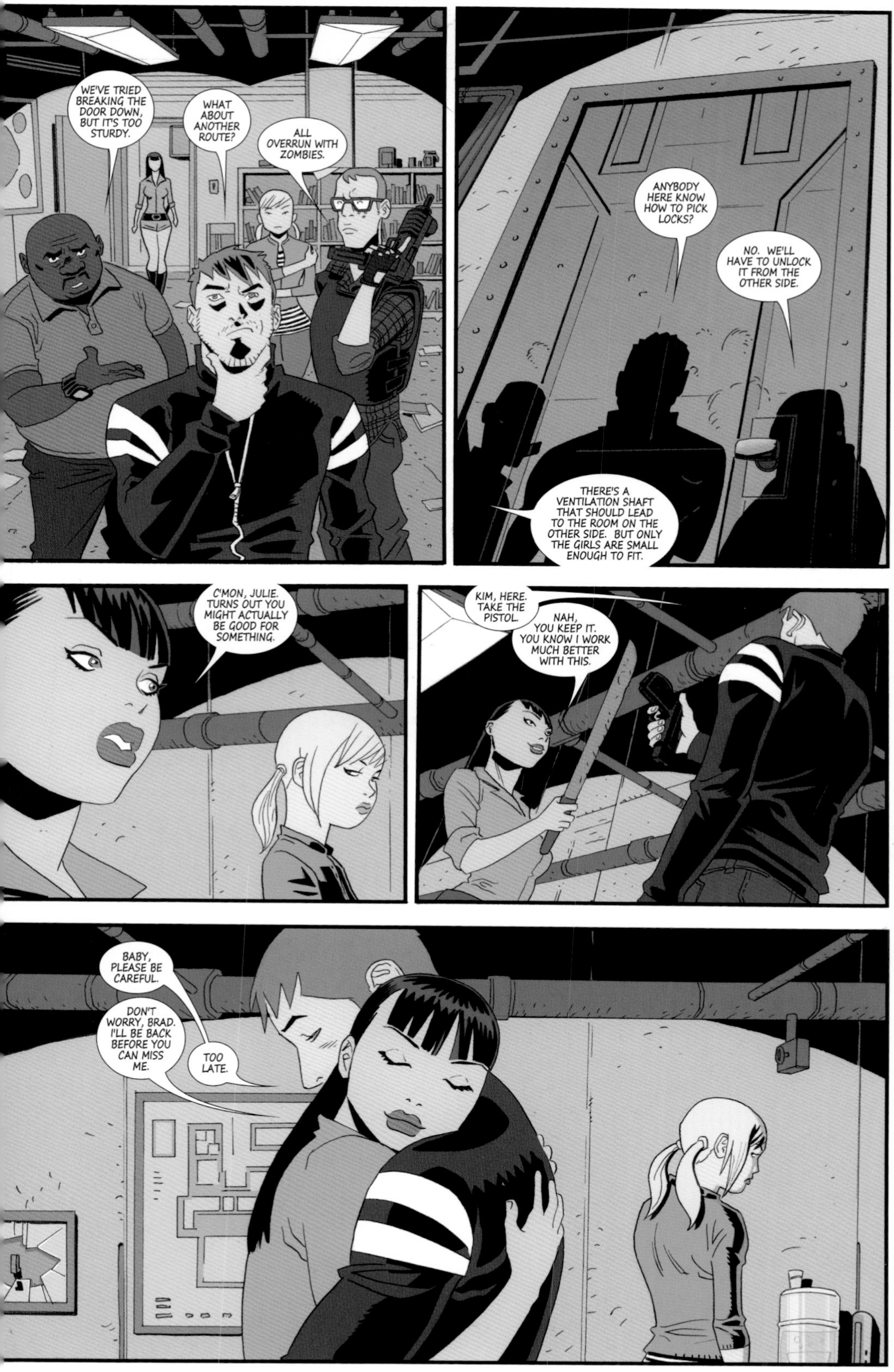
WE'VE TRIED BREAKING THE DOOR DOWN, BUT IT'S TOO STURDY.
WHAT ABOUT ANOTHER ROUTE?
ALL OVERRUN WITH ZOMBIES.
ANYBODY HERE KNOW HOW TO PICK LOCKS?
NO. WE'LL HAVE TO UNLOCK IT FROM THE OTHER SIDE.
THERE'S A VENTILATION SHAFT THAT SHOULD LEAD TO THE ROOM ON THE OTHER SIDE. BUT ONLY THE GIRLS ARE SMALL ENOUGH TO FIT.
C'MON, JULIE. TURNS OUT YOU MIGHT ACTUALLY BE GOOD FOR SOMETHING.
KIM, HERE. TAKE THE PISTOL.
NAH, YOU KEEP IT. YOU KNOW I WORK MUCH BETTER WITH THIS.
BABY, PLEASE BE CAREFUL.
DON'T WORRY, BRAD. I'LL BE BACK BEFORE YOU CAN MISS ME.
TOO LATE.

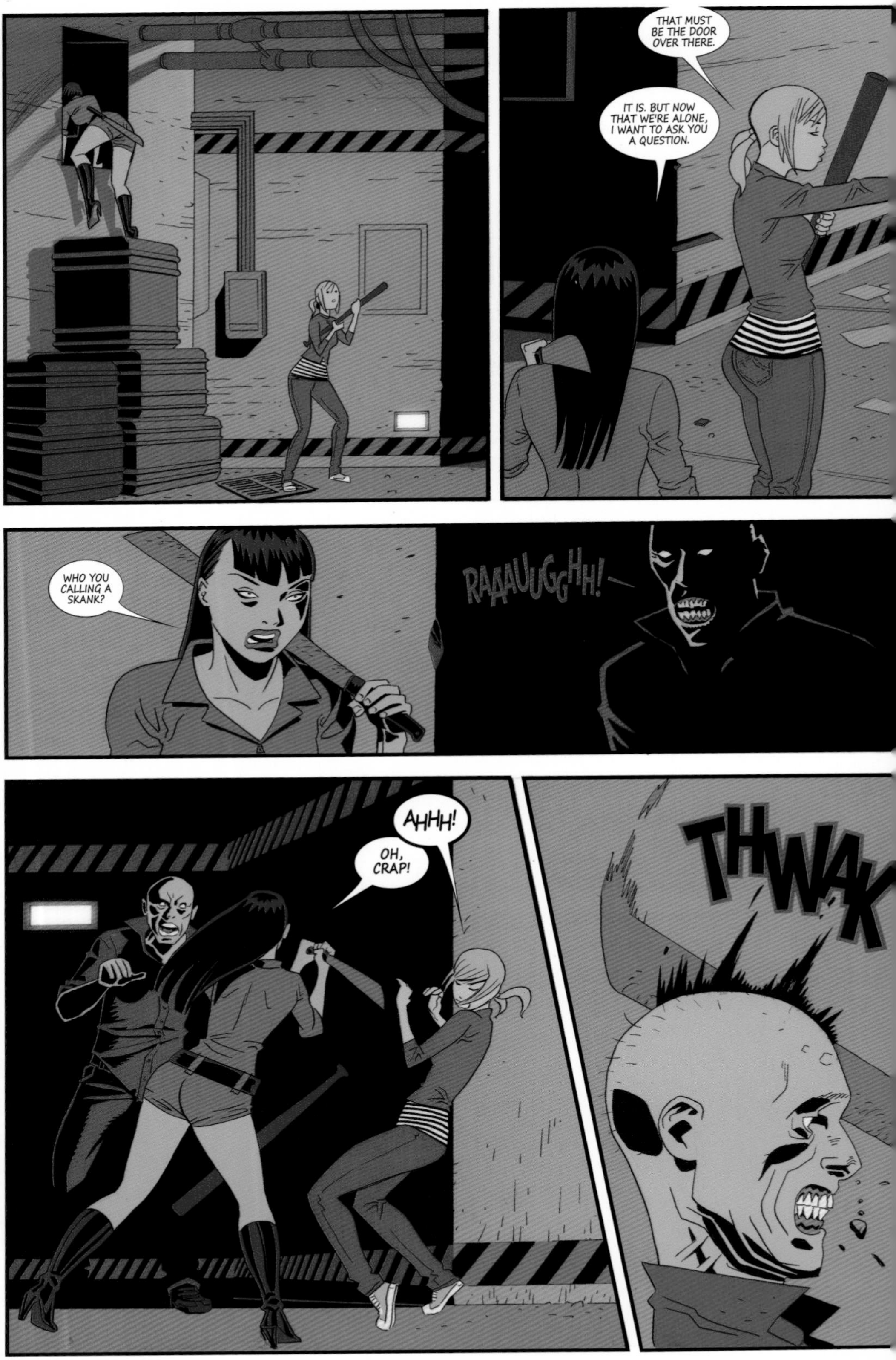

THAT MUST BE THE DOOR OVER THERE.
IT IS. BUT NOW THAT WE'RE ALONE, I WANT TO ASK YOU A QUESTION.
WHO YOU CALLING A SKANK?
RAAAUUGGHH!
AHHH!
OH, CRAP!
THWAK

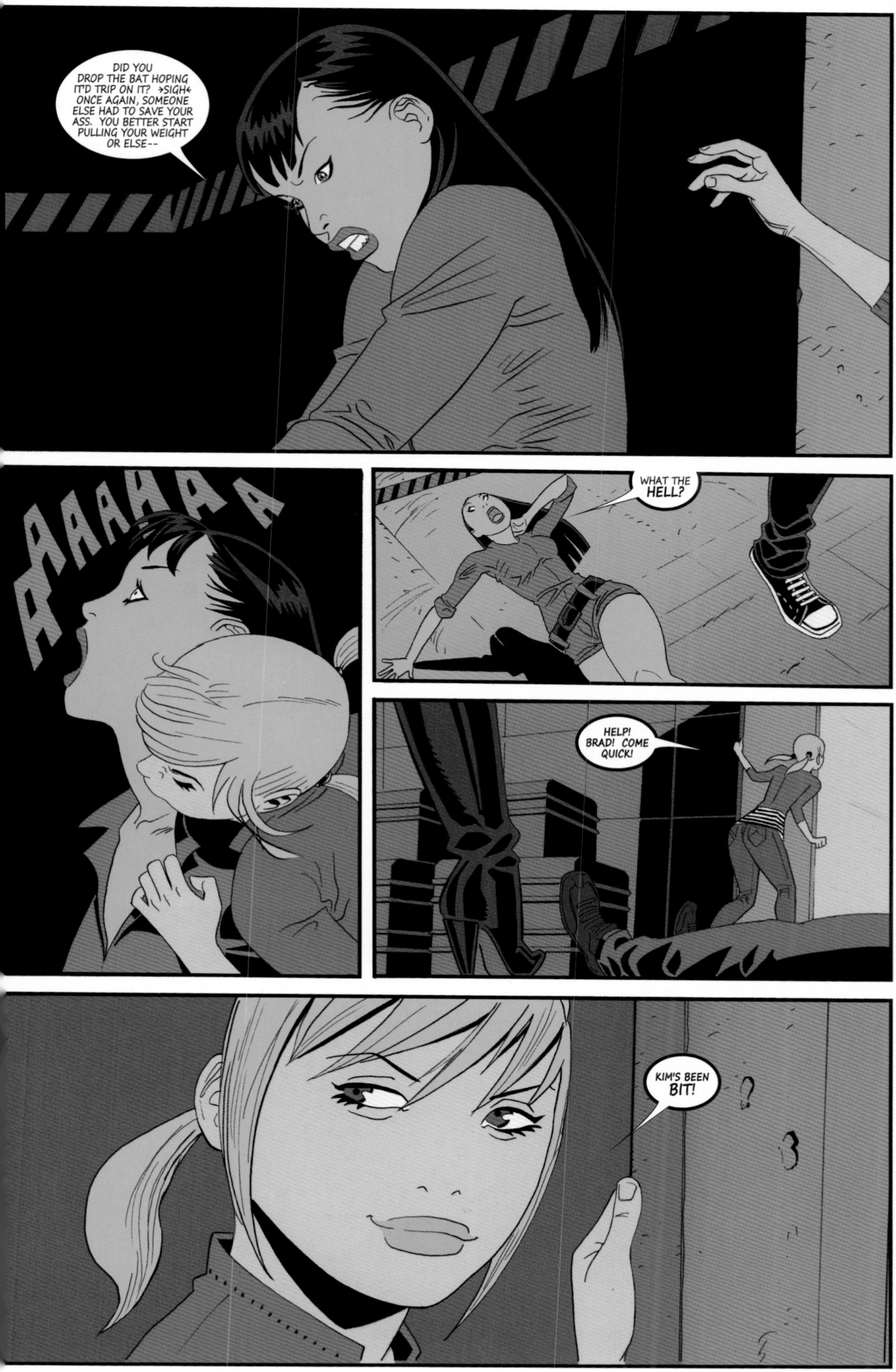
DID YOU DROP THE BAT HOPING IT'D TRIP ON IT? →SIGH← ONCE AGAIN, SOMEONE ELSE HAD TO SAVE YOUR ASS. YOU BETTER START PULLING YOUR WEIGHT OR ELSE--
AAAAAAA
WHAT THE HELL?
HELP! BRAD! COME QUICK!
KIM'S BEEN BIT!

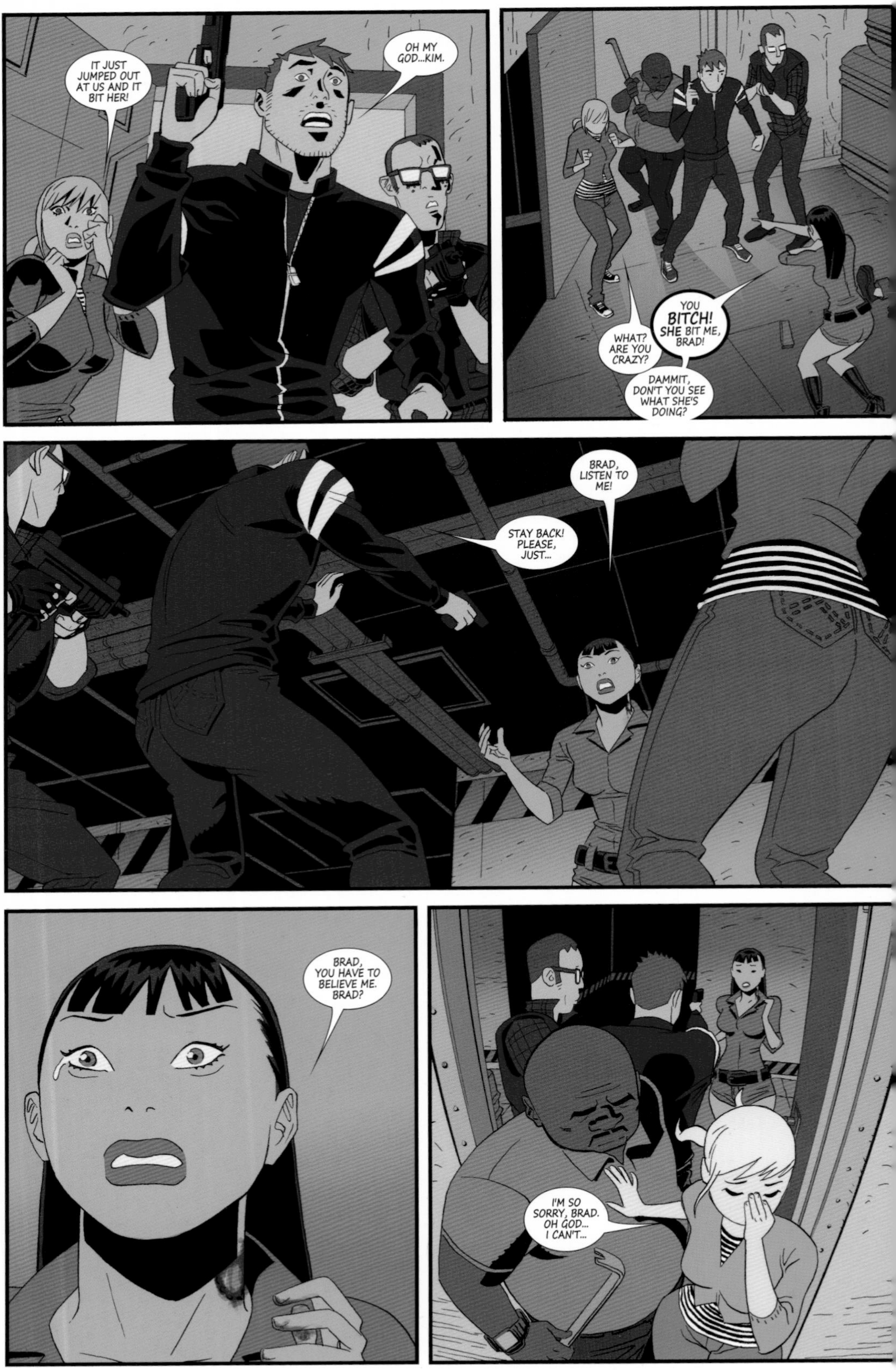
IT JUST JUMPED OUT AT US AND IT BIT HER!
OH MY GOD...KIM.
WHAT? ARE YOU CRAZY?
YOU BITCH! SHE BIT ME, BRAD!
DAMMIT, DON'T YOU SEE WHAT SHE'S DOING?
BRAD, LISTEN TO ME!
STAY BACK! PLEASE, JUST...
BRAD, YOU HAVE TO BELIEVE ME. BRAD?
I'M SO SORRY, BRAD. OH GOD... I CAN'T...

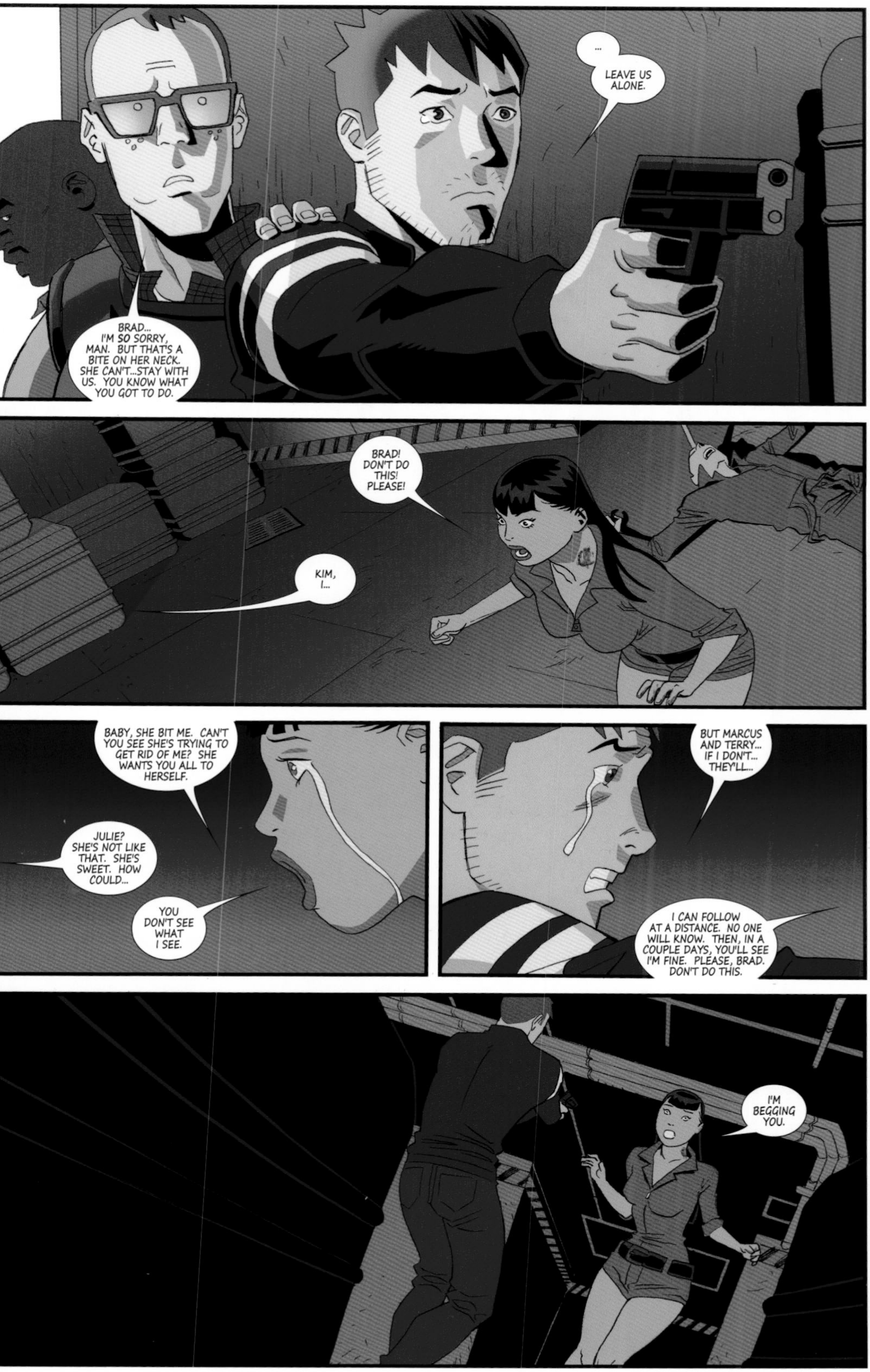
...
LEAVE US ALONE.
BRAD... I'M SO SORRY, MAN. BUT THAT'S A BITE ON HER NECK. SHE CAN'T...STAY WITH US. YOU KNOW WHAT YOU GOT TO DO.
BRAD! DON'T DO THIS! PLEASE!
KIM, I...
BABY, SHE BIT ME. CAN'T YOU SEE SHE'S TRYING TO GET RID OF ME? SHE WANTS YOU ALL TO HERSELF.
JULIE? SHE'S NOT LIKE THAT. SHE'S SWEET. HOW COULD...
YOU DON'T SEE WHAT I SEE.
BUT MARCUS AND TERRY... IF I DON'T... THEY'LL...
I CAN FOLLOW AT A DISTANCE. NO ONE WILL KNOW. THEN, IN A COUPLE DAYS, YOU'LL SEE I'M FINE. PLEASE, BRAD. DON'T DO THIS.
I'M BEGGING YOU.

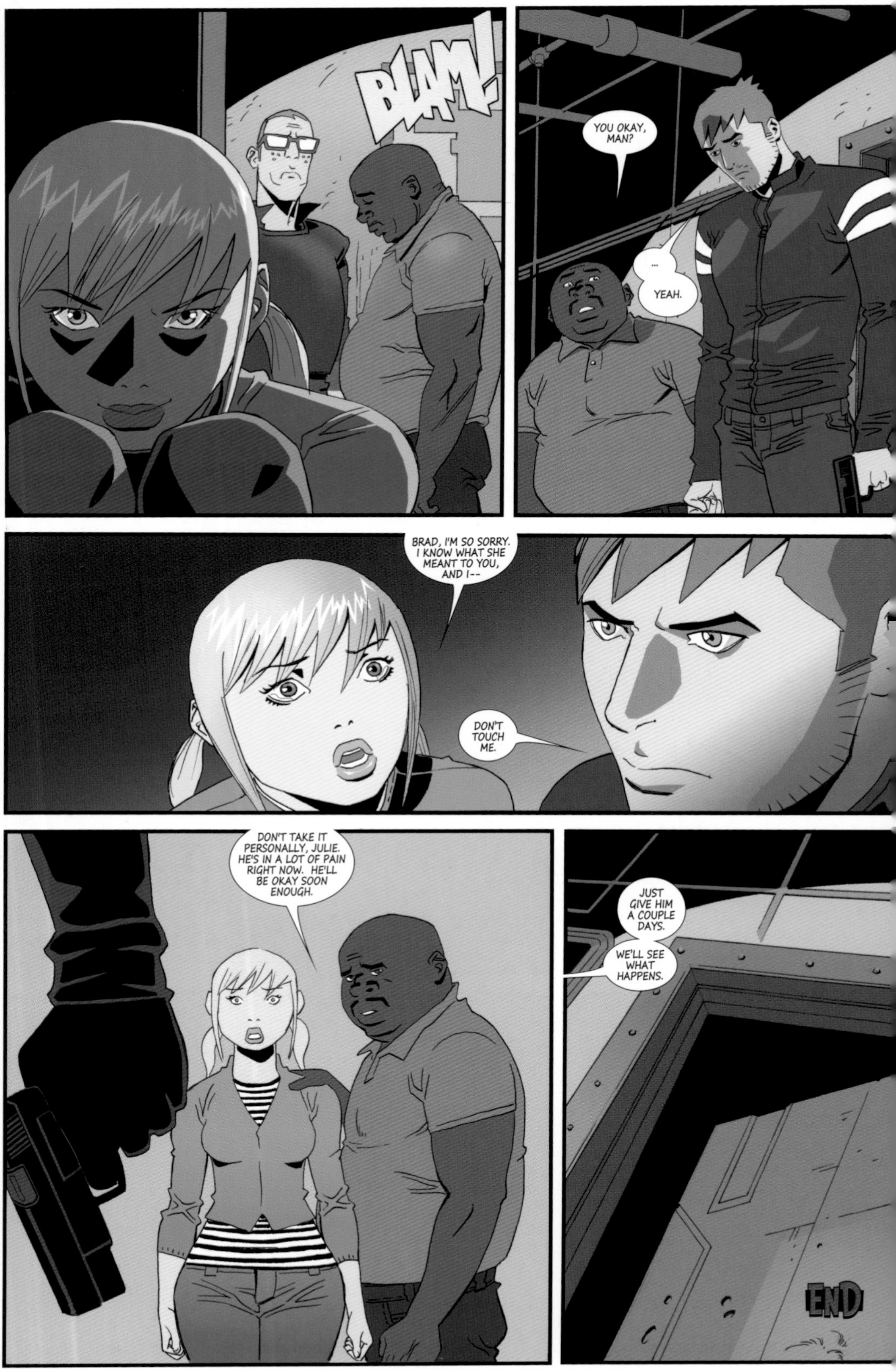
BLAM!
YOU OKAY, MAN?
...
YEAH.
BRAD, I'M SO SORRY. I KNOW WHAT SHE MEANT TO YOU, AND I--
DON'T TOUCH ME.
DON'T TAKE IT PERSONALLY, JULIE. HE'S IN A LOT OF PAIN RIGHT NOW. HE'LL BE OKAY SOON ENOUGH.
JUST GIVE HIM A COUPLE DAYS.
WE'LL SEE WHAT HAPPENS.
END

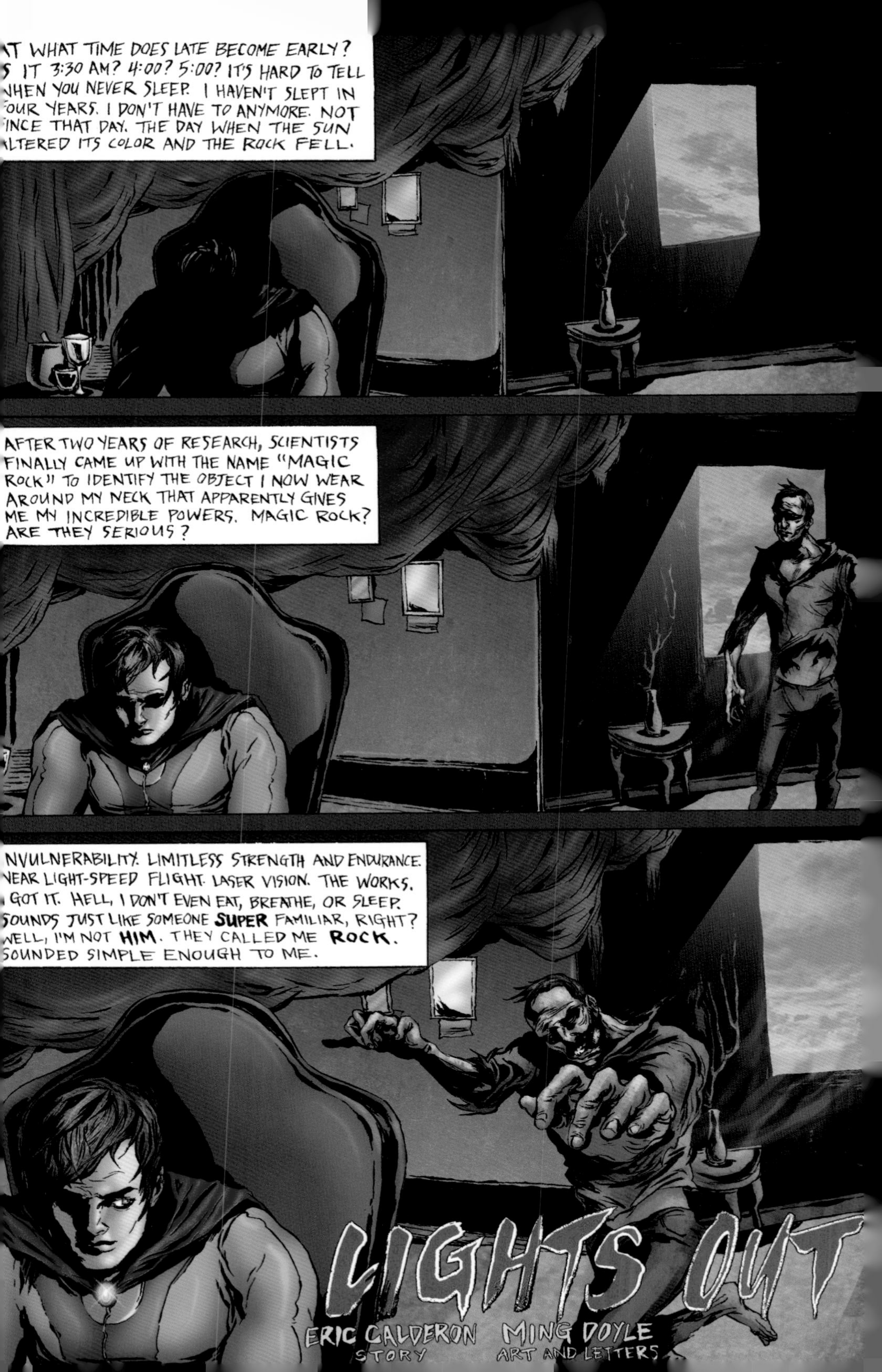
AT WHAT TIME DOES LATE BECOME EARLY? IS IT 3:30 AM? 4:00? 5:00? IT'S HARD TO TELL WHEN YOU NEVER SLEEP. I HAVEN'T SLEPT IN FOUR YEARS. I DON'T HAVE TO ANYMORE. NOT SINCE THAT DAY. THE DAY WHEN THE SUN ALTERED ITS COLOR AND THE ROCK FELL.
AFTER TWO YEARS OF RESEARCH, SCIENTISTS FINALLY CAME UP WITH THE NAME "MAGIC ROCK" TO IDENTIFY THE OBJECT I NOW WEAR AROUND MY NECK THAT APPARENTLY GIVES ME MY INCREDIBLE POWERS. MAGIC ROCK? ARE THEY SERIOUS?
INVULNERABILITY. LIMITLESS STRENGTH AND ENDURANCE. NEAR LIGHT-SPEED FLIGHT. LASER VISION. THE WORKS. I GOT IT. HELL, I DON'T EVEN EAT, BREATHE, OR SLEEP. SOUNDS JUST LIKE SOMEONE SUPER FAMILIAR, RIGHT? WELL, I'M NOT HIM. THEY CALLED ME ROCK. SOUNDED SIMPLE ENOUGH TO ME.
LIGHTS OUT
ERIC CALDERON STORY
MING DOYLE ART AND LETTERS

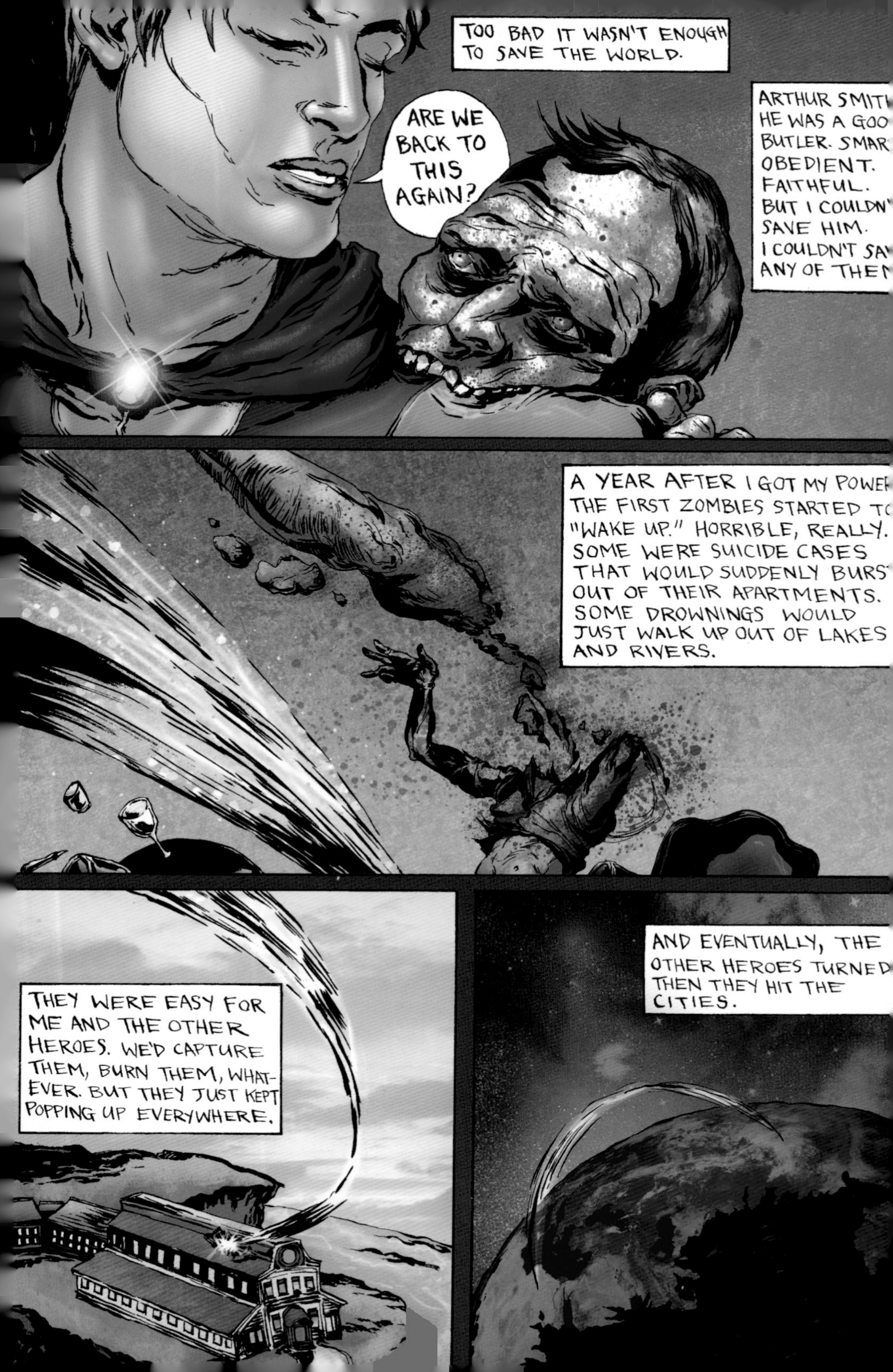
TOO BAD IT WASN'T ENOUGH TO SAVE THE WORLD.
ARE WE BACK TO THIS AGAIN?
ARTHUR SMIT HE WAS A GOO BUTLER. SMAR OBEDIENT. FAITHFUL. BUT I COULDN' SAVE HIM. I COULDN'T SA ANY OF THE
A YEAR AFTER I GOT MY POWE THE FIRST ZOMBIES STARTED T "WAKE UP." HORRIBLE, REALLY. SOME WERE SUICIDE CASES THAT WOULD SUDDENLY BURS OUT OF THEIR APARTMENTS. SOME DROWNINGS WOULD JUST WALK UP OUT OF LAKES AND RIVERS.
THEY WERE EASY FOR ME AND THE OTHER HEROES. WE'D CAPTURE THEM, BURN THEM, WHAT-EVER. BUT THEY JUST KEPT POPPING UP EVERYWHERE.
AND EVENTUALLY, THE OTHER HEROES TURNED. THEN THEY HIT THE CITIES.

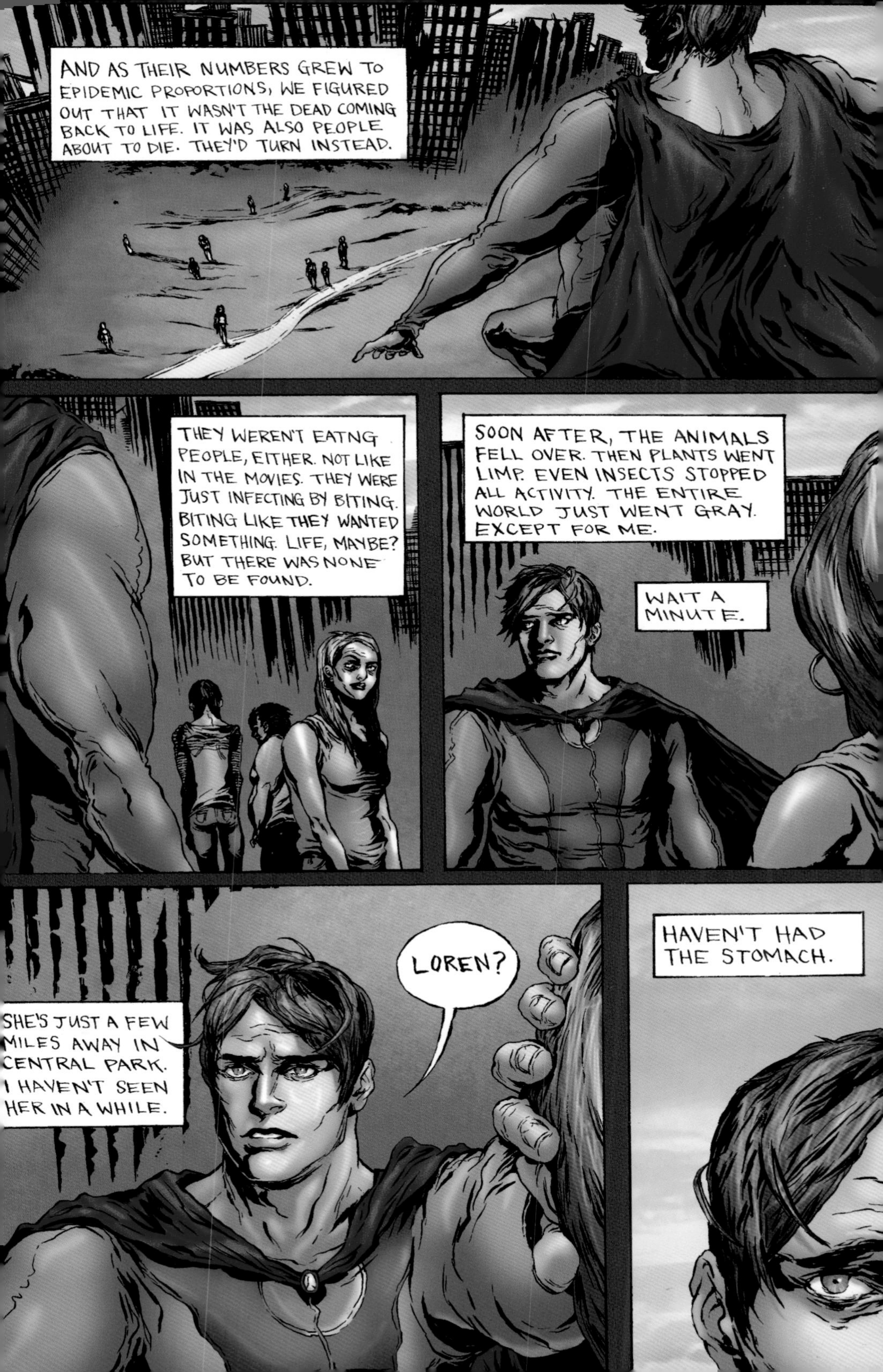
AND AS THEIR NUMBERS GREW TO EPIDEMIC PROPORTIONS, WE FIGURED OUT THAT IT WASN'T THE DEAD COMING BACK TO LIFE. IT WAS ALSO PEOPLE ABOUT TO DIE. THEY'D TURN INSTEAD.
THEY WEREN'T EATNG PEOPLE, EITHER. NOT LIKE IN THE MOVIES. THEY WERE JUST INFECTING BY BITING. BITING LIKE THEY WANTED SOMETHING. LIFE, MAYBE? BUT THERE WAS NONE TO BE FOUND.
SOON AFTER, THE ANIMALS FELL OVER. THEN PLANTS WENT LIMP. EVEN INSECTS STOPPED ALL ACTIVITY. THE ENTIRE WORLD JUST WENT GRAY. EXCEPT FOR ME.
WAIT A MINUTE.
LOREN?
SHE'S JUST A FEW MILES AWAY IN CENTRAL PARK. I HAVEN'T SEEN HER IN A WHILE.
HAVEN'T HAD THE STOMACH.

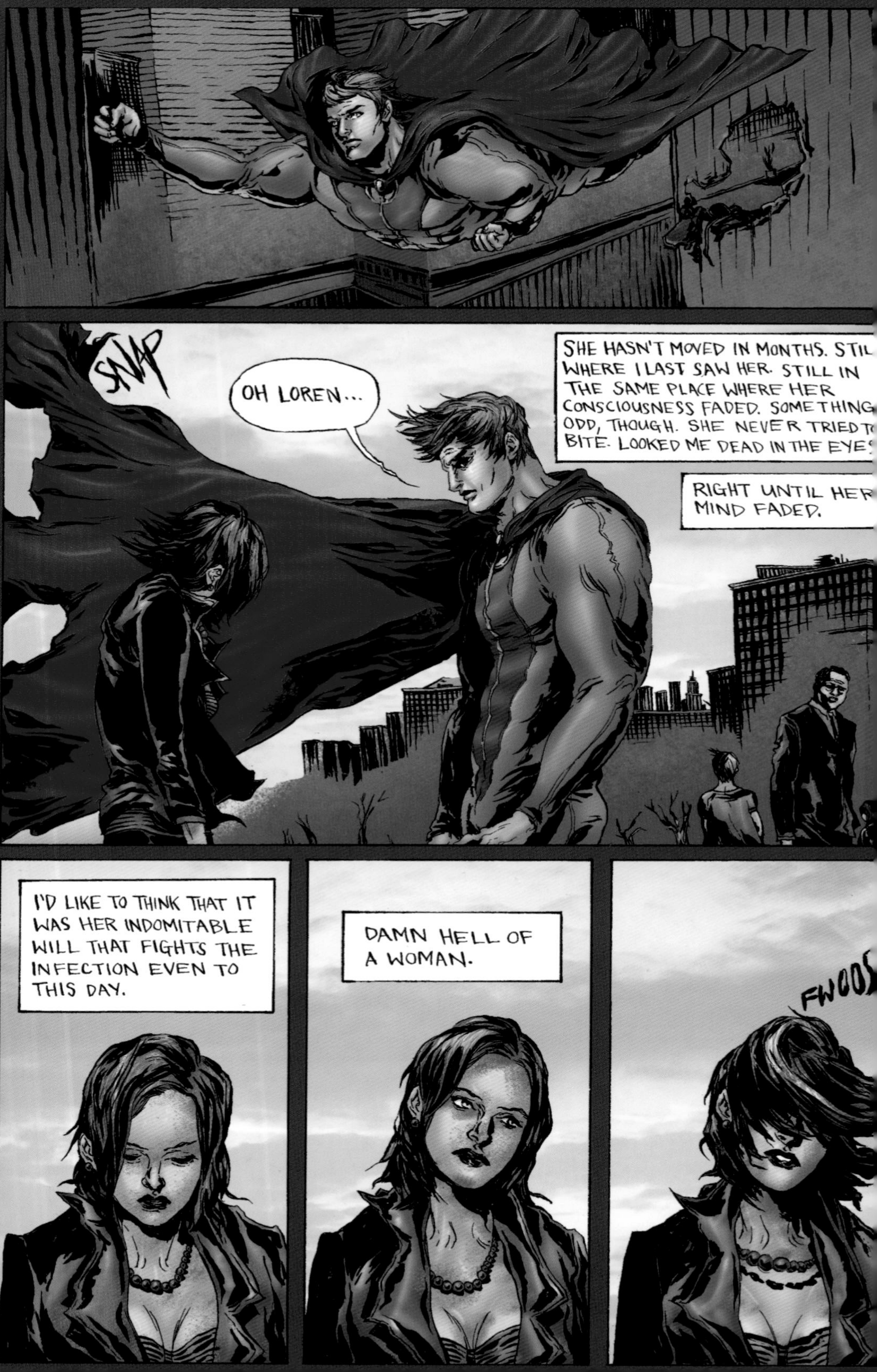
SNAP
SHE HASN'T MOVED IN MONTHS. STIL WHERE I LAST SAW HER. STILL IN THE SAME PLACE WHERE HER CONSCIOUSNESS FADED. SOMETHING ODD, THOUGH. SHE NEVER TRIED T BITE. LOOKED ME DEAD IN THE EYES
OH LOREN...
RIGHT UNTIL HER MIND FADED.
I'D LIKE TO THINK THAT IT WAS HER INDOMITABLE WILL THAT FIGHTS THE INFECTION EVEN TO THIS DAY.
DAMN HELL OF A WOMAN.
FWOOS

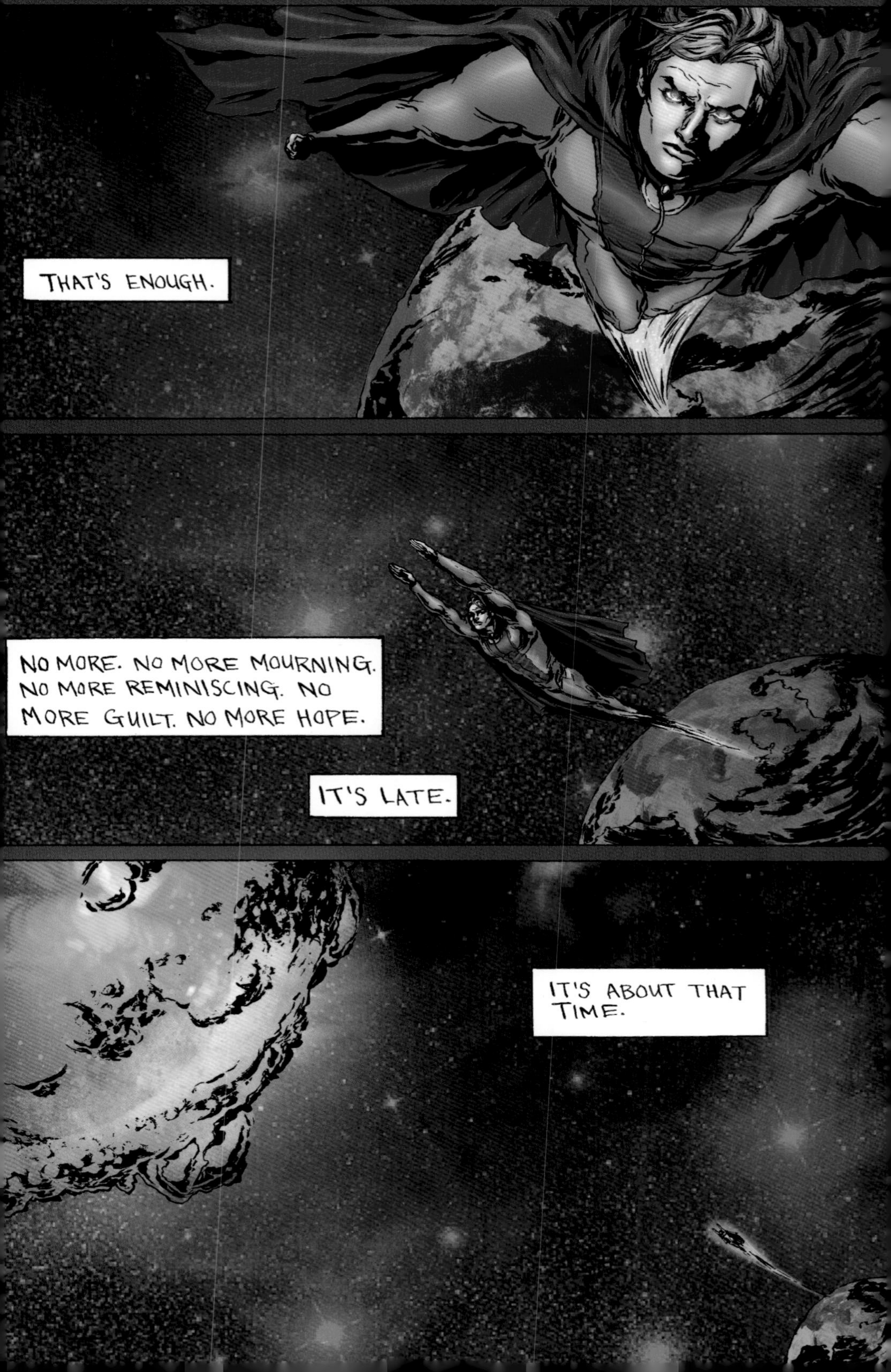
THAT'S ENOUGH.
NO MORE. NO MORE MOURNING. NO MORE REMINISCING. NO MORE GUILT. NO MORE HOPE.
IT'S LATE.
IT'S ABOUT THAT TIME.

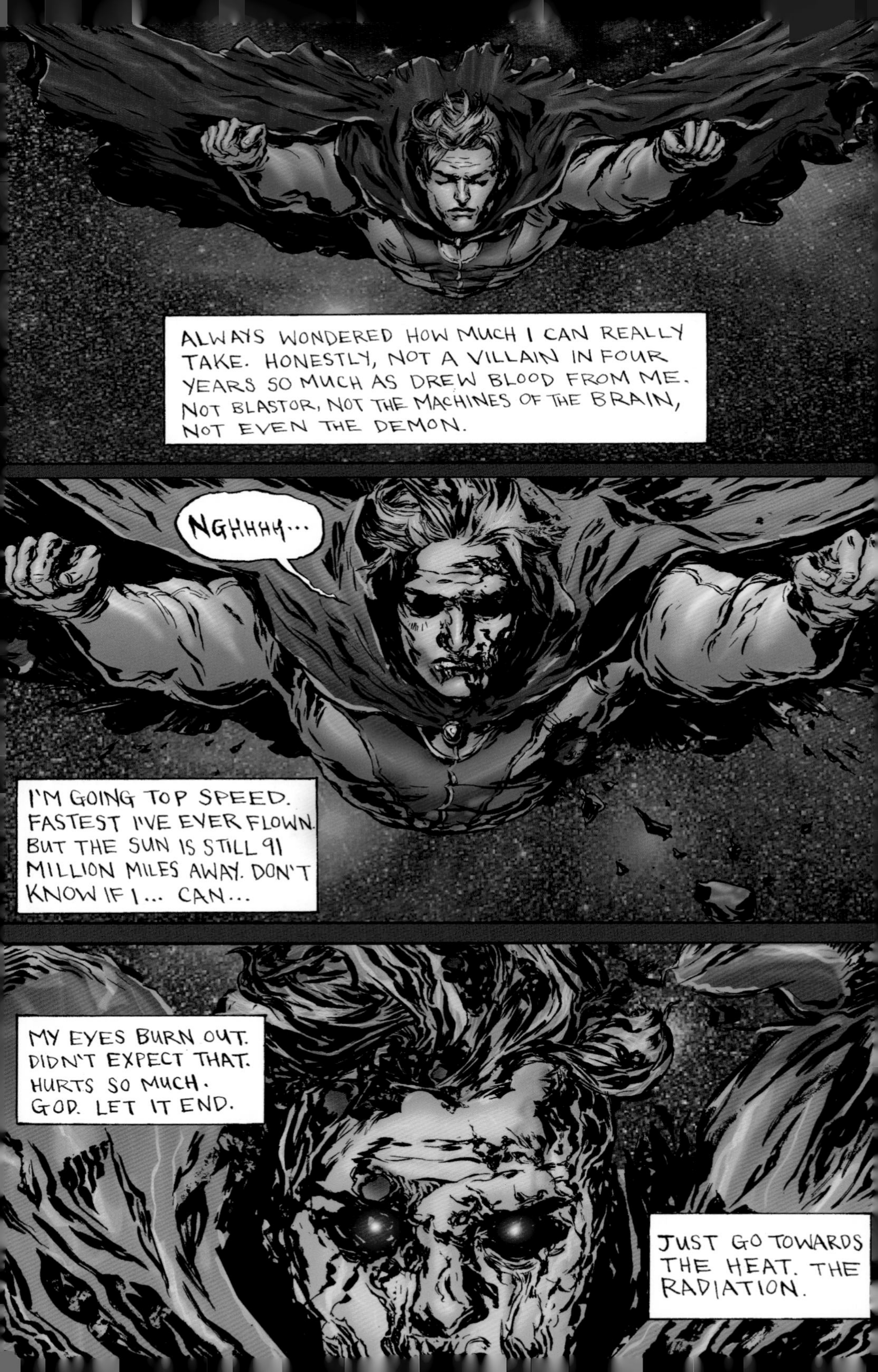
ALWAYS WONDERED HOW MUCH I CAN REALLY TAKE. HONESTLY, NOT A VILLAIN IN FOUR YEARS SO MUCH AS DREW BLOOD FROM ME. NOT BLASTOR, NOT THE MACHINES OF THE BRAIN, NOT EVEN THE DEMON.
NGHHHH...
I'M GOING TOP SPEED. FASTEST I'VE EVER FLOWN. BUT THE SUN IS STILL 91 MILLION MILES AWAY. DON'T KNOW IF I... CAN...
MY EYES BURN OUT. DIDN'T EXPECT THAT. HURTS SO MUCH. GOD. LET IT END.
JUST GO TOWARDS THE HEAT. THE RADIATION.

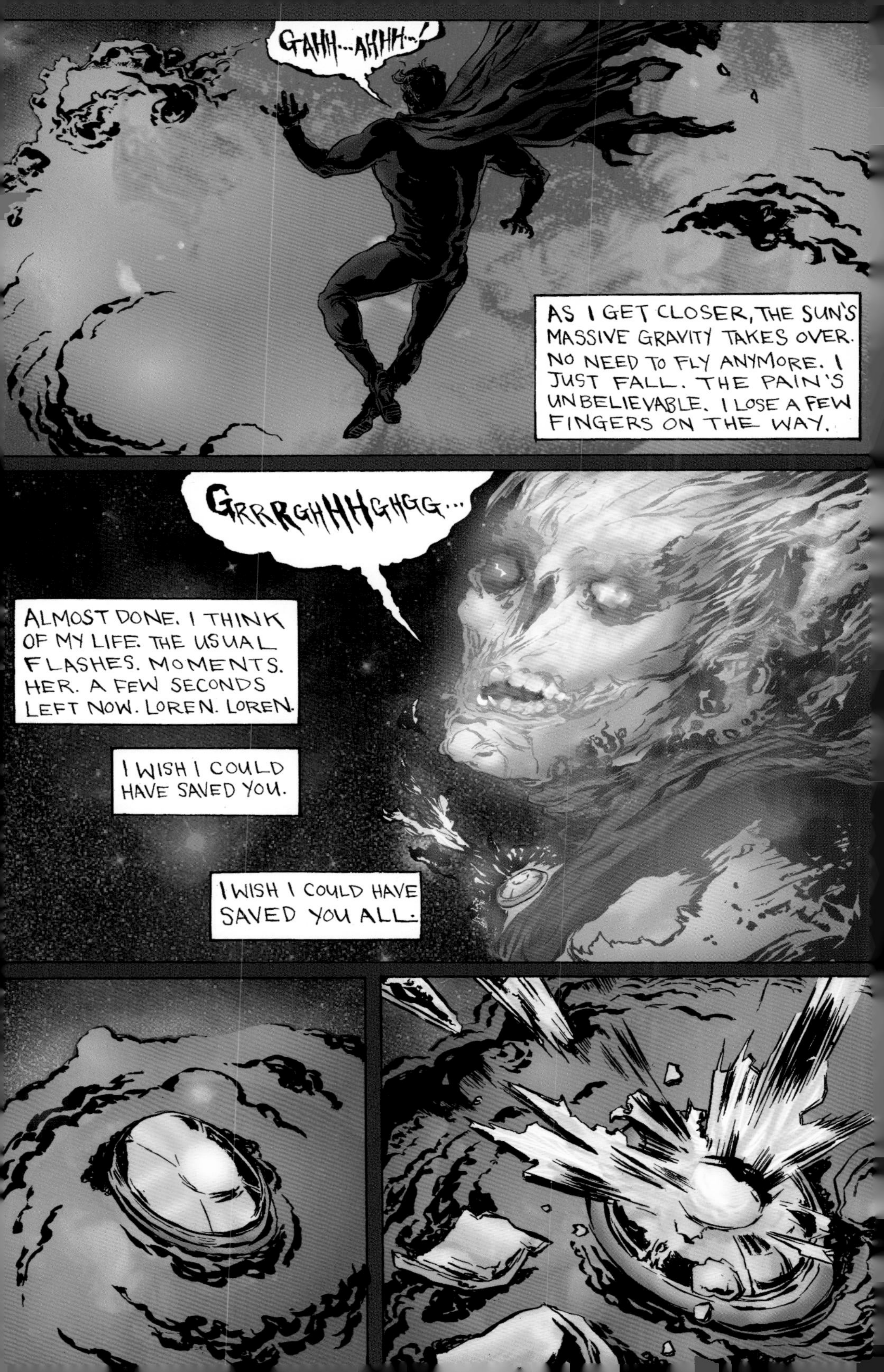
GAHH--AHHH--!
AS I GET CLOSER, THE SUN'S MASSIVE GRAVITY TAKES OVER. NO NEED TO FLY ANYMORE. I JUST FALL. THE PAIN'S UNBELIEVABLE. I LOSE A FEW FINGERS ON THE WAY.
GRRRGHHHGHGG...
ALMOST DONE. I THINK OF MY LIFE. THE USUAL FLASHES. MOMENTS. HER. A FEW SECONDS LEFT NOW. LOREN. LOREN.
I WISH I COULD HAVE SAVED YOU.
I WISH I COULD HAVE SAVED YOU ALL.

DAYS.

WEEKS.

YEARS.

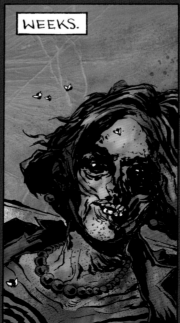

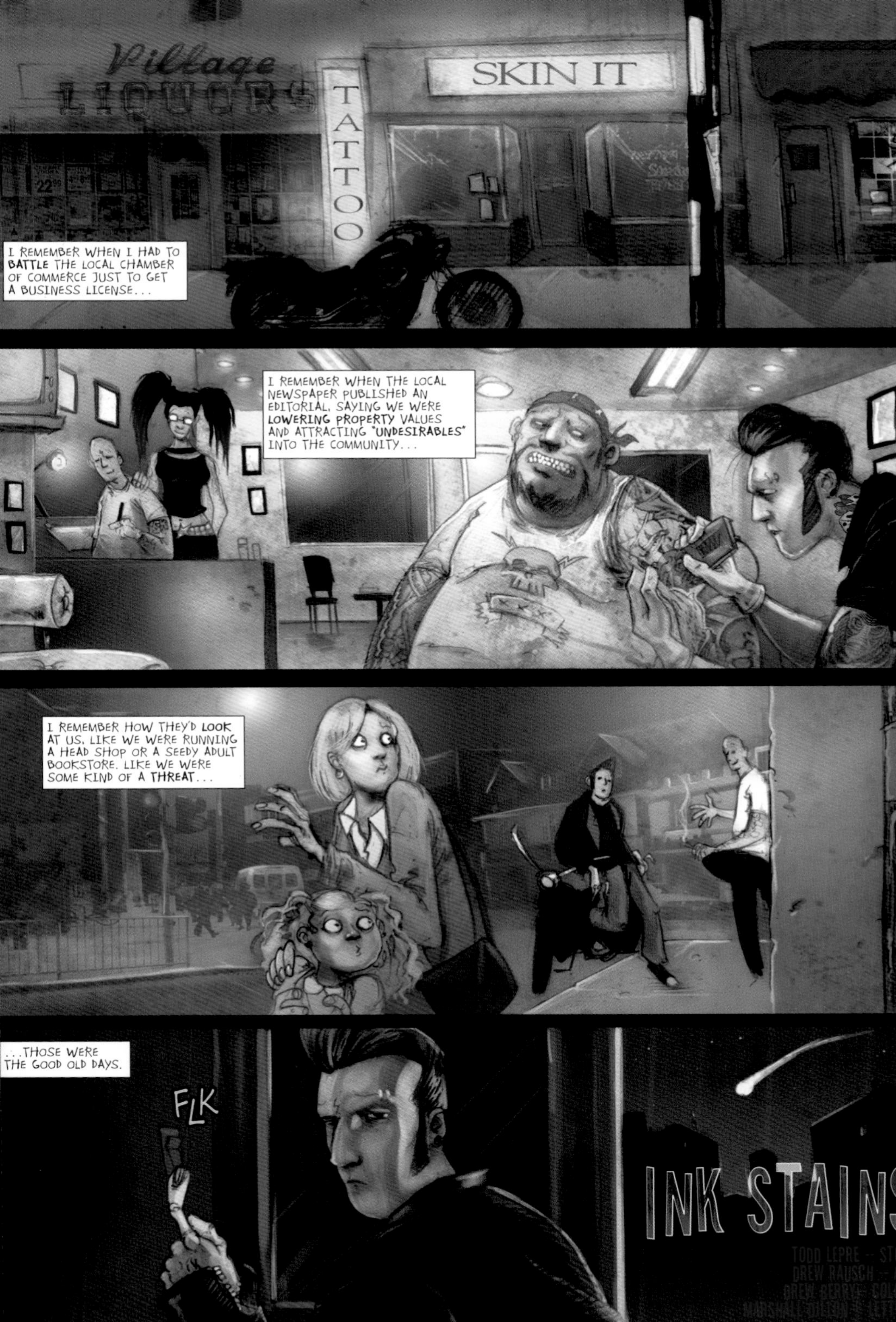
Village
LIQUORS
TATTOO
SKIN IT
I REMEMBER WHEN I HAD TO BATTLE THE LOCAL CHAMBER OF COMMERCE JUST TO GET A BUSINESS LICENSE...
I REMEMBER WHEN THE LOCAL NEWSPAPER PUBLISHED AN EDITORIAL, SAYING WE WERE LOWERING PROPERTY VALUES AND ATTRACTING "UNDESIRABLES" INTO THE COMMUNITY...
I REMEMBER HOW THEY'D LOOK AT US, LIKE WE WERE RUNNING A HEAD SHOP OR A SEEDY ADULT BOOKSTORE. LIKE WE WERE SOME KIND OF A THREAT...
...THOSE WERE THE GOOD OLD DAYS.
FLK
INK STAINS
TODD LEPRE --
DREW RAUSCH --

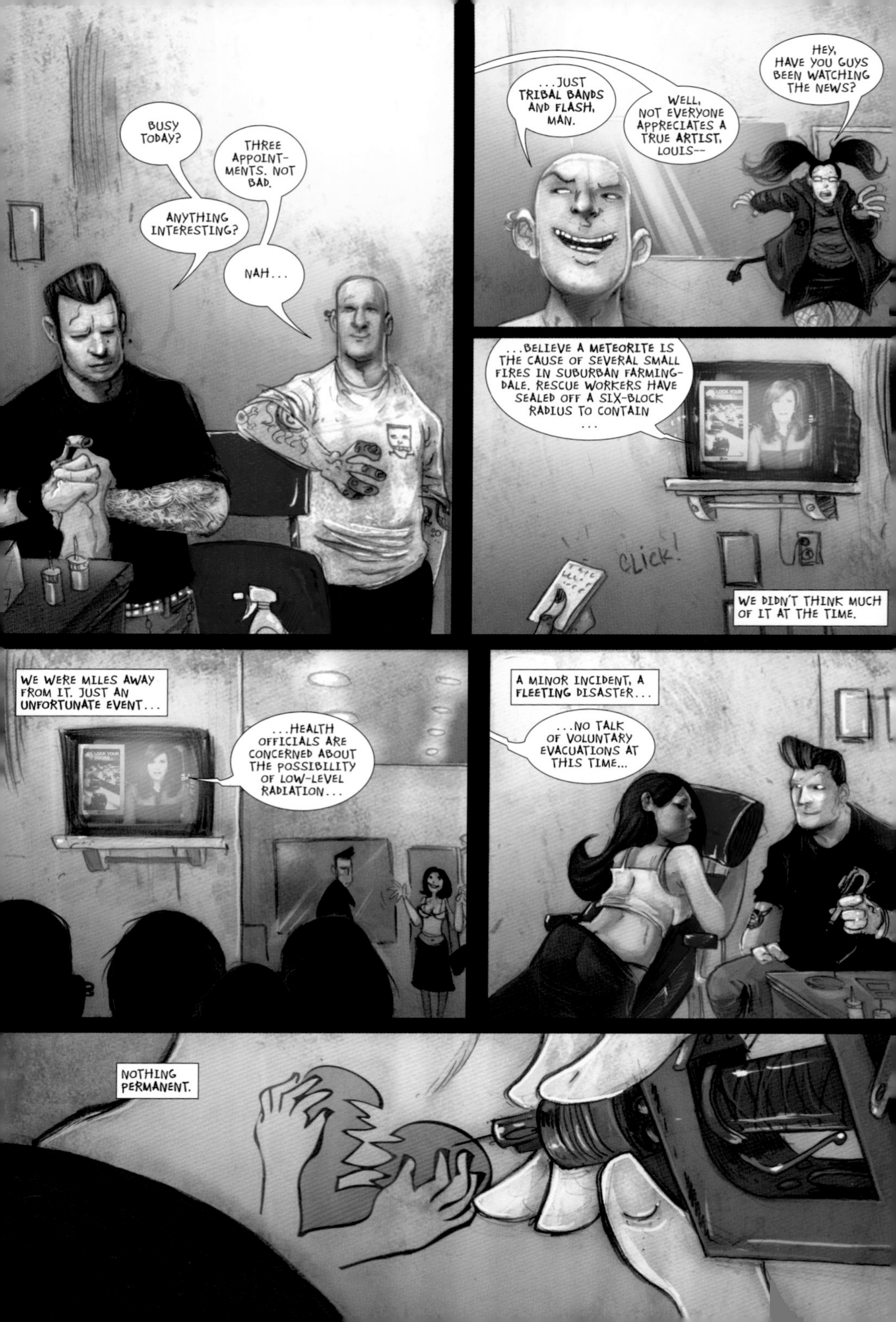
BUSY TODAY?
THREE APPOINT-MENTS. NOT BAD.
ANYTHING INTERESTING?
NAH...
...JUST TRIBAL BANDS AND FLASH, MAN.
WELL, NOT EVERYONE APPRECIATES A TRUE ARTIST, LOUIS--
HEY, HAVE YOU GUYS BEEN WATCHING THE NEWS?
...BELIEVE A METEORITE IS THE CAUSE OF SEVERAL SMALL FIRES IN SUBURBAN FARMING-DALE. RESCUE WORKERS HAVE SEALED OFF A SIX-BLOCK RADIUS TO CONTAIN ...
CLICK!
WE DIDN'T THINK MUCH OF IT AT THE TIME.
WE WERE MILES AWAY FROM IT. JUST AN UNFORTUNATE EVENT...
...HEALTH OFFICIALS ARE CONCERNED ABOUT THE POSSIBILITY OF LOW-LEVEL RADIATION...
A MINOR INCIDENT, A FLEETING DISASTER...
...NO TALK OF VOLUNTARY EVACUATIONS AT THIS TIME...
NOTHING PERMANENT.

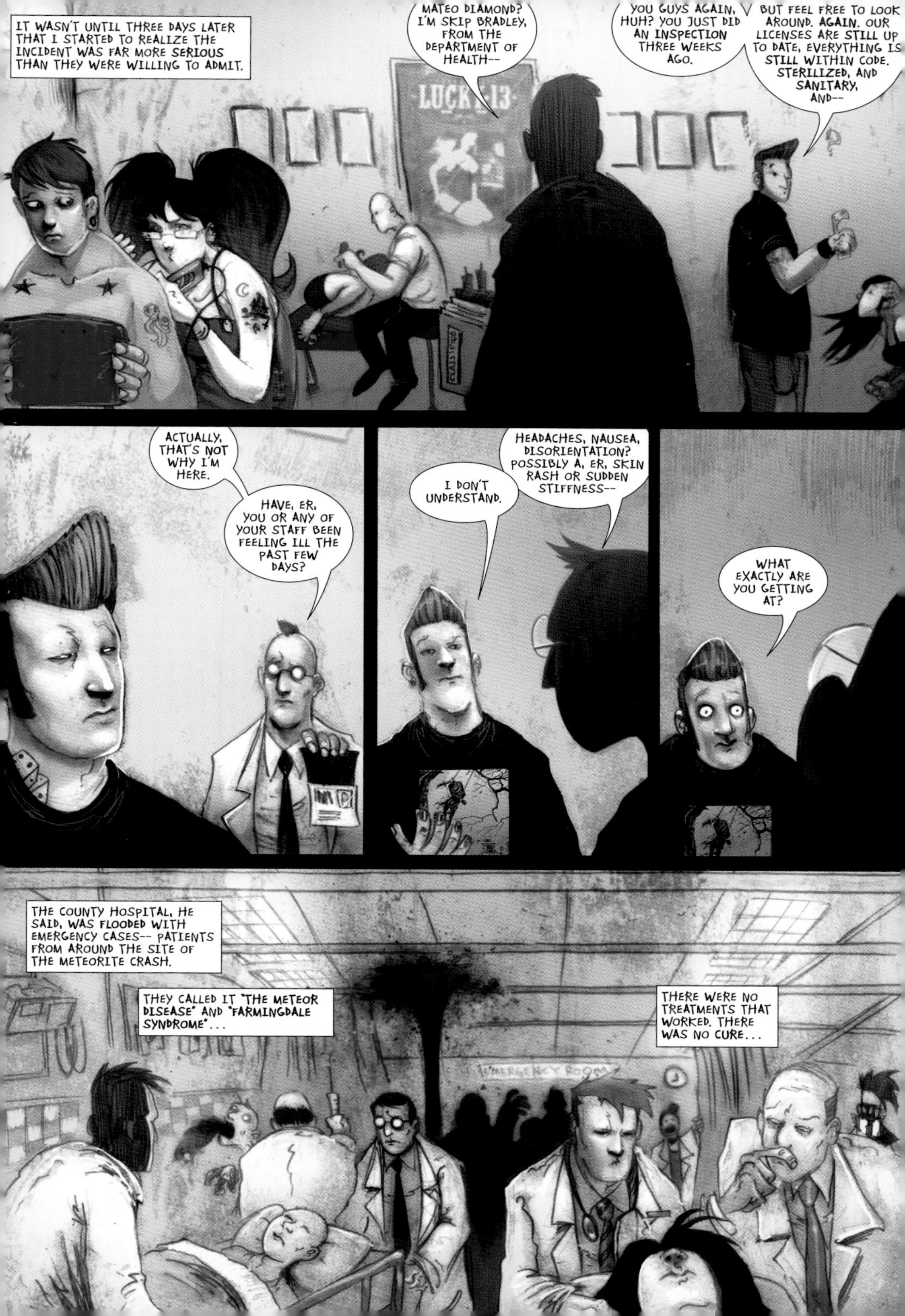

IT WASN'T UNTIL THREE DAYS LATER THAT I STARTED TO REALIZE THE INCIDENT WAS FAR MORE SERIOUS THAN THEY WERE WILLING TO ADMIT.
MATEO DIAMOND? I'M SKIP BRADLEY, FROM THE DEPARTMENT OF HEALTH--
YOU GUYS AGAIN, HUH? YOU JUST DID AN INSPECTION THREE WEEKS AGO.
BUT FEEL FREE TO LOOK AROUND. AGAIN. OUR LICENSES ARE STILL UP TO DATE, EVERYTHING IS STILL WITHIN CODE. STERILIZED, AND SANITARY, AND--
LUCKY 13
ACTUALLY, THAT'S NOT WHY I'M HERE.
HAVE, ER, YOU OR ANY OF YOUR STAFF BEEN FEELING ILL THE PAST FEW DAYS?
I DON'T UNDERSTAND.
HEADACHES, NAUSEA, DISORIENTATION? POSSIBLY A, ER, SKIN RASH OR SUDDEN STIFFNESS--
WHAT EXACTLY ARE YOU GETTING AT?
THE COUNTY HOSPITAL, HE SAID, WAS FLOODED WITH EMERGENCY CASES-- PATIENTS FROM AROUND THE SITE OF THE METEORITE CRASH.
THEY CALLED IT "THE METEOR DISEASE" AND "FARMINGDALE SYNDROME"...
THERE WERE NO TREATMENTS THAT WORKED. THERE WAS NO CURE...
EMERGENCY ROOM

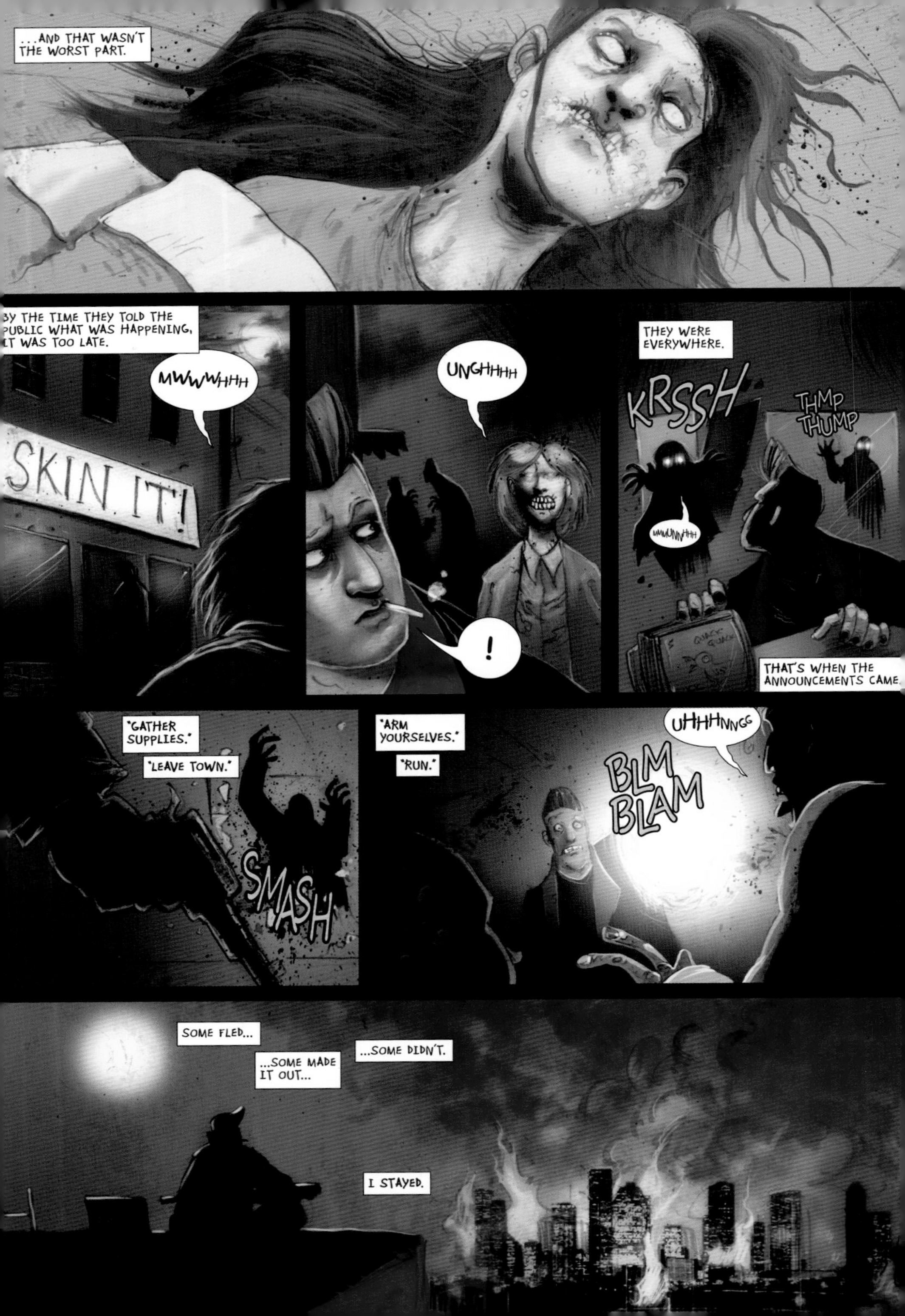
...AND THAT WASN'T THE WORST PART.
BY THE TIME THEY TOLD THE PUBLIC WHAT WAS HAPPENING, IT WAS TOO LATE.
MWWWHHH
SKIN IT!
UNGHHHH
!
THEY WERE EVERYWHERE.
KRSSH
THMP THUMP
MMMUNNHHH
THAT'S WHEN THE ANNOUNCEMENTS CAME.
"GATHER SUPPLIES."
"LEAVE TOWN."
SMASH
"ARM YOURSELVES."
"RUN."
UHHHNNGG
BLM BLAM
SOME FLED...
...SOME MADE IT OUT...
...SOME DIDN'T.
I STAYED.

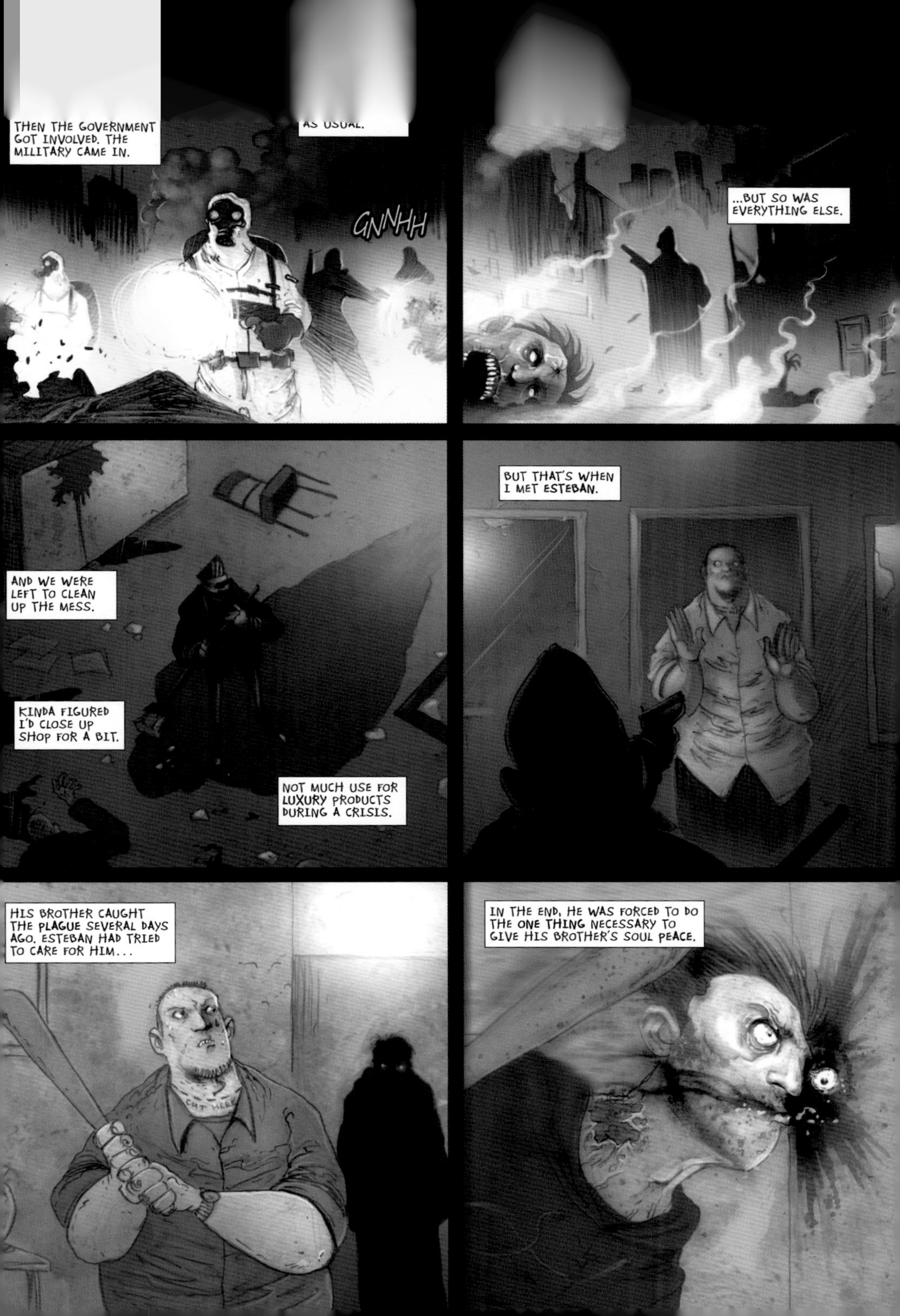
THEN THE GOVERNMENT GOT INVOLVED. THE MILITARY CAME IN.
AS USUAL.
GNNHH
...BUT SO WAS EVERYTHING ELSE.
AND WE WERE LEFT TO CLEAN UP THE MESS.
KINDA FIGURED I'D CLOSE UP SHOP FOR A BIT.
NOT MUCH USE FOR LUXURY PRODUCTS DURING A CRISIS.
BUT THAT'S WHEN I MET ESTEBAN.
HIS BROTHER CAUGHT THE PLAGUE SEVERAL DAYS AGO. ESTEBAN HAD TRIED TO CARE FOR HIM...
IN THE END, HE WAS FORCED TO DO THE ONE THING NECESSARY TO GIVE HIS BROTHER'S SOUL PEACE.

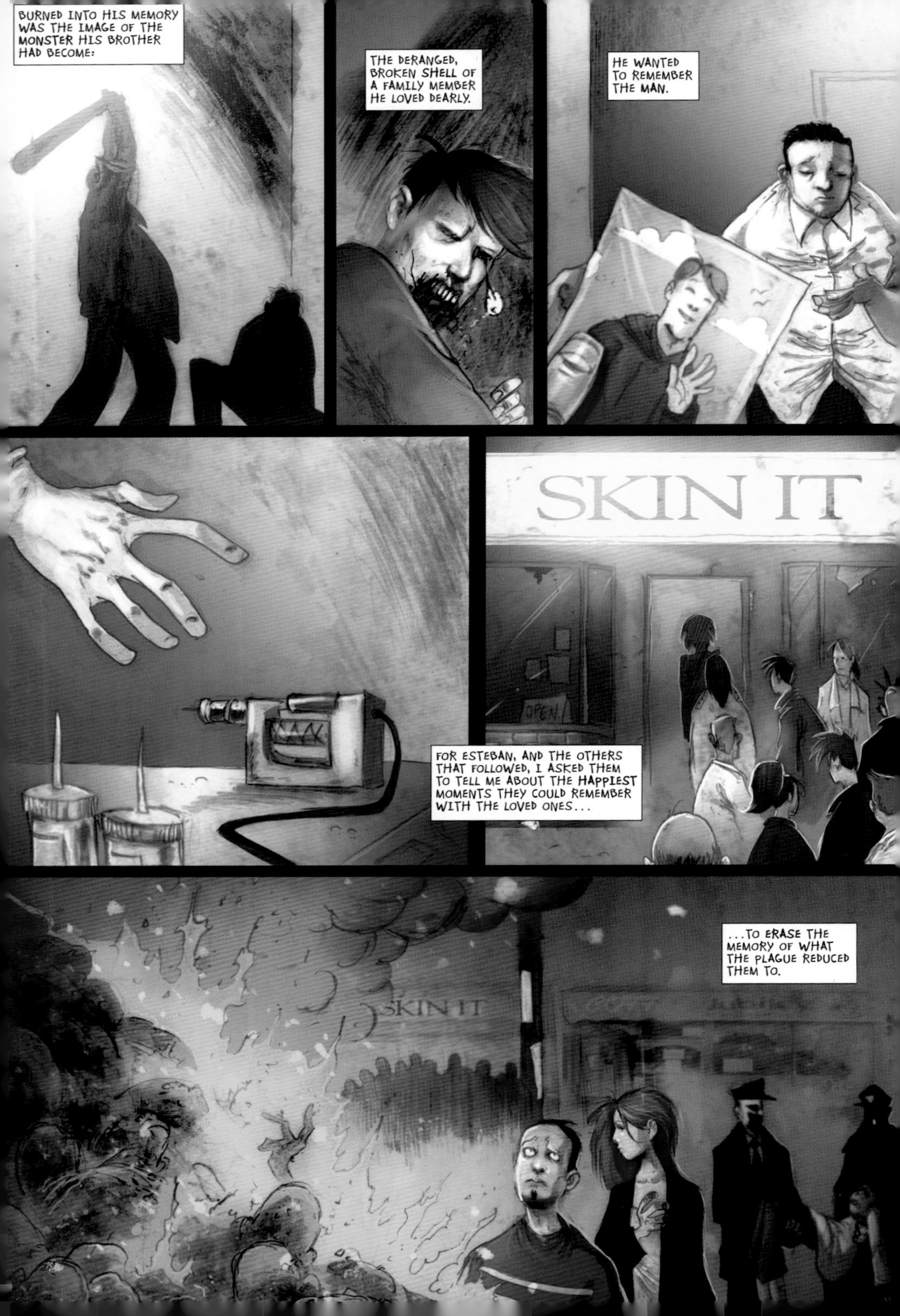
BURNED INTO HIS MEMORY WAS THE IMAGE OF THE MONSTER HIS BROTHER HAD BECOME:
THE DERANGED, BROKEN SHELL OF A FAMILY MEMBER HE LOVED DEARLY.
HE WANTED TO REMEMBER THE MAN.
SKIN IT
OPEN
FOR ESTEBAN, AND THE OTHERS THAT FOLLOWED, I ASKED THEM TO TELL ME ABOUT THE HAPPIEST MOMENTS THEY COULD REMEMBER WITH THE LOVED ONES...
SKIN IT
...TO ERASE THE MEMORY OF WHAT THE PLAGUE REDUCED THEM TO.

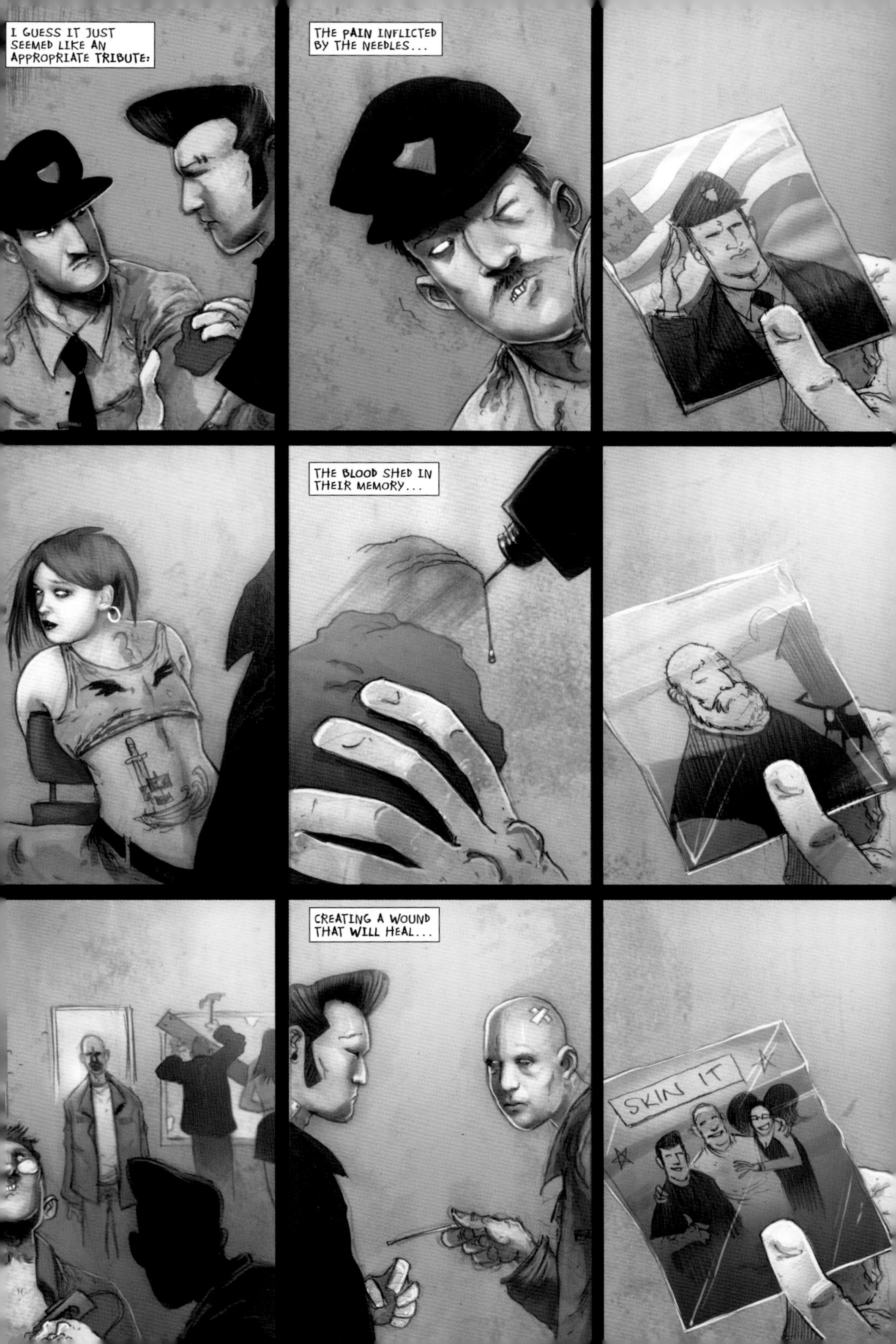
I GUESS IT JUST SEEMED LIKE AN APPROPRIATE TRIBUTE:
THE PAIN INFLICTED BY THE NEEDLES...
THE BLOOD SHED IN THEIR MEMORY...
CREATING A WOUND THAT WILL HEAL...
SKIN IT

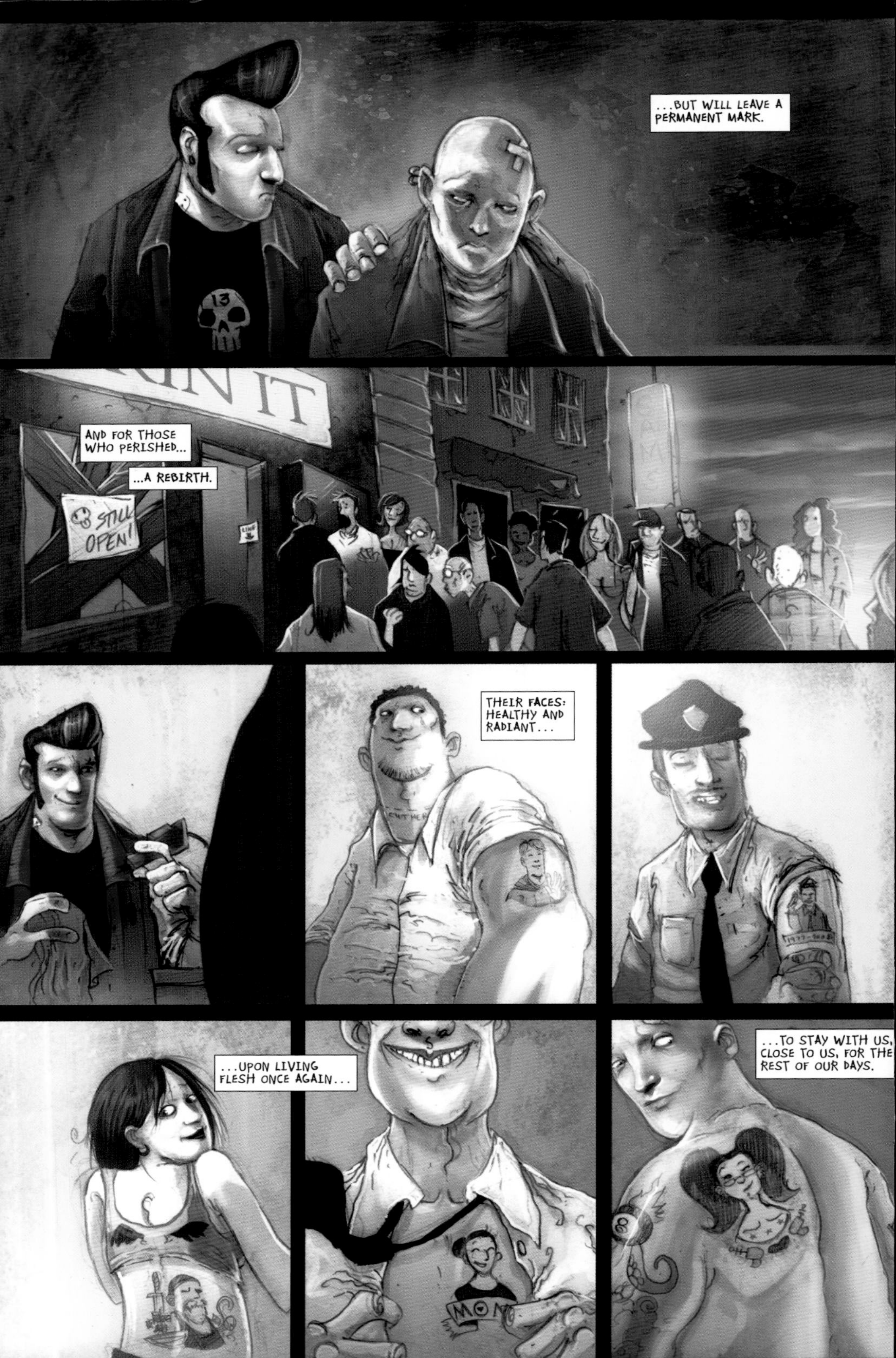
...BUT WILL LEAVE A PERMANENT MARK.
AND FOR THOSE WHO PERISHED...
...A REBIRTH.
STILL OPEN!
THEIR FACES: HEALTHY AND RADIANT...
...UPON LIVING FLESH ONCE AGAIN...
MOM
...TO STAY WITH US, CLOSE TO US, FOR THE REST OF OUR DAYS.